TILLICH

OUTSTANDING CHRISTIAN THINKERS

Series Editor: Brian Davies, OP, Professor of Philosophy at
Fordham University, New York

Paul
C.K. Barrett

The Cappadocians
Anthony Meredith SJ

Augustine
Mary T. Clark RSCJ

The Venerable Bede
Benedicta Ward SLG

Aquinas
Brian Davies OP

Catherine of Siena
Giuliana Cavallini OP

Teresa of Avila
Rowan Williams

Kierkegaard
Julia Watkin

Karl Barth
John Webster

Bultmann
David Fergusson

Reinhold Niebuhr
Kenneth Durkin

Paul Tillich
John Heywood Thomas

Hans Urs von Balthasar
John O'Donnell SJ

Lonergan
Frederick E. Crowe SJ

TILLICH

John Heywood Thomas

Continuum
London and New York

Continuum
Wellington House, 125 Strand, London WC2R 0BB
370 Lexington Avenue, New York, NY 10017–6503

First published 2000

British Library Cataloguing-in-Publication Data
A catalogue record for this book is available from the British Library.

ISBN 0 8264 5082 2 (Hb)
0 8264 5083 0 (Pb)

Typeset by Paston PrePress Ltd, Beccles, Suffolk
Printed and bound in Great Britain by Biddles Ltd
www.biddles.co.uk

Contents

Editorial Foreword

St Anselm of Canterbury (1033–1109) once described himself as someone with faith seeking understanding. In words addressed to God he says 'I long to understand in some degree thy truth, which my heart believes and loves. For I do not seek to understand that I may believe, but believe in order to understand.'

This is what Christians have always inevitably said, either explicitly or implicitly. Christianity rests on faith, but it also has content. It teaches and proclaims a distinctive and challenging view of reality. It naturally encourages reflection. It is something to think about; something about which one might even have second thoughts.

But what have the greatest Christian thinkers said? And is it worth saying? Does it engage with modern problems? Does it provide us with a vision to live by? Does it make sense? Can it be preached? Is it believable?

The Outstanding Christian Thinkers series is offered to readers with questions like these in mind. It aims to provide clear, authoritative and critical accounts of outstanding Christian writers from New Testament times to the present. It ranges across the full spectrum of Christian thought to include Catholic and Protestant thinkers, thinkers from East and West, thinkers ancient, mediaeval and modern.

The series draws on the best scholarship currently available, so it will interest all with a professional concern for the history of Christian ideas. But contributors also write for general readers who have little or no previous knowledge of the subjects to be dealt with. Its volumes should therefore prove helpful at a popular as well as an academic level. For the most part they are devoted to a single thinker, but occasionally the subject is a movement or school of thought.

Brian Davies OP

Bibliography

Books by Tillich

Biblical Religion and the Search for Ultimate Reality (London: Nisbet, 1956).

Christianity and the Encounter of the World Religions (New York: Columbia University Press, 1963).

Love, Power and Justice (London: Oxford University Press, 1959).

On the Boundary (introduction by J. Heywood Thomas) (London: Collins, 1967).

Political Expectations (ed. James Luther Adams) (New York: Harper & Row, 1971).

The System of the Sciences (Cranbury, NJ: Bucknell University Press, 1981).

Systematic Theology (3 vols; Welwyn: Nisbet, 1953–68).

Theology of Culture (ed. Robert C. Kimball) (New York: Oxford University Press, 1957).

The Courage to Be (New Haven: Yale University Press, 1952).

The Future of Religions (ed. Jerald C. Brauer) (New York: Harper & Row, 1966).

The Interpretation of History (London: Scribners, 1936).

The Protestant Era (ed. James Luther Adams) (London: Nisbet, 1951).

The Religious Situation (New York: Meridian Books, 1956).

The Shaking of the Foundations (London: SCM Press, 1949).

Visionary Science (ed. Victor Nuovo) (Detroit: Wayne State University Press, 1987).

What is Religion? (ed. James Luther Adams) (New York: Harper & Row, 1969).

Books about Tillich

James Luther Adams, *Paul Tillich's Philosophy of Culture, Science and Religion* (New York: Harper & Row, 1965). In many ways, this is the definitive study of Tillich. Luther Adams was not only Tillich's earliest translator and editor but remained one of his closest friends and colleagues. Because of its very wealth of information and scholarship, this book is best read after really familiarizing oneself with Tillich.

John P. Clayton, *The Concept of Correlation: Paul Tillich and the Possibility of a Mediating Theology* (Berlin and New York: de Gruyter, 1980). An excellent detailed study of this central concept in Tillich and a very penetrating discussion of it as a problem of theological method. This too is a book to be read as a piece of advanced study of Tillich.

Kenneth Hamilton, *The System and the Gospel: A Critique of Paul Tillich* (London: SCM Press, 1963). This is, as its title says, a critique of Tillich. Arguing on the basis of Kierkegaard's critique of 'the system' from a generally Barthian perspective, Hamilton contends that Tillich's system is incompatible with the Christian Gospel.

John Heywood Thomas, *Paul Tillich: An Appraisal* (London: SCM Press, 1963). The first book-length study of Tillich produced in Britain sought to offer an appraisal rather than a critique, elucidating Tillich as well as highlighting some of the basic confusions in his thinking.

Charles Kegley and Robert W. Bretall (eds), *The Theology of Paul Tillich* (New York: Macmillan, 1952). The first volume of the Library of Living Theology was, and remains, an outstandingly valuable collection of essays on aspects of Tillich's theology by some of the most distinguished twentieth-century theologians. It is also very important as showing Tillich in conversation with other theologians.

David Kelsey, *The Fabric of Paul Tillich's Theology* (New Haven: Yale University Press, 1957). Beautifully lucid, this is an anatomy of Tillich's theology seen as a deliberately Christian articulation of New Testament faith. It remains one of the most penetrating and judicious appraisals of Tillich's theological method.

Thomas O'Meara and Celestin Weisser (eds), *Paul Tillich in Catholic Thought* (London: Darton, Longman and Todd, 1964). A valuable collection of essays by Catholic theologians offering sympathetic but critical comment on Tillich's theology. Although some are technical, others provide very significant impressions of the theologian. The book includes a Foreword from Heywood Thomas and an Afterword from Tillich himself.

Wilhelm and Marion Pauck, *Paul Tillich: His Life and Thought*, vol. 1 (London: Collins, 1977). The first volume of a projected two-volume study of Tillich is an account of his life: his struggles from earliest infancy, his agonies and triumphs. It is a minutely detailed although not over-lengthy narrative and is, in every way, a monumentally significant book by two of Tillich's friends and colleagues.

Adrian Thatcher, *The Ontology of Paul Tillich* (Oxford: Oxford University Press, 1978). Broadly sympathetic to Tillich's theological aims and methods, this is a study of the relationship between ontology and theology. It shows the various philosophical influences on Tillich and analyses his doctrine of God and his doctrine of Christ in that light.

Ian E. Thompson, *Being and Meaning: Paul Tillich's Theory of Meaning, Truth and Logic* (Edinburgh: Edinburgh University Press, 1981). This rather specialist study presupposes much philosophical background, but it is a highly individual contribution to Tillich studies. It places him in philosophical context, teasing out his metaphysics of meaning and truth, and bringing the insights of logic to show how he could have achieved more.

Abbreviations

LPJ   *Love, Power and Justice*
OB   *On the Boundary*
PE   *Political Expectations*
ST   *Systematic Theology*
VS   *Visionary Science*

To my grandchildren

1

Tillich's Life and Career

Paul Tillich was a remarkable and, in the view of many, a unique theologian because he was as much at home in a philosophical discussion as he was in the pulpit and seemed as keenly interested in art and politics as he was in his life-work as a professional theologian. An invitation to a gathering of artists pleased him as greatly as the innumerable invitations he had to address church occasions. He was a teacher of extraordinary influence, but his first commitment was to the production of his theological system. He was an amazingly learned man and yet he never seemed concerned with details of scholarship, so that often students would joke that they followed his lectures on Luther or Calvin to learn about Tillich rather than the particular Reformer. For all his stature as a scholar, thinker, teacher and public figure Tillich was very anxious about his authority and standing, so that he would never take kindly to criticism of any kind. However near to vanity this sensitivity became, it did not make him insensitive to his fellow-man, and his efforts on behalf of other refugees were some of his unsung glory.

This figure of worldwide renown was born the son of a manse in a village near Berlin on 20 August 1886. Starzeddel is now part of Poland but it was then part of the district of Guben in the German province of Brandenburg. Paul's father, Johannes Oskar, was the pastor of the Evangelical Church of Prussia in the village. Despite rather desperate struggles in his first hours as he lay between life and death, Paul survived and was baptized by his father a month later.

Tillich recalled his earliest childhood as an almost idyllic enjoy-

1

ment of rural life; and rural indeed his life was in those first years in the parish house of Starzeddel. He played in the garden or in the park with the other village children and life was one long happy game. Even when the family moved to Schonfliess his life still had a rustic charm and dreamy quality—the beautiful little mediaeval town with its nearby lake, surrounded by farms, having the character of a traditional county town (especially because of its famous horse market). It was of Schönfliess that Tillich was thinking when in *On the Boundary* he described the typical German small town:

> Towns of this kind have a decidedly rustic character. Many of the houses have yards, barns and gardens attached to them, and it is only a few minutes' walk out into the fields. Cattle and sheep are herded through the streets morning and evening...
> The sheltered, protective quality of the town with its hustle and bustle, its contrast to the eeriness of the forest at night and the silent fields and sleepy hamlets is one of the earliest and strongest of my childhood impressions. (*On the Boundary*, p. 16)

The dream remained with him for life. There, in Schonfliess, Tillich first attended school: the grammar school which faced his father's church. He seems to have been very happy in school. He recalled the religious instruction given there as the foundation of his entire theological thought ('Autobiographical reflections', p. 6). However, they were not completely untroubled years, because Tillich's comparatively privileged position created a certain tension. As the son of a parson he was friendly with the son of a noble family, but he felt that his real friends were the boys of the local school, and identifying with them he shared their animosity towards the upper classes.

In 1898 the Tillich family moved to Berlin because Tillich senior had been appointed minister and superintendent of the Bethlehem-gemeinde and also a member of the consistory of the province of Brandenburg. So deeply moved was Paul by his early experience of life in the city that he later spoke of some of his works as expressing its myth. The brilliant celebration of the dawn of the new century and the ceremonial parades would obviously have been an unforgettable experience; but so also was the daily savouring of the sophistication and variety of a great city and capital. His grammar school or Gymnasium education was continued in Königsberg (now

Kaliningrad in Russia), where he was sent to board, and then from 1901 in the Friedrich Wilhelm Gymnasium in Berlin.

If life in the city had special attraction for the young Tillich, his ties to the country were even stronger and remained throughout his life a source of special inspiration. Probably even as a youth that attachment was rather remarkable, though one can readily appreciate how landscape, soil, weather, the fields of grain and the smell of the potato crop in autumn would remain powerfully nostalgic memories for him. The sea in particular became very important to him. Every year from the age of eight he spent weeks (later months) by the sea. As a youth he delighted in building sandcastles and, later, as a married man, when he took his family on holiday to the seaside, the construction of an elaborate sandcastle was his contribution to the entertainment. The sea was a significant inspiration for him, for he found in its contemplation the suggestion of the infinite bordering on the finite. There indeed, he tells us (*On the Boundary*, p. 18), was the likely source of his theory of the human boundary situation. Similarly, the way the sea breaks in on the sand made him think of religion as the Eternal breaking in on the Temporal. Ideas such as his theory of the 'dynamic mass' and the Absolute as the ground and abyss of dynamic truth were conceived under the influence of the constantly moving sea.

The young Tillich was something of a romantic and inclined, indeed, to fantasy—a tendency powerfully strengthened by the tragic death of his mother when he was seventeen. So great was his sorrow that he often spoke as if he had lost her when he was only a child. He had a capacity for identifying himself completely with particular characters and his mood would often be determined by whatever literary work he was reading. He enjoyed the garden his mother had created and tended; but his peace was increasingly troubled by the independent attitude he developed towards his father. His lonely home and solitary father made him more and more reflective, so that it is not surprising to find him described by the Gymnasium as 'interested in philosophy'. That was the world that now beckoned him as he entered university, to which he went set on following his father in an ecclesiastical career.

Tillich entered the University of Berlin in the winter semester of 1904 to pursue theological studies in preparation for ordination. As was customary in the German system, he was able to move from Berlin to Tübingen, where he spent one semester, and to Halle, where he spent two whole years. These years at Halle seem to have been the most influential part of his university career. In Berlin, he heard lectures on the history of philosophy by the distinguished Hegelian Adolf Lasson, and that early exposure to a very schematic history of philosophy doubtless left an abiding impression on his thinking. Yet it was a casual discovery in a bookshop that can be described as the fateful event of his university days of intellectual development: he came across and bought the *Collected Works* of F. W. J. Schelling. Schelling (1775–1854) was the early inspiration of Hegel (1770–1831), though he later became Hegel's great opponent. Tillich fell in love with Schelling and became so imbued with his thought that late in his life, when we were discussing a quotation from Schelling, he commented 'But I said that, not Schelling'.

It was to the University of Halle that he owed his intellectual formation in a social as well as an academic context. Here he was taught by two great thinkers, Martin Kähler and Fritz Medicus (1835–1912) and here too he joined and became a leading member of the Wingolf Society ('Wingolf' meaning 'Friendship House'). This was a non-residential society which aimed to provide university students with a sense of community, fostering this by formal social evenings. Tillich's father had been a member of the society and it was a great joy to Paul to take part in one of the national conventions together with him. The presence of Kähler and Medicus in Halle meant that academically Halle gave Tillich's theological development a decisive slant. Kähler was the most popular of the theological lecturers and Tillich was tremendously enthusiastic about him, remarking that it was to Kähler he was indebted for his understanding of the 'all-embracing character of the Biblical-Lutheran idea of justification'. The relief of seeing doubt as something encompassed by justifying faith was cathartic: at the same time he felt that this theology rescued him from any kind of moralism or easy mysticism. There were very distinctive lessons to be learnt in Christology and the whole field of dogmatics from a teacher who distinguished between the Christ of faith and the Jesus of history. In philosophy he was guided perhaps decisively by the younger lecturer, Fritz Medicus, who had already established a great reputation for his scholarly work on the German Idealists. Later generations of Schelling scholars refer to his works as classical, and it is very likely that Medicus confirmed and reinforced Tillich's love of Schelling.

After returning to Berlin at the end of his fourth semester in Halle, Tillich began to prepare for the theological examination required for ordination. At the same time, he followed courses leading to the doctorate of philosophy. Though his studies were interrupted by his acceptance of the position of pastoral assistant in a village near Berlin, he passed his first theological examination in 1909. Then he spent a year in the Berlin Cathedral Seminary, during which time he wrote his licentiate of theology dissertation on Schelling, 'Mysticism and guilt-consciousness in Schelling's philosophical development'. By August 1910 he had completed and successfully submitted his doctoral dissertation on Schelling, 'The conception of the history of religion in Schelling's positive philosophy: its presuppositions and principles'. Passing his final church examinations in July 1912, he was ordained in Berlin in August of that year. From 1912 to 1914 he served as assistant preacher with the Evangelical Consistory of Berlin.

At this time too, on a visit to his sister's house in Butterfelde (now part of Poland), Tillich met a lively young woman two years his junior, Grethi Wever. He fell in love with her and their engagement was announced in January 1914. They were married on 28 September but were soon separated by the Great War. Filled with patriotic zeal and a sense of the religious sanction of the war, Tillich volunteered for military service as an army chaplain. Brim-full of romantic notions of glorious battle and devotion to the fatherland, he went to the war a young chaplain politically naive and socially inexperienced. Recent studies of this period of his life show that he believed the successful outcome of the German offensives to be the will of God. When he joined his division it had been withdrawn from the front for a rest period; but when it was moved back again to the front Tillich volunteered to go too. In December 1914 he was awarded the Iron Cross, though it was the period of October 1915 onwards that made him a real front-line soldier. These were difficult and dangerous months in which he discharged his duties with courageous thoroughness. Often he would act as a gravedigger as the danger settled into carnage, carnage which robbed him of some of his best friends. This agony filled him with a sense of all-embracing death. Writing to his father at this time he wondered whether, when peace eventually came, he would himself be intellectually productive, or indeed whether the German economy would be able to sustain a university system.

In early 1916 Tillich obtained leave to go to Halle to deliver a trial lecture which he had been composing in the trenches. He was not able to do that until the following June; for, after the comparatively

5

tranquil opening of 1916, he was involved in the battle for Verdun with its hellish struggle and enormous loss of life. Comforting the wounded and the dying and burying the dead, Tillich suffered seemingly endless anguish and—not surprisingly—his first nervous breakdown. Even so, he made a rapid enough recovery to be able to visit Halle in July to deliver his lecture, and as a result he was appointed *Privatdozent* of theology. By October 1916 he was back in the thick of the fray and once again was as much an ambulanceman as a chaplain as he saved the wounded and scurried to and fro in the heat of the battle to tend the wounded and the dying. There was no peace or respite and he preached almost nothing except 'the end'— 'experiencing the actual death of this our time', as he put it in one of his letters. Again he broke down and this time it was serious enough for him to be sent to hospital. The only relief he had was the contemplation of the pictures he pasted into books—and his constant philosophizing.

It was a time not only of agony but of growing intellectual self-assurance. Tillich had never been quite conventional theologically, but his experience of living with and preaching to such a variety of men as was found in his division made him seem more of a freethinker. Certainly he managed to shock some of his fellow-officers; but more significant was his own awareness of a decisive change in his outlook. Not only had the naive romantic been shell-shocked into realism, but the more or less traditional believer found his idea of God changed. He could no longer believe in the kind of God he had always imagined. Liberation from that came with his reading of Nietzsche (1844–1900), who remained one of his favourite authors for the rest of his life. Reading *Thus Spake Zarathustra* in a French forest was for him an 'ecstatic experience', as he found in it an affirmation of existence which contrasted with the death he found around him. Exulting in this affirmation of life, he began to think of God as the possibility of life being born afresh. He was not persuaded by either Nietzsche's rejection of Christianity or his idea of the superman; but the notion of will to power entered not only his general philosophy of life but also his view of God. Perhaps it was another, very different, great classic that helped balance this influence of Nietzsche: Rudolf Otto's *Idea of the Holy*. Otto's description of religion as the sense of the numinous, the 'beyond' that is in experience, moved him deeply and must have resonated with his experience of death in the midst of life and hope at the very heart of despair. For Otto (1869–1937) it was not the rational but the

6

irrational (that is, the feeling) element of religion which was its essential nature, and all religious ideas were attempts to articulate what was beyond thought. They were ideograms which pointed to a deep experience. Such contrasting thoughts seemed to the young chaplain to catch exactly the contradictions of his life in the trenches. They were ideas that he then expressed as his paradoxical faith without God—justification by faith indeed but without the old idea of a God who guaranteed a happy ending.

After America entered the war in 1917, German fortunes seemed more desperate and Tillich reflected on the betrayal of German society by the church's support of the war. Where did that leave him? He had always thought of himself as destined for the church, but now that seemed unthinkable. More and more his interest had turned to philosophy—this in fact was the time when he read Husserl (1859–1938), a thinker whose influence on himself and his generation he described as being their salvation from naturalism. Yet he could not feel happy with the abandonment of an ecclesiastical future any more than he could feel entirely happy with his new and rather disturbing ideas about God and religion. For all his radicalism, he still yearned for the peace and unity he remembered as the world of his youth. When late in life he was criticized as a nineteenth-century figure, he used to be very annoyed, saying that it was only his big toe that was in the nineteenth century. That may well have been footing enough to establish an attitude. Yet it was not an attitude which he could easily maintain as the war came to its agonizing close. The final year of the war was a year of mixed fortunes for Tillich, as it was a year of impatient waiting for his eventual return to civilian life. In April, he suffered his third nervous breakdown, which, though not as serious as the Verdun breakdown, did make him feel that this must be the end of his war. The horror of what he had seen and endured was so great that he felt close to insanity or the seductive peace of suicide. Then in May he was once more back in his earlier sense of romantic patriotism—and this fresh joy was heightened even more when in June he was awarded the Iron Cross First Class. In August he was moved to Spandau, where he remained for the rest of the war.

Returning from the war, Tillich entered a broken world of disappointment, despair and near-anarchy. The German economy was in ruins, the old social order gone, and workers were organizing a revolution. His mood at this time was aptly captured in the graphic phrase he later used in the famous lecture of 1919—'the whole house

7

was in ruins'. What he had increasingly felt during the war was now the powerful conviction of a new policy which transfigured all the hurt of his (and indeed his generation's) disappointment with the pre-war establishment as it also transcended his dreadful pessimism. Looking back he thought that it was 'practically impossible for a people educated as Lutherans to move from religion to socialism' (*On the Boundary*, p. 75). There was opposition to religious socialism within the Lutheran church: yet he was more and more convinced that the demand of the moment was for a socialist restructuring of society. In the last stage of the war he had discussed political issues with friends and he had pondered problems of society and history— his usual method being that of teasing out the philosophical issues that underlay even the most practical problem. It was at this time that he used the New Testament notion of *kairos*, the fulfilled time or the time of fulfilment, the fullness of time as distinct from a simple chronological moment of history. On his return from the war, Tillich became active in the kind of feverish political engagement that dominated those early post-war years as the Weimar Republic settled into its uneasy course. In May of 1919 he gave a lecture to the Independent Socialist Party on Christianity and Socialism, thereby incurring the displeasure of the consistory (see p. 13 below). It is very interesting that he wrote a circular letter in the following September to emphasize that he had not joined the Independent Socialist Party. Active in politics he was, but a political activist he was not. He was, as he says (*On the Boundary*, p. 32), 'very much alive to the political situation', whereas previously he had been 'rather indifferent to politics'. He associated with political theorists but he insisted that their goal was not his. Later on he joined the Social Democratic Party; but for the moment he joined no party. Anxious to help bring about a new order of society that would be both Christian and socialist, he threw his weight behind the religious socialist movement and so joined the 'Kairos Circle', also called the Berlin Group (see p. 14 below).

The iron of the war's disappointment had entered deep into Tillich's soul in a more intimate way than this great change in his political sensitivity and outlook. When he went to war, he had been a young bridegroom who was more or less sexually innocent—something that perhaps needs to be emphasized, in view of his wife's salacious memoirs published after his death. As a member of the Wingolf Fraternity, he had observed its rule of chastity, being a priggish and almost puritanical upholder of it when in a position of authority. That was his attitude in the early days of his marriage to Grethi, but hers was very different, and finally she left him in the spring of 1919. The years that followed were years of chaotic encounters with women. (Much has been said about Tillich's womanizing, and the prominence given to this in the memoirs of Hannah Tillich has confused rather than clarified our understanding of his attitude to women.) There was little satisfaction in the 'bohemian' existence he led at this time. Escape came, he felt, in the shape of his second marriage, in 1924, to Hannah Werner (see p. 15 below).

One very important feature of the way Tillich's life and outlook changed during the war years has been mentioned all too briefly. He sought refuge from the horrors of war in looking at pictures and collecting them for reflection. As we have seen, he had eagerly looked at the pictures he could get from the military bookstore whilst at the front and had tried to make some study of art by way of relief from the agonies of life in the front. Then on his final furlough of the war on a visit to Berlin he experienced what he describes as 'almost a revelation' when he saw a Botticelli painting—the 'Madonna with Singing Angels'. It was for him not only a representation of angels but essentially a manifestation of the holy (*On the Boundary*, p. 28). Again and again he referred to this experience, insisting that what gave it a revelatory character was not the nature of the subject but the nature of the painting itself. It was *great* art— and, as such, had a depth that was beyond anything definable even in terms of the theology with which he was familiar. On his return from the war, that expansion of his spiritual horizons and of his cultural knowledge was taken further through the influence of his old friend Eckart von Sydow. Hannah Tillich's phrase is that he 'educated Paulus in modern art' (*From Time to Time*, p. 100). It was von Sydow who introduced him to Expressionism, and there can be no doubt that this was one of the formative influences on his developing theology. It is crucial to remember that we are now talking of the young theologian who had moved far from the jingoism of his early months as a chaplain, and even beyond the rather volatile sentiments that characterized his last months of service. Now he was thoroughly disillusioned and one thing was clear: the nineteenth-century unities had been shattered. If intellectually he now found a kinship with Kierkegaard (1813–55) and Nietzsche, then artistically what stated that same conviction was the painting of the Expressionists. As Tillich was rejecting the world of bourgeois religion, so these painters were rejecting the domination of art by bourgeois taste: they were nothing less than fellow-combatants in the same mental strife. Unlike the religious art of capitalist society, here was art that was indeed religious, but religious precisely because it revealed a broken world. These paintings were not concerned with the perceptible form of nature; but by exaggerating certain forms even to the point of destroying the visible unity they sought to penetrate to the metaphysical significance of that piece of nature. Cézanne, says Tillich, had thus penetrated to the real metaphysical meaning of things by struggling with the form. This stress on the revelation of metaphysical meaning was what Tillich saw as the mystical element in Expressionism. This was what was revealed as something that broke through the meaninglessness of the picture's obvious representation. The importance of this artistic movement for his theology lies deeper than its obvious role in his famous lecture on culture. Contributing as it does to his understanding of revelation and even of religion itself as a state of being grasped by a power that breaks through our finite concerns, it becomes one of the decisive concepts in Tillich's interpretation of the New Testament picture of Jesus.

Tillich had qualified as a *Privatdozent* in the University of Halle; but before the war ended he was advised to transfer that qualification to the University of Berlin, where he might well find an academic opportunity. For the first year after the war, he was employed by a friend of his father's, Bishop Gustav Haendler of Berlin, as one of his vicars. So in January 1919 he gave his inaugural lecture at Berlin ('The existence of God and the psychology of religion'), and started teaching. The topic of the course was 'Christianity and the present social problems', and Tillich addressed it with passion and verve. As well as lecturing to his students, he met several of them regularly every other month in some kind of seminar. There he would expound his own ideas based on his voluminous reading and would question the students, not only about what he had expounded but more especially about what they had read or gleaned about current ideas and developments. This was for him a source of what he would have to say in his projected book on the System of the Sciences, published in 1923 as *Das System den Wissenschaften nach Gegenständen und Methoden*. Lecturing was his great joy and remained so throughout his life. It was one of his greatest pleasures, filling him with nervous anticipation and, as he spoke, with unqualified delight. Partly to earn some money but even more for the sheer joy of doing it and for the pleasant satisfaction of success, he lectured whenever he could. The greatest lecture of this period was his paper to the Kant Society in Berlin in April 1919, 'On the idea of the theology of culture'. This remarkable paper, which pleads for a new beginning in theology and rejects the separation of the religious from the secular, marked out both a programme within theology and a programme for the substance and style of Tillich's life-work in theology. Tillich was now launched as a theologian and the interest the Kant Society took in him showed that he would be a philosophical theologian.

Soon after his marriage to Hannah came the move to Marburg, where Tillich had been appointed as the successor of Rudolf Otto, the renowned theologian and philosopher of religion. There he taught for three semesters. It was an important period for him and he never forgot his close contact with Otto. During their long walks they discussed problems of Christian theology, Oriental religion and basic ideas of religion (such as the demonic). Otto's influence on Tillich was profound: he responded so readily to Otto's stress on the crucial importance of religious experience. About the same time, two other thinkers had come to Marburg: the New Testament critic Rudolf Bultmann (1884–1976) and the philosopher Martin Heidegger (1889–1976). While the former could be said to have confirmed some of Tillich's views on the nature of the New Testament, Heidegger could be said to have had a more significant influence in that he proved to be one of the forces that shaped Tillich's theology. Tillich's own description of that influence is that he was attracted by Heidegger's ideas, struggled with them and finally learnt from them, making them, to some extent at least, his own.

Two things are worth remembering as we note this acknowledgement of a debt to Heidegger. First, Tillich tells us that he was prepared for Heidegger's philosophy by his reading of Schelling—so that there is a real sense in which for him Heidegger's ideas were filtered through Schelling. In trying to understand Tillich's philosophy it is very important always to bear in mind that his study of Schelling (for both his philosophy and theology higher degrees) was probably the greatest single influence on his philosophical outlook and his view of the development of modern philosophy. Towards the end of his life, Tillich appeared to change his views, but the remarkable feature of his thought is its extraordinary consistency. Up to 1935, he did not discuss the same issues as later; yet the earlier more general philosophical work coheres easily with the later more theological thinking. In the same way, the writings of the American period have a remarkable unity. It would be wrong to think of Schelling as the only key that one needs to Tillich's thought; but there is no doubt that this still unpopular thinker is the most important key. Secondly, it is equally necessary to remember that we are dealing with the living and developing thought of someone who had just come through the traumatic experience of World War I. Rollo May describes how Tillich used to relate the impact made on him by a battle on the Marne.

> His fellow officers were brought in on stretchers, chopped to pieces by gunfire, wounded or dead. That night 'absolutely transformed me', he used to say. 'All my friends were among those dying and dead. That night I became an existentialist.' From then on he could not separate truth from the human being who acts on it: right and wrong were no longer decided at purely ethereal heights of thought; the living, pulsing, committing, suffering and loving human being must always be taken into account. (Rollo May, *Paulus*, p. 18)

That said, one is forced again to qualify this characterization because Tillich not only used to insist that he was as much of an essentialist as an existentialist; but, again and again, he used to argue that existentialism had its origin in the work of Schelling.

There are two respects in which Heidegger did have a decisive influence on Tillich—even though that influence was not as thoroughgoing and dramatic as it was on Karl Rahner. The first has to do with a view of human life as tragedy. The existentialist philosophers in general, and Heidegger in particular, put themselves in a literary tradition which has its roots in Greek tragedy. Whatever one might say about any redeeming features of Heidegger's call to a heroic existence in *Being and Time*, the general tone—and indeed the precise description of the human situation—is tragic. My situation is one of estrangement, and salvation comes with the recognition that what gives my life its meaning is the fact that I shall die. Throughout Tillich's writings, the note of tragedy sounds like the theme of a great symphony. Secondly, there are some metaphysical notions derived from Heidegger which he uses to develop his doctrine of man (the area where he said that existentialism had been an important influence in twentieth-century thought). The most obvious is that of finitude and temporality. One of Tillich's greatest triumphs as a theologian was his analysis of the theological mystery of time, showing how the categories of existence all have a temporal significance and, as such, are categories of finitude. He was enabled to achieve that clarification by the influence of Heidegger's analysis of human existence as characterized by temporality. Then, as he sought to define what constituted finitude, Tillich once again had recourse to one of Heidegger's concepts: Nothing. What makes his doctrine of creation in *Systematic Theology* so difficult for English readers is the perplexing way in which he speaks of 'Nothing' as if it were something. The explanation is to be found in Heidegger's analysis of the idea of being in which being something, nothing and notness are the most important features. For Heidegger, the problem of the nothing was at the very heart of philosophy. Towards the end of his life, Tillich would insist that, by contrast with empiricist philosophy which dismissed such language as meaningless, this was his ontology.

Launched on an academic career, Tillich still had little by way of a livelihood and it was the generosity of family and friends that ensured his financial well-being during those early post-war years. The war had changed his outlook profoundly, and in no respect more than his attitude to social and political affairs. Having gone to the war a political innocent—and probably a monarchist in his father's mould—he returned an ardent socialist. The Social Democrats were in power; but Tillich's political position was clearly more radical than that. This is clear from his opposition to the continued church–state alliance: he was one of the signatories of a statement in 1918 by one of the minor groups, the New Church Alliance, advocating the separation of church and state. By the following spring, he was sufficiently active to be attending political gatherings, and in May he addressed a meeting of the Independent Socialist Party, which occupied a position to the left of the Social Democratic Party. This put him in bad odour with the church authorities and he received a request from the President of the Protestant Consistory of Brandenburg for a report on the matter. In reply, Tillich supplied a summary of the paper 'Christianity and Socialism' to show that, while he emphasized the duty of Christianity to create justice and liberty, he rejected any attempt to identify Christianity with a particular social order. Though no action was taken against him, Tillich was severely reprimanded and ordered by the hierarchy not to speak at any more rallies. Characteristically, he continued to attend meetings with other intellectuals who had organized themselves for the discussion of the relation of the church to socialism. At the same time, he sent a circular letter to his friends to explain that he had neither joined nor intended to join the Independent Socialist Party, though he now intended to cast his vote for it.

Tillich was in fact becoming more and more political. Not only was he lecturing on Christianity and the social problems of the day, but he had already shown his radical attitude and nailed his revolutionary colours to the mast in his lecture of April 1919 on the idea of a theology of culture. He spoke of the 'idealistic socialists' whose message of love distinguished their position from Marxism. His own vision of the state was of a socialist organization from which the capitalist spirit would be quite absent. In tones reminiscent of Luther's *Address to the German Nobility*, he says that the concepts of 'the poor' and of 'charitable giving' would be annulled on the soil of socialism. The lecture's closing remarks emphasize the unity of a theology of culture and the aims of socialism. The pattern of Tillich's political attitude and of his political engagement was thus already set when, in 1920, he joined a group known as the 'Berlin Group' or the 'Kairos Circle' organized by Karl Mennicke, but of which Eduard Heimann and Adolf Löwe were the more prominent members. They met fortnightly, and after a while Tillich became their leader. Increasingly dissatisfied with the churches, especially the Lutheran, because of their vested interest in power and the status quo, the group was strongly socialist in attitude though not in fact associated with any socialist party. It was opposed to any utopian faith in some alliance of Christianity and socialism, whatever its source or political hue. Yet it was also a group united in hope before the unique opportunity of the critical situation facing them. The group's members fiercely resisted the unrealistic hopes (of groups or individuals) that the Kingdom of God would soon be established. On the other hand, they were just as much opposed to the Marxist prophecy of an inevitable proletarian victory. Their conviction that the postwar world was one in which there was an opportunity of crucial renewal occasioned Tillich's contribution to the group—the reinterpretation of the New Testament idea of *kairos*, the time of fulfilment when the eternal breaks in on the time (*chronos*) of human history. Until he left Berlin in 1924, Tillich was not only active as leader of the group but, as one of the main exponents of its ideas, he contributed many articles to the small journal which Mennicke edited, *Blätter für den religiösen Sozialismus* (Pages for Religious Socialism). So the shape of his political existence had then been drawn before Tillich ever became an academic figure of consequence—let alone a theologian of national or international renown.

With the success of his lecture to the Berlin Kant Society on the idea of a theology of culture, Tillich's academic career was well and truly guaranteed. This was, however, also a time of great personal tragedy. The war had killed for him not only the blissful innocence that had sent him to the front as a good son of the Fatherland (only to send him back home with shattered illusions and full of disappointment), but also the bliss of his brief married life. His wife Grethi had not only had an affair: the affair had been with his friend Richard Wegener, who had been Tillich's soul-mate in the years preceding the war, when Tillich, an inexperienced student, was a raw assistant pastor. (The story recalls Somerset Maugham's *Cakes and Ale*, for early in their marriage Tillich and his young wife had lost a child in infancy.) Grethi left Tillich in 1919 but when she had a child in June of that year, Tillich gave the boy his name. He went on to show even more generosity towards his friend by not citing him in the divorce that followed, and also ensured that Wegener should be financially responsible for the child's support during the early years.

The divorce and the bitter blow of Grethi's desertion threw Tillich into what he called the 'bohemian' period of his life. Bohemian or not, it was certainly the life of a lively young bachelor; as he frequented theatres, cafés and balls, he met several young women, falling in love, but not finding his true love. Such a change in his behaviour made his friends very concerned, and it was feared that the women in his life would lead to his being excommunicated. Probably the most accurate as well as the shrewdest assessment of this period was that of his pupil and friend Rollo May, who in his memoir *Paulus* speaks of the many women with whom Tillich had relations of different degrees of intimacy. He speaks of Tillich loving one or two of these women 'authentically and deeply'; but his final judgement is that his relations with them were 'sensual rather than sexual'. For such a man, the desolation of a solitary existence after the joy of consummated love was too great an agony to bear. Indeed, Tillich convinced himself that he could not work without the stimulus of erotic experience.

This frantic pursuit of a relationship came to a head in 1920 when he met a *femme fatale* in green stockings, Hannah Werner. Their courtship was tempestuous. An art teacher ten years his junior, Hannah was engaged, then married, to Albert Gottschow, but left him two years later; she was divorced in 1923 and married Tillich in March 1924. While he was alive, she sought to show that what was sauce for the goose was sauce for the gander. A remarkable woman, she wreaked energetic vengeance on Tillich for the slights and hurts she felt he had inflicted on her; she told this tale and various scurrilous stories about Tillich himself in her extraordinary books *From Time to Time* and *From Place to Place*. Even so, she was his anchor and he described her as the only woman he could ever have married. In his final years, when he was often in danger of being socially lionized to death, she guarded him as attentively and effectively as the second Mrs Thomas Hardy had guarded her famous husband.

Tillich's real academic career began in 1924 with his appointment to the prestigious chair of theology in the Philip's University of Marburg (so called because it was founded by Philip of Hesse in 1527). The position could hardly have been more distinguished for two reasons. One, as has been said, was that he was succeeding the renowned Rudolf Otto, author of the classic work *The Idea of the Holy*. The other was that the university itself had for centuries enjoyed a great reputation as the first Protestant university. Even so, Tillich was extremely reluctant to accept because of the invidious comparison he made between the excitement of Berlin and the provincialism of Marburg. Accept, however, he did because it was, after all, a step forward in his career. Once there, he was thrown into a context of fierce theological debate represented by his students who were either rabid Barthians or else enthusiastic followers of Bultmann and Heidegger. Tillich remained in Marburg for only three semesters, but this was a period of immense importance in his development. We have already seen how the encounter with Heidegger's thought was influential; and so it is all the more important to understand the importance of the period, as it were, from inside Tillich's own mind. It was here that he first set about creating a systematic theology, lecturing on it in his final semester after his initial teaching of philosophy of religion. The distinctive feature of this systematic theology, which struck his students at first as frustrating and then as exciting, was Tillich's individual way of speaking of God. Many years later, he was to profess his immense debt to Otto but at the time he obviously thought it important not to use Otto's language. So, instead of speaking of God as 'wholly other', he referred to 'the Unconditioned' and, with a military flourish, used to say that if we are grasped by faith in God (already for him a decisive way of putting things) we march forward to the beat of the divine.

Attractive as Marburg was, with the lovely countryside and the fulfilment born of a successful teaching career, it was too provincial a context for Tillich—and certainly for Hannah. However, as we have seen, the intellectual stimulus was of decisive importance, though perhaps even this is best understood against the background of personal unease and dissatisfaction with the atmosphere of Marburg. We have already seen how Heidegger proved so influential a contact; therefore it is rather surprising to recall that it was Otto rather than Heidegger who was Tillich's great friend and inspiration during these months at Marburg. This is an interesting example of the way in which the number and variety of Tillich's points of contact with the history of philosophy and theology make it almost impossible to analyse exactly his relation to this or that particular figure. He himself left us in no doubt about his great indebtedness to the stimulating friendship that Otto generously showed him at this time.

Already now a successful university teacher, Tillich had the good fortune to be singled out for appointment as Professor of Religious Studies in the department of humanities at the Dresden Institute of Technology, largely on the strength of his reputation as a Schelling scholar. The combined attractions of a full professor's salary and of the cultural opportunities of a large city were irresistible. An interesting footnote can be added to the story here: Tillich was helped to this position by Richard Kroner, who was already in Dresden. Years later, when Tillich had been established in New York, he was able to repay that kindness by encouraging Kroner's appointment to Union Seminary.

Tillich took to Dresden like a duck to water. The innovative outlook of the Institute was very much to his taste; the students were enthusiastic and attentive; and his working brief had the kind of openness and breadth of scope that pleased him greatly. By this time he had established himself as a successful author with the publication of *The Religious Situation* (*Die religiöse Gegenwart*, Berlin, 1925) and such important papers as his 'Philosophy of religion' (*Lehrbuch der Philosophie*, ed. Max Dessoir, Berlin, 1925). Evidently it was not only his Dresden students who came to see Tillich as a rising star in the theological firmament; for during his first years in Dresden he was awarded the honorary degree of doctor of theology by the University of Halle. It was a happy time with much social entertainment and cultural refreshment. Tillich became interested in dance, seeing in modern dance as exemplified in the work of the Steinweg Dance Group a link with Expressionist painting. He wrote an essay, 'Dance and religion', in which he deplored the lost unity of worship and drama, wondering how it could be revived in 'the stony dry earth of Protestantism'. His long-standing interest in painting also flourished in Dresden, where art was encouraged and developed by wealthy patrons of modern painting.

Up to this point, Tillich's career had been much in the borderland of theology rather than in the field of theology proper. What inaugurated his professional career as a systematic theologian was his appointment to the University of Leipzig in 1927. However, it was a short-lived appointment; for in 1929 he was elected to the chair of philosophy in Frankfurt once held by Max Scheler (1874–1928). Now a full professor, he was to enjoy a generous financial reward which would help wipe out the debts accumulated by privation and instability over the years. There being no faculty of theology in this relatively new university, Tillich saw the filling of this gap as one of his tasks: his formal duty, however, was to teach social education. His appointment was greeted with enthusiasm by his former teacher Fritz Medicus, the important Fichte and Schelling scholar who had visions of Tillich ushering in a new period of philosophy by recreating Schelling's philosophy as a meaningful philosophy of life. Though that was not exactly what happened, a new period was created as Tillich proved a great success in Frankfurt, attracting large and increasing numbers of students who in turn came to regard this least bigoted of men as a guide, friend and inspiration. An intimate friend of this period was Theodor Adorno (1903–1969) who wrote his doctoral dissertation on Kierkegaard under Tillich's supervision. In the rarefied atmosphere of Frankfurt's illustrious university, which boasted such distinguished and renowned members of staff as Karl Mannheim, the sociologist whose work was to be quoted by a whole generation, Tillich breathed the free air of debate and quickly won respect for his unusual expression of Christian faith. He already had his life-long reputation for great scholarship and erudition; but with this he displayed his nimbleness of intelligence and his love of system and organization. In a conversation with him the summer before he died, he responded very positively to the suggestion that his theology bore the imprint of Kantian architectonic. What above all else characterized his years at Frankfurt was the sense of their being 'secular years', as he used to say—the enjoyment of nature as much as of culture and the feeling that he was able now to savour the essential delights of good living such as wine, good food and society. Neither an epicurean nor a gourmet, he nevertheless regarded these as things which ought to be enjoyed.

For Tillich, the great success of his early years in Frankfurt presaged a happy and secure future of academic labour which would bring with it an increasingly pleasant social existence. The storm clouds that spelt the end of his days in Germany had, however, already appeared on the horizon. As the 1920s wore on, the National Socialist Movement grew in strength and influence. By the end of the decade, the threat it posed was sufficient to persuade Tillich that he could no longer afford to keep the Social Democrat Party at arm's length and in 1929 he became a member, though never a very active one. Parallel with this was his other piece of political involvement: together with others he supported the creation of a new journal, *Neue Blätter für Sozialismus* (New Pages for Socialism). He contributed an article to its first issue under the title 'Socialism'. From this point on, he was on a collision course with National Socialism, however much his capacity for, and love of, theory and abstraction made him seem to be living in an ivory tower. He showed his colours in 1932 in a letter he sent to the Berlin Wingolf Fraternity in which he criticized their ostracism of left-wing students and Jews as anti-Christian. The letter had no effect and Tillich resigned from the fraternity. By this time, he was already a power in Frankfurt, having been made Dean of the philosophical faculty. In July 1932, Nazism revealed its horrible character all too publicly, as Stormtroopers and Nazi students created a disturbance and attacked Jewish students. Theodor Adorno had been appealing to Tillich for a clearer and more definite rejection of Nazism than his hitherto rather theoretical and vague pronouncements. This stimulated him to produce what became his significant contribution to the political debate in pre-war Germany: his book *The Socialist Decision*. It was the decisive public expression of what he had been saying in different ways and in various contexts: it declared his opposition to the political romanticism of both Communism and National Socialism. Throughout the 1920s, he had described capitalism as demonic; now he pronounced it to be beyond redemption. The need was for a Socialism that would prevent the collapse of European civilization into barbarism. Seeing the European world whole and seeing it clearly, he said that both faith and realism called for 'the socialist decision'.

After Hitler's rise to power in 1933, *The Socialist Decision* and *New Pages for Socialism* were banned, and, by March, Tillich was specifically listed by the government as 'unreliable'. The following month, he was listed amongst the professors to be dismissed. Suddenly he was without employment or any prospects of employment. He decided, however, to stay in Frankfurt, hoping against hope that he could influence developments and perhaps help to restore some sanity. He was sufficiently frightened to make plans for the security of his daughter, and his situation became more ominous with the threat posed by an official instruction that he should not leave Germany. In May, the books on the Nazi blacklist were publicly burned.

At that very time, his American future was being planned. American academics were alive to the dangerous turn of events in Germany, and in New York a group of intellectuals discussed the plight of their German counterparts. The President of Union Theological Seminary, Henry Sloane Coffin, seeing Tillich's name on a list of these Nazi victims, offered to give him a temporary post in Union Seminary if the Columbia University philosophy department would also employ him. Reinhold Niebuhr, whose brother Richard had translated Tillich's *Beyond Socialism*, was deputed to extend the invitation and it was accepted. The nerve-racking flight from Germany has been recounted by Hannah Tillich: after months of uncertainty and fear which had driven them from Dresden to Berlin for their last few weeks, the end of October saw Tillich and his family leaving Germany. The Atlantic crossing was stormy but they arrived safely in New York on 3 November 1933. The following morning, they were taken to Union Seminary to be welcomed by Ursula Niebuhr (Reinhold's wife) and President Coffin. Though he had been forced to flee from Germany, Tillich had hoped that his academic position was secure. So it was with deep disappointment that he received a letter from the Nazi Minister of Culture informing him that he was deprived of any official position. He protested at some length, but in June 1934 he was informed that the decision was final. By late summer, it was clear that he could no longer hope for an improvement in the German situation—Germany was completely in the Nazi grip. Loyal German as he was, Tillich threw himself into vocal protest against Nazism and support of its opponents. Many find something of a contradiction between the very political figure that Tillich was during his German period and the vague, even ambiguous, attitude he exemplified throughout his American years. They can justly point to the Hamlet side of his character—thought more than conscience crippling his motivation to act. There is no doubt too that Tillich demonstrated a rare chameleon-like quality, to a very large extent taking his colour from his context. Yet the easy criticism fails to grasp the profound sorrow of this latter-day Abraham and his keen sense that, welcoming as America was, it was not *his* land.

Early in 1934, Tillich began to teach in New York. Though his position in Union was only on an annual basis until 1937—and even then only for a three-year tenure—he was gradually established in the city, largely through the interest and good offices of John Herman Randall Jr. His lectures were popular with students. One suspects that their appeal was largely to curiosity; for dimly as the students grasped the interest of his reinterpretation of doctrine, expressed in language that would be utterly strange to them, they could not fail to register the excitement of this strange mixture of passion and abstraction.

Visiting Europe in 1936 for the first time since his emigration, Tillich had the opportunity of making contact with many friends and also the last opportunity of a long telephone conversation with his father, who died the following year. He later published the diary he kept of this visit and *My Travel Diary 1936—Between Two Worlds* gives one of the fullest pictures of Tillich the man and the thinker. In those pages, the whole man is found: his love of food and wine, his delight in friends old and new, in places visited and, above all, in the lectures and speeches he delivered. Then, more than ever, he tried to rally European thought and opinion in opposition to Nazism, warning afresh that Nazism could spell the death of European culture. On his return to America, he felt saddened as he reflected on the inevitability of war; but, characteristically, he looked forward to the possibility of reconstruction after another European destruction. An example of this confidence in the future is to be found in his work on behalf of German émigrés with the organization called Self-help for Emigrés from Central Europe, which continued for many years. As the war clouds lowered, he made a rare public appeal for German Americans to support the destruction of Nazism. He became an American citizen in 1940, and was made a full Professor at Union Theological Seminary, and the long succession of American honours began with an honorary DD from Yale. In the early 1940s, he regularly broadcast to Germany on the need for religious resistance to Nazism and the hope for a new order. The same urgent effort was seen in his chairmanship of the Council for a Democratic Germany, which published a statement urging the disarmament of Germany and the economic and political reintegration of Germany with Europe. He tried to persuade President Roosevelt of the desirability of German reconstruction; but neither during nor after the war was Roosevelt prepared to accept such a policy.

Once the war ended, Tillich looked forward to revisiting Germany, and the opportunity came with the invitation from the Universities of Marburg and Frankfurt to give lectures there and elsewhere. He lectured there and in several places, visited France, Switzerland and England, and enjoyed many reunions with friends such as Karl Barth (1886–1968), K. L. Schmidt and Emmanuel Hirsch. The reunion with Hirsch was probably the most moving, for Hirsch was a friend of very long standing; but Tillich had broken with him because of Hirsch's support of Hitler (there had in fact been a bitter exchange of open letters between them on this subject). Now Hirsch had been forced to retire and Tillich's visit was a kindness the memory of which Hirsch long cherished. Being in Germany once more, Tillich pressed home the problem of anti-Semitism as a special one for German Christianity. That particular discussion apart, he was enormously popular, and, not surprisingly, there were several invitations to return to one or other university in Germany. Despite his anxiety to play a part in the political development of Germany, however, he decided to return to America.

When he made this return visit to Germany, Tillich was already a well-established literary figure: he was now indeed an English author. Since 1934, he had published quite regularly in American periodicals and journals and in 1936 *The Interpretation of History* had been published in New York and London. Thanks to the efforts of the late James Luther Adams, a similar collection of papers, including his American productions, was published in 1948 as *The Protestant Era*. In the same year *The Shaking of the Foundations* was published, a work which revealed Tillich's remarkable power as a preacher and one which was to have a powerful influence on popular theology in Britain as a result of John Robinson's use of Tillich's thought in his celebrated little book *Honest to God*. From this point onwards, almost to the very end of his life, Tillich was a prodigious, if not indeed a prolific, writer known on both sides of the Atlantic. After a spate of articles in various kinds of periodicals, the first volume of *Systematic Theology* appeared in 1951; and it did not have to wait until its publication in London two years later in order to be known in Britain. My own knowledge of Tillich was minimal indeed when in 1952 I went to New York and began my studies in Union Seminary. Because volume 1 of *Systematic Theology* was available,

Tillich gave the first part of his course in systematic theology as seminars rather than lectures. Thus it was that I and many others (the class numbering something like a hundred, some of whom had come from the four corners of the world) studied those topics.

Early in 1952, the Terry Lectures, which Tillich had given in Yale in 1950, were published as *The Courage to Be*. This very interesting analysis of the ontology of ethics reveals the extent to which Tillich's views had changed. Profoundly influenced as he had been by the Marxist background to the political engagement of his early career in Germany, he had now for a long time been as interested in other formative influences on contemporary thought beside Marx— notably Freud (1856–1939). In the 1940s, he had become friendly with Karen Horney and at the same time sought a more consistent and humane application of Freud's psychology as a method of historical analysis—once again one sees the way in which his thinking was naturally and inevitably a generalization. In a sense, *The Courage to Be* shows Tillich standing where he stood in his preaching: that is, he spoke in prophetic and not merely in philosophical mode. This was his prophetic word to America. Pondering the word 'courage' (his theology being very often launched in this way by a quasi-etymological study of words), he made free with his erudition before launching into a historical analysis of anxiety and a characterization of modern anxiety. The state of anxiety is to be overcome by courage; at which point in his general argument Tillich produces an analysis of the individual and society which is a remarkable amalgam of sociology, psychology and philosophy. Here, more than anywhere, he appears as the Existentialist philosopher he was often taken to be.

Almost every following year saw a new book by Tillich. The Firth Lectures (a series he inaugurated in Nottingham in 1952) appeared as the slim volume *Love, Power and Justice* in 1954. This brief but highly suggestive ontological analysis revealed Tillich's extraordinary capacity for plunging into concrete issues as he marched forward in abstract argument. As a result, though it was hardly influential, this little book was found by many to be a most useful introduction to his thought. The book that followed in 1955, *Biblical Religion and the Search for Ultimate Reality* (the James W. Richard Lectures, given in the University of Virginia in 1951–52), was in many ways much the more accessible and is probably the clearest statement Tillich gave of the position he had established in volume 1 of *Systematic Theology* concerning the necessary interrelation or 'complementarity' of philosophy and theology. The success of *The Shaking of the Foundations* led to the publication of more sermons in the volume *The New Being*, which appeared in 1955. Meanwhile, Tillich had delivered the Gifford Lectures in the University of Aberdeen in 1953 and had for this purpose been engaged in the final formulation of the remainder of his *Systematic Theology*. Part III of the system was published as volume 2 in 1957 and Part IV was published as volume 3 in 1964. In the same year as volume 2's publication, Tillich published *The Dynamics of Faith*; and this, like *Ultimate Concern: Tillich in Dialogue*, which had appeared the year before (1956), was a popular summary of his basic theology.

It is interesting to reflect that towards the end of his career Tillich once more returned to the theme of culture. 'Theology of culture' was the umbrella under which an important collection of articles was gathered: *Theology of Culture*, published in 1959.

The final work to be mentioned to complete this account of Tillich's career as thinker and writer is *Christianity and the Encounter of the World Religions* (1963), a work which for many represents yet another turning-point in Tillich's life. He delivered the Bampton Lectures at Columbia University, New York in autumn 1961. They appear here in the form that they were delivered, as he decided when he prepared them for publication. The book was dedicated 'To Professor Yasaka Takagi who made my trip to Japan possible', and in the Preface's concluding paragraph, Tillich expressed the hope that his ideas 'would arouse critical thoughts not only with respect to the relation of Christianity to the world religions but also with respect to its own nature'. Some scholars have suggested that, as a result of his Japanese experience, Tillich was led to a radical rethinking of his theology and that, had he lived, he would have progressed to a quite new position. What lends this view the little credibility it possesses is the fact that Tillich's last public words comprise the lecture delivered only ten days before his death entitled 'The significance of the history of religions for the systematic theologian'. This is a matter to which I shall return later.

The story is nearly concluded, and the catalogue of Tillich's publications has nicely indicated how he had become something of a globe-trotter in the last ten years of his life. He himself felt some unease about this, being moved by a reference in *Time* magazine to Harvard's 'wandering professors' to justify himself in a letter to Dean Pusey. This was one aspect of the great fame he had now achieved and there is no doubt that it was one of its many benefits which he greatly enjoyed. Honours had been heaped upon him, including the University Professorship at Harvard, to which he was appointed on his retirement from Union Seminary in 1965 (he had already been granted an honorary DLitt by Harvard in the previous year). As well as the many honorary degrees granted by American universities, honorary doctorates were also conferred on him by the Universities of Glasgow and Berlin. Prizes and medals were also gathered: the Goethe Medal of Frankfurt; the Great Order of Merit of the West German Republic (presented to him personally in Washington by the German Ambassador in 1956); the Hanseatic Goethe Prize in 1958; and in 1962 the coveted Peace Prize of the German Publishers' Association.

Tillich's travels were most often associated with his lecturing engagements, such as the Schelling centenary celebrations, the Gifford Lectures, the Tokyo and Kyoto exchange lectures. He visited many parts of the world during these years, and it goes without saying that his experience of Japan was the most impressive and also the most meaningful. Visits to temples gave him the opportunity of not only cultural but also religious experience, as he took part in the ritual and had discussions with monks and spiritual masters, especially the Zen Master Hisamatsu Shin'ichi, with whom he had had conversations in Harvard in 1957. Without going any further into the question of whether his travels in Asia and experience of Asian religion led Tillich to change his theological perspective, it can be said that he came away with a profound appreciation of what he had seen. It confirmed what he had always advocated: that understanding religion meant destroying the concept of 'religion'. In an article in *Christian Century* which was typically entitled 'On the boundary line', he reaffirmed his rejection of any attempt to divide the world's religions 'into one true and many false religions' because the criterion of religion's truth was 'a love which unconditionally affirms, judges and receives the other person'.

As honour followed honour, so celebrations jostled with public appearances. To a very large extent, Tillich's last years were ones of social lionization. There is no doubt too that the pride which had always been as characteristic of him as his gentleness became more obvious. He had always been very quick in expression of self-defence and very sensitive to criticism. My own first experience of him revealed this, as he responded to a critical article with the outburst 'You are personally hostile to me'; but at the close of that discussion he inscribed my copy of *The Courage to Be* with the quotation from Nietzsche 'A good fight justifies every cause'. In that whirligig of lectures, celebrations and entertainment which constituted his final years, he was more and more prone to vanity, greedily accepting the plaudits and overblown praise which people heaped on him. Yet the gentleness shone through, as I discovered in my final conversation with him in Union Seminary in September 1965. He remained ambiguous and paradoxical to the end. On the one hand, he displayed that quite unconscious and certainly un-self-conscious egocentricity which had always been typical of him. On the other hand, he showed himself to be extremely generous. With a rare touch of humour, he said that he wanted to compliment me on being one of the few people to understand his thought, adding 'The trouble with you is that you do not agree with me'. As we parted, he promised that if I sent him an invitation to visit Durham he would come and said 'All I want is the invitation and I shall be there. I do not need to be paid'. All was in place when the news came that he had died on 22 October 1965. His ashes were first buried in East Hampton but were finally re-interred in the Paul Tillich Park which had been created by Mrs Kenneth Dale Owen, the wife of Robert Owen's great-grand-son.

Tillich was many things: a political fighter and not simply a political thinker, a preacher of extraordinary charisma and power (who often boasted that he did not go to church), a strangely attractive teacher, a profound scholar whose learning was so imbued with the dynamic of his own thought that, Midas-like, whatever he touched was turned into the gold of his systematic vision. Above all, to all who ever saw and knew him, he will remain a presence. In a review of Rollo May's compassionate memoir, and of Hannah Tillich's pained account of her life with Tillich, Harvey Cox remarked that they recreated for him Tillich's amazing presence and his capacity to invest simple words with huge meaning. He recalled that, having arrived late at the seminar Tillich held in Harvard, he explained that his first child had just been born. Tillich stopped the class and, with unusual warmth, asked the child's name. On being told that it was Rachel, he nodded and, his face now wreathed in smile, said 'Rachel. Ah, yes, the breath of God'. He paused and added 'That is a good name, a good name'. As Cox said, what from anyone else might have been a trivial remark, from Tillich 'sounded like a benediction'. That presence is felt in so much of his work and it gives life to his thought that is so often formal, abstract and even contrived. He once remarked that he could not understand why people found his book *The Courage to Be* difficult because, having re-read it, he thought it read like a novel. This probably says more about the kind of novels he read than it does about anything else.

2

Theology, Revolution and Culture

When Tillich began his theological studies, his view of the nature and purpose of theology would have reflected the very traditional and conservative notions of his father. But by the time he began his career as a professional theologian, he was a changed man with a changed outlook. He had returned from the war with the scars of mental suffering and with a quite radically changed social outlook. Also changed was his perception of the area of revelation: that great 'one moment of beauty' had taught him that a religious revelation was to be found in any great art, not merely art which had as its subject something religious. It is this double extension of Tillich's own spiritual horizons that gives his earliest work its peculiar thrust and flavour of radicalism. His first public lecture was the famous lecture to the Kant Society in Berlin, 'On the idea of a theology of culture'; and it was typical of him that he should have chosen that context for his definition of the programme which he wanted to map out not simply for his own career as a theologian but also for the very discipline of theology itself. Throughout his life's work he remained very much in thrall to Kant (1724–1804), so that in a conversation with me during the last summer of his life he remarked 'Of course I am a Kantian—scratch any German and you will find a Kantian'. Typical too is his concentration on the idea; for, as has been pointed out by commentators, the title reflects the Platonic sense of 'idea' (what something really is, the proper exemplification of whatever it is that we have in mind). Already he was displaying how his wide learning was being refashioned in his own thinking to produce a world of thought so complex in its composition and so diverse in its sources that it could easily be dismissed as contradictory. Abstractly intellectual its subject might be, but it was for Tillich very concrete and of immediate practical relevance. His intention was to address the situation in which he and his generation now found themselves. A bloody war had ended and the innocent hopes and beliefs of those who had gone happily to war had been bitterly betrayed. Now 'the whole house was in ruins'; and if the church had been partly responsible for that, the problem of how to construe the task of theology was as urgent as it was difficult. What was equally important was that Tillich's cast of mind was now very different: intellectually as well as spiritually he had gained a clearer vision of things. In the trenches he had read Nietzsche's *Thus Spake Zarathustra* and it had not only restored his flagging spirits but had also confirmed his growing distaste for bourgeois hypocrisy. All this was evidently in his mind, as the pages of the lecture show.

It is tempting to begin characterizing Tillich's theology by describing it as a theology of culture, to be distinguished as such from the theology of his friend Karl Barth. In many ways, that has, in fact, been his fate as a theologian and this fundamental contrast has led to a misinterpretation of both theologies. This simple opposition of the two theologies has been an unfortunate misinterpretation of both—Barth's as much as Tillich's. As was pointed out by Barth's best British expositor, T. F. Torrance, Barth's protest was not against culture but against a simplistic correlation of Christianity and culture. Likewise Tillich was as concerned to spell out a theological critique of culture as he was to rediscover the vitality of theology in an engagement with culture. Therefore it is necessary to look carefully at Tillich's argument in this lecture.

In the first of its four sections, he is concerned with theology and philosophy of religion. These are systematic cultural sciences and in such sciences the standpoint of the thinker is integral to the very object of the enquiry. Here, says Tillich, the thinker is part of the very history of culture and he distinguishes between a purely *a priori* philosophy and what Kant would have called the *a priori* synthetic knowledge where attention is focused on the concrete particular. That is, philosophy pure and simple is not concerned with what kind of world confronts us, but the theologian and the student of religion must obviously be so concerned. But there is too a third kind of study: 'normative-cultural science which brings the concrete study to a systematic expression' (VS, p. 20). Throughout his life Tillich showed a fondness for threefold distinctions and, as is often the case, that is not particularly helpful here. Implicit in the title of this section is a distinction between two kinds of intellectual activity: doing theology is different from doing philosophy of religion. Fortunately Tillich goes on to clarify his understanding of that distinction by invoking the analogy of moral philosophy. Just as, he thinks, one can discuss morality by asking 'What is morality?' or by asking the different question 'What is moral?', so the philosopher of religion asks a different question from that asked by the theologian. It would seem then that he is distinguishing between a descriptive account of some behaviour and the kind of discussion which evaluates this or that piece of behaviour in the way that is typical of that whole pattern of behaviour. 'Theology therefore is the concrete normative science of religion' (ibid.).

What is important for Tillich is to reintroduce Kant's rejection of the idea that theology is some super-science which can yield knowledge of something which is otherwise unknown because it is heavenly rather than earthly. That notion of theology, he thinks, has gone: theology has been made concrete. In the sense, then, that theology is a science of religion it is concerned with something in the world but it is concerned with it as a systematic study of the norm of religion. So, from this stress on the empirical, Tillich turns to the very life-blood of religion, its conviction that there is a revelation. But once more he insists that we must remember that both logic and religion make the flight to an unworldly abstraction quite wrong. That is to say, theology after Kant cannot proceed as if it were some kind of observational account of the supernatural. Kant had insisted that our knowledge is limited to the world of sense and all claims about what can be known about a world beyond that were a misunderstanding of the scope of reason. Equally, a theology which had been taught by Schleiermacher (1768–1834) and Wilhelm Herrmann (1846–1922) that its roots lay in that inner movement of the soul would reject any notion of its object as purely other-worldly.

In protesting against a supernatural understanding of theology, Tillich would seem to be talking very much as the product of Liberalism. The Liberal theologians could be said to be heirs of Kant, for they saw the essence of Christianity to be ethical: for several of them this meant that it was concerned with social change, and for all of them it meant that Christianity had to be reinterpreted in terms consistent with modern science. The contention that the theologian does not go beyond his own standpoint would not have seemed very different from the Liberal stress that theology was concerned with human experience and its apparently other-worldly assertions capable of being understood as a new morality. However, Tillich soon makes clear that his view of theology is not at all the same as this rationalist theology. Indebted to Kant his theology might be; but it is not, as with Kant, subservient to morality. By the same token, he wanted to distinguish his view of theology from Hegel's, according to which theology is some crude form of rational speculative thought which finds its proper expression in metaphysics. Theology is more than rationalism because it is controlled by the concrete standpoint of history. 'History' is the refrain that sounds through all this first section of Tillich's lecture. Without such a concrete basis, every philosophical concept is empty. Philosophy of culture and the normative systematics of culture 'belong together and stand in correlation' (VS, p. 21). This concept of correlation is one we shall meet again; but it is worth emphasizing that this too would have sounded to his audience the kind of thinking made familar by Liberalism.

It is important to recognize that Tillich does not offer any explanation of the term 'correlation' here, so that it is probably a mistake to look for any understanding of correlation as the methodological principle which was to characterize his developed theology. A more likely meaning of what he says is that he was anxious to present theology as a discipline which belonged equally to the class of reflective investigations like philosophy and among those practical disciplines such as ethics and politics. The use of the word 'empty' is, I feel, an echo of Kant. Just as Kant had seen knowledge to be the combined activity of the categories of understanding and the manifold of sense, so Tillich is insisting that merely manipulating the concepts that had been traditionally the stuff of theology was to produce a variety of rational abstraction that had nothing to do with concrete religion. It is not easy, if indeed possible, to clarify this understanding of theology. What is clear is that here Tillich is protesting against what he sees to be the besetting sin of theology, that it becomes entirely occupied with its own concepts and ceases to have any relevance to the social situation which is its context. He is pinning his colours to the mast, saying that he wants to stand where his fellows stand and do theology as an intellectual activity that is itself a cultural creation as well as a cultural inspiration.

Not surprisingly, then, Tillich goes on to discuss the way in which theology had in the recent past been understood: theology was a tripartite study—apologetics, dogmatics and ethics. Likewise, it is theological ethics which engages his attention. This he declares to be passé, made out of date by cultural change which had reduced the significance of the church as a social community. Such a study would now be as much of a cultural curiosity as a theological aesthetic. So he says boldly that his claim is: '*what until recently was the intention of theological ethics can only find fulfillment in a theology of culture which is related not only to ethics but to every cultural function*' (VS, pp. 22–3). In passing, it is worth noting that while he is consciously advocating a departure from the traditional style of a theological ethics, he does not reject its *intention*. Interesting too is his silent dismissal from consideration of apologetics and church dogmatics, not least because when he comes to write his *Systematic Theology*, he presents his system of theology as both apologetic in intention and ecclesiastical in point of departure and content. This confirms us in our view that the 1919 Tillich was seeking a radically new kind of *theology*. This theology, as a theology of culture, will fulfil the intention of theological ethics because it will show that necessary overlap of theology and social existence which theological ethics as ethics reveals. That is, instead of the theologian attending to the thought and concerns of a separated group, he will look upon every cultural function as relevant. Mention has already been made of the way in which Tillich's understanding of revelation had been changed and widened by the 'one moment of beauty'. If revelation is thus possible outside some narrowly delimited ecclesiastical context, so the *religious* function of theologizing must be similarly unconfined. The theologian must discover his discipline's determinative concept 'outside the camp', as the phrase of Scripture puts it.

We are led on to what has generally been taken to be Tillich's main argument about a theology of culture: the relation of religion to culture. Here again he harks back to Kant and Schleiermacher but this time couples them with Hegel (1770–1831). The three represent misleading ways of understanding the nature of religion and its relation with culture. For Hegel, religion belonged to the theoretical faculty; for Kant, it belonged to the practical, while for Schleiermacher it was a matter of feeling. Of these, Schleiermacher's seems to Tillich the most plausible, but even he was wrong. Religion is no simple feeling but the complex unity of feeling, theory and practice. Tillich does not argue this point but contents himself with a brief exposition of what he means by religion; and this suggests that he realized that his description of it so far had been neither precise nor well-defended. It is, he says, 'the experience of the unconditioned and this means the experience of absolute reality, founded on the experience of absolute nothingness' (VS, p. 24). This is not an experience of something extra, a particular thing that is unlike the rest of the things we know in being absolute. It is the experience of the reality of the world as something so fundamental that compared with it the very elements of the world can only be described as nothing—'throughout everything the reality forces itself upon us that is simultaneously a No and a Yes to things' (VS, pp. 24–5). Tillich expressly uses the language of mysticism: 'what is beyond being, what is simultaneously and absolutely nothing and some-thing' (VS, p. 25). From this it is clear that we cannot speak of a particular or special religious sphere of culture. This releases us from the old conflict between science and religion and between ethics and religion. The very possibility of conflict has been removed.

What, then, is this theology of culture? In defining this, Tillich uses concepts that will become very important for his developed theological system—the concepts of autonomy, heteronomy and theonomy. As always, Tillich proceeds in an idiosyncratic manner; and rather than indicating that his use of the opposition of autonomy and heteronomy is derived from Kant's moral philoso-phy, he merely says that the autonomy of cultural forms is estab-lished in their forms. So for him the difference between autonomy and theonomy is in the relation between their basis in form and, on the other hand, in substance. Having said this, he later enunciates the principle: 'the more form the more autonomy, the more substance the more theonomy'. However, to gain some grasp of what he means, we need to remember that for Kant the very nature of morality was its being a free response of obedience to the Categorical Imperative (the Command of Duty) which we rationally recognize. Hence, he says, morality can be construed as a law that I lay upon myself and so it can be defined as autonomous (the self's own law). Heteronomy, by contrast, is the command that the other person (*ho heteros*) lays upon me and is the kind of thing that we readily recognize as the law of the land. That I should drive my car at no speed higher than 30 miles an hour is what the law of the land enacts; but my duty to relieve the suffering of humanity is something which no government or social group or anyone other than myself requires of me. With that distinction in mind, Tillich seems to regard autonomy as the characteristic of any *free* action—not just moral action but any action that is my choice and so expressive of my human creativity. Perhaps it is because of this preoccupation with creativity that he views autonomy as a matter of form: 'the autonomy of the cultural functions is established in their form' (VS, p. 26). With this is contrasted the relation of theonomy to substance; but this contrast does not afford any clarification of what is meant by theonomy. To grasp that we need to remember the distinction between autonomy and heteronomy and its Kantian roots. If that lies in the difference between a law which is my own enactment and one which has nothing to do with my nature and interests (with the former being alone a moral law), then we can see that there might be a law which, though it is another's, is nevertheless that of my own nature. In other words, though this would be a law enacted by God because it is God's creation, it is identical with my nature, so that whether or not it is my creation becomes an irrelevant issue.

Rather like an abstract painter, Tillich reduces these three possibilities to the relations of pattern. Whereas Kant had been anxious to point out simply that no action was moral unless it was my own free response as a rational being to the Categorical Imperative of Practical Reason, Tillich is concerned with the character of the more general activity of humanity that we call culture. Kant is often, indeed generally, criticized as having developed a system of ethics that is too formal; but in a sense, though he considers only the rational person as such by contrast with Tillich's emphasis on cultural functions, Tillich's concern with the latter is even more formalist than Kant.

To return to the distinction, what we should note is that Tillich has little to say about heteronomy; but in the development of the argument up to this point, and also here, it is clear that for Tillich, just as much as for Kant, heteronomy is the mark of an action that is not properly moral. Furthermore, just as he has widened Kant's concept of autonomy, so he significantly widens that of heteronomy by concentrating on the aspect of domination by an extraneous authority. For Kant, any consideration other than the rational demand of duty was not a proper moral motive. That can be seen as Tillich's starting-point for his equally negative estimate of heteronomy; and then he goes on to reject any such external authority. This is what makes these pages read like a revolutionary manifesto despite the very formalism that has just been noted. By presenting some kind of purely formal account of man's creative world, Tillich is nevertheless appealing to all men as free spirits to assume the responsibility of the free creation of their cultural world. The formal description is, then, the enunciation of some kind of scientific law: 'the more form, the more autonomy, the more substance the more theonomy' (VS, p. 26). The two aspects are for Tillich interrelated because—again like Kant's conceptual forms—pure form without substance is empty and there can be no substance which does not have form. For this reason, his own analogy of a line at one end of which is pure form, and at the other end pure substance, is quite wrong. There is no such thing as pure form. His point, however, is that sometimes the form is inadequate as an expression of the reality it contains, so that the very strains and tensions of expression are the form that properly express the substance.

The task of the theology of culture is not essentially different from what had classically been identified as theology's task; but Tillich defines it with reference to the essential structure of the cultural expression of religion. That is, whereas the traditional starting-point had been a particular ecclesiastical confession reference to which gave theology its distinctive character, he sees theology emerging from the fact of religion within culture. If form and substance are the polarities of the life of freedom, what the theologian must seek to do is to map and indeed express that tension; and one clear difference between the theologian and the philosopher of culture is that the theologian does this from the standpoint of substance as the theonomous element. In a trinitarian fashion that is very characteristic of his approach, Tillich describes this task thus: '(1) A general religious analysis of culture, (2) A religious typology and philosophy of the history of culture, (3) A concrete religious systematization of culture' (VS, p. 27). The language is somewhat academic and forbidding—but there is no mistaking the very human and catholic thrust of this thinking. Theology is no longer to be thought of as concerned with only the history of the church or even of some wider aspect of Christian history. It is culture as a whole that is the object of study, and religion in general, not a particular confession that is the inspiration of that study. What is perhaps even more radical is the apparent suggestion that the traditional method of validating theology must give way to a more anthropological methodology.

At this point in his argument, Tillich makes a distinction that has caused great difficulty. Substance, he says, is different from content. No explanation of this distinction is given beyond saying that substance signifies the meaning, 'the spiritual substantiality, from which alone form receives its significance' (ibid.). Characteristic of

Tillich's method of argument throughout his whole work is this intuitive grasp of a principle which then becomes the basis for further assertions, all of which are perfectly valid assertions as inferences from that basic premiss. The relation of content, substance and form seems to be something like this: the content of any culture is whatever happens to be the case at any particular time; but the substance of that culture is something that belongs not to the accidents of history but to the eternal nature of spiritual existence. Inevitably and necessarily that is given a form—and this in and by the content. Just as the very title of the lecture had a Platonic ring to it, so here there is a view of the nature of thought and reality that echoes Plato's notion of eternal verities of which this world is a shadow. Yet perhaps it is more to the point to grasp that what animates Tillich's vision of theology of culture is exactly that sense of abiding presence which is expressed in the text 'Jesus Christ the same yesterday today and for ever'. Moreover, it is the same global and cosmic vision as that of the Epistle to the Hebrews, where it must be said that there is the same Platonic understanding of the relation between the shadows of this world and the realities of the eternal world. What becomes clear then is that content is to be viewed as something ephemeral in relation to the substance, and the first task of the theologian of culture is seen to be that of demonstrating this dialectic of form and substance. Theology of culture must show the way in which the content of culture is not the necessary form of the substance. This negative task, however, is counterbalanced by the positive one of discerning the 'substance' of religious reality. It must, in short, take up the dominical challenge of reading the signs of the times even to the point of recognizing that the servant of the Lord is a heathen emperor and not the chosen nation.

Moving on to the second task, Tillich once again offers a trinitarian formula by saying that three points could be distinguished on the linking line between form and substance. In its task of constructing a typology of cultural creation, theology of culture distinguishes three types. First, there is the completely secular kind of cultural creation which lies as it were on the form end of the line— that is, it emphasizes form. Secondly, there is the cultural creation which is typically a religious matter and is to be seen as a predominance of substance. Finally, there is the classical type of culture where form and substance are balanced in harmony. The model of the line thus gives Tillich his view of 'the three decisive points'. Despite its mathematical terminology, the model owes more to chemistry than to mathematics and Tillich himself seems to have appreciated that the model was rather confusing when he admits that the variety of forms of concrete religion must make the typology 'unusually diverse'. Because it is more chemistry than mathematics and is thus really the model of classifying what might be called organic types, the model of the line is not really very helpful. If we leave this refinement of the argument to one side, it is clear that what Tillich wants to emphasize is the contemporary nature of theology of culture. The theologian of culture relates the general typology to the present and so takes up a more concrete issue than the formal one of classification. Distinguishing between types is indeed part of what he has to do; but primarily he has to decide, when confronted with possibilities, where he himself stands in relation to the culture of the present.

The third task is the religious systematization of culture which is clearly the distinctively theological contribution to the cultural sciences; for theology has already been defined as the formal expression of a concrete religious standpoint. Immediately, however, Tillich raises queries and problems. How can the theologian do this? He explains the problem by reverting to his distinction between form and substance. If the theologian were to effect a systematization from the point of view of form, this would be an illicit rejection of other forms, what Tillich calls a 'heteronomous encroachment upon culture' (VS, p. 28). Indeed, he seems to view this as nothing short of a betrayal of the theologian's vocation: the theologian's standpoint must relate to substance. Yet substance, as we have seen, can only appear in form as substance with a particular form, something which is expressed in this or that form. That being so, says Tillich, we must concede that 'the theologian of culture is not directly culturally creative' (ibid.). This is not very clear because Tillich is spelling out what would appear to be a cultural activity rather than denying the possibility of such. He seems to suggest that a theology of culture would not be a discipline like the science of physics or ethics or jurisprudence, and his point can then be construed as an emphasis on the methodological nature of this study. That is, it is a matter of saying not that there is no such study, but that the study does not produce new information or knowledge but is concerned with how some such knowledge is gained. Yet while very obviously emphasizing the critical role of theology of culture, he is anxious to affirm its positive contribution.

The theologian of culture looks at a particular culture and points to the mirage of possibility which it presents because it is not a proper expression of the substance that it contains. The theologian of culture is indeed very much like Matthew Arnold's picture of Goethe as the physician who takes the sick nineteenth century in his hand and says 'Thou ailest here! Thou ailest there!' The important thing for Tillich is that in this way the theologian is showing the possibility of a theonomous culture, but is not elevating a particular creation to that status merely on the basis that it has a religious source. It must earn its authority as theonomous culture. The systematic task of the theologian of culture is thus very circumscribed; but it is precisely that limitation, says Tillich, which gives universal significance to his work. That universal significance is more than the cultural range of his work as he comprehends any and every culture within his purview. The importance of this for Tillich is that, in this way, the opposition of religion and culture, which has been so culturally destructive, will be overcome. In other words, by abdicating from the status of some external authority that judges culture, and by taking its place alongside other cultural forms, thus accepting its own cultural formation, the theology of culture can be seen to have the right to pronounce on culture from its own proper standpoint.

Conscious of the revolutionary attitude he was expressing, toward the end of his lecture Tillich faced the question of the relation of a theology of culture to a theology of the church or a church-based theology. To what extent, he asked, did there remain a special sphere of the sacred? His answer is that there does and there will remain such a separate sphere; but while that assertion is clear enough, his reasons for the judgement are complicated and unclear. One argument is that, though we never find the sacred apart from its concrete expression in the secular, the two are quite distinct concepts. In that case, he is saying that though we are talking about the same facts and situation we must still ask whether and where the concept of the sacred applies. A slightly different argument is that culture, however secular it may be, will contain substance and will thus gain a religious quality and become a religious culture. The discussion is complicated still further by Tillich's attempt to spell out the brave new world of theology in which it is faithful to its heritage as well as its vocation but lives in and speaks to the newly-changed world of the post-war period. The first two arguments are probably Tillich's very abstract way of working out some formal description of this final argument, which is very clearly the kind of vision that animated Tillich as he worked within the contexts of church and university— not forgetting the social situation which was increasingly in his mind. As against either some simple opposition of church and world, or what was for him the now untenable position of traditional Protestantism, which distinguished between the relativity of history and the absolute knowledge of supernatural revelation, the future belongs to a third way. This too is explained in rather a complicated fashion; but essentially it is a positive relation of complementarity between a theology of culture and a church theology. The church theologian is more conservative, controlled by his inheritance, whereas the theologian of culture 'stands freely within the living cultural movement, open not only to every other form but also to every new spirit' (VS, p. 37).

Perhaps, as he thus expressed his vision of the future theologian as some Ariel-like spirit or almost a Scholar Gipsy, Tillich took fright, for he instantly spoke of the danger that the theologian of culture faced. The danger was that he would become a fashionable prophet of dubious development. However, though Tillich thus conceded that this vision of theology was capable of being self-destructive, he was convinced that the correlation should be a unity. In other words, the future of theology for him was the development of a new kind of theology which was more open in its attitude to culture and not confined to some rigidly defined horizon. It is in that spirit that he concludes the lecture by speaking of the theological faculties. Other faculties naturally mistrust them, he says, for two reasons: the definition of theology as scientific knowledge of a supernatural being, and the authoritative claims of a limited ecclesiastical confession. These two objections disappear if religion and theology are understood in the way he has sought to clarify. The theological faculties would be a powerhouse for the regeneration of culture. In a fine closing peroration, Tillich contrasts the unhappy history of the previous two centuries with the challenge that confronted theology.

Theology ... must once more take the offensive after abandoning the last remaining of its indefensible culturally heteronomous positions. It must fight under the standard of theonomy, and under this standard it will triumph, not over the autonomy of culture, but over the secularizing, emptying and ruin of culture that has taken place during the most recent human epoch. It will conquer, for, as Hegel says, religion is the beginning and the end of everything just as it is the centre that gives life, soul, and spirit to all things. (VS, p. 39)

So Tillich confronted the ruined world of Europe with a vision of theology as free, radical and decidedly constructive intellectual force.

One very important feature of the new stance which he adopted and advocated was Tillich's welcome of what he called 'the new cultural unity that is arising on socialist soil' (ibid.). There was such a unity, he thought, because for socialism, just as much as for religion, an individualism that ignores the demands of the community is to be rejected as destructive of culture. As we have seen, Tillich was by this time much involved with the Independent Social Democrats and was part of the groundswell in the movement for Christian Socialism. Dissociating himself from the armchair liberal reform which he saw amongst intellectuals, he called for something more than reform and identified himself with the work of the Kairos Circle, of which he became a leading theorist for the next few years. It was a time of urgent engagement with problems which he recognized were matters of cultural life and death. *Kairos* was the subject of the essay he published in 1922 outlining the importance of this concept for a philosophy of history. In line with the view of religion that he had now come to hold, he protests that anything can be the vehicle of the sacred in history and all realms of reality could be holy. While the past two centuries had removed God from the powers in the field of man's activities, the response of the church had been either an introverted theology of crisis or a submissive liberal theology. The former made God an enormous abstraction, quite divorced from human experience; but the latter sold out to the current social situation, selling the message of the new reality for a mess of cultural pottage. Tillich's essay was a deliberate attempt to avoid these mistaken theological extremes on the one hand and also, on the other hand, to effect a similar mediation between the political extremes of a Marxist determinism and a romantic enthusiasm. It is a call to the consciousness of history that is itself born of the experience of the unconditional because it sees the symbols that express the unconditional as answers to the questions of the historical present. Listening to the prophetic voices outside itself, the church judges both culture and itself as part of culture. By revealing dogmatic structures in society, it asserts the meaning of history and by remaking them within the church it bridges that gap between church and society which makes religion irrelevant.

Kairos is clearly the decisive concept of Tillich's thinking at this point as he reflects on the problem of a philosophy of history, the evangelical task of the church and the challenge of Europe's cultural house ruined by the shaking of its foundations in the recent cataclysm. It is a concept, of course, derived from biblical theology, where this finely felt distinction between 'the right time' and 'formal time' found its 'most pregnant and most frequent image' (PE, p. 38). The distinctive features of a philosophy of history which recognizes the validity of *kairos* as its key concept is the paradox that 'what happens in the *kairos* should be absolute and yet not absolute but under the judgement of the absolute' (PE, p. 48). Continuing this effort to see the scope of the holy beyond the boundaries of the church, Tillich insists that an age which is open to the unconditional (and so ready to accept the *kairos*) is not necessarily one in which the majority of people are formally religious. That is, the kairotic or prophetic character of a particular age is not constituted by the social institution of religion, but rather by its awareness of the transcendent significance of any and every institution and activity. We can see in this emphasis the same understanding of the essential nature of religion developed in his earlier work, and indeed Tillich goes on to use the now familiar concepts of theonomy, autonomy and heteronomy to explain what he means. Autonomy is not necessarily a turning away from the unconditional. A new theonomy does not reject the autonomous, nor does it, like heteronomy, seek to dominate its freedom of creativity. Theonomy, in this view of history, is thus a situation where there is no tension between the recognition of God's will as the call for man's obedience and the fulfilment of man's own will—what indeed Kant had regarded as the highest form of morality. A very interesting parallel could be drawn between this avowedly dialectical philosophy of history which Tillich was developing and Karl Barth's prophetic work as the radically political parson in Safenwil when, as he says, with the Bible in one hand and the newspaper in the other he had battled against social injustice. Little wonder that, both in these early years and towards the end of his life, Tillich was so anxious to hail Barth as a friend.

What he had explained *kairos* to mean is what Tillich declared to be discernible in the cultural situation and its critique of the 1920s. The movement 'most strongly conscious of the *kairos*, was socialism' and the political theology he was advocating was a 'religious socialism'. So far was this from being some softening of the socialist critique that it was in fact more radical and more revolutionary than the normal secular forms of socialism. Neither 'a church-political movement nor a state-political party', it was a purely prophetic attitude proclaiming a message that was conscious of the *kairos* precisely because it saw itself under the judgement of the unconditioned.

These principles of a religious socialism are the ideas that Tillich developed further in the various political writings of the next ten years. Fundamental to them is the notion of theonomy which was such an important concept in his analysis of culture and his understanding of the relation of theology to culture. A theonomy unites autonomy and heteronomy by transcending them, so that, for Tillich, religious socialism united the sacramental and the historical in an ethic of justice which found its basis in theonomy rather than the power of the state. That rare combination of a sense of historical tradition and conceptual analysis which we have seen in Tillich's life and thought is very obvious here. Looking back from the 1920s, he seeks a more profound *rapprochement* of church and culture than the flawed outlook which had brought about the disaster of the war, and yet he felt that a mediaeval sacramentalism was an attitude and a policy that the modern world found impossible to adopt. So he pleaded for a new basis for society and for the conquest of the demonic in education, state and culture as a preparation for that.

Although there seems something very theoretical if not indeed utopian about this, we need to remember that not only was Tillich always very critical of utopianism, but at this time he was a theorist active in practical politics. It would then be quite wrong to dismiss these writings as either purely abstract theory or the outpourings of an armchair socialist. There is something very characteristic of Tillich's outlook and habit of thought in the way in which his thinking at this time seemed to wander back and fore from theology to sociology. Certainly the sociologist Max Weber (1864–1920), and the great historical theologian Ernst Troeltsch (1865–1923) were powerful influences on the development of his thought during this period, as is clear from his book *The Religious Situation*. There, Tillich begins in his usual way by contextualizing the religious situation within the broader culture and historical background, analysing that cultural history in terms of its expression of the eternal. The book is a plea for 'belief-ful realism' as the perspective not only for metaphysics, ethics and art but for politics as well. In his Preface to *Political Expectations*, James Luther Adams—who knew Tillich better than almost anyone—speaks of Tillich's 'persistent efforts for more than a decade (before 1931) to combat the forces that were now bringing on dark night and destruction'. The title Luther Adams gave to this collection of essays—most of which were published in the Germany of the 1920s and 1930s—is very apt. Tillich's attitude as a theologian was one of political expectation and his thought was fashioned for the purpose of political action as the response to the ever-changing actual situation, but more particularly to the demand of the eternal.

The Socialist Decision, which was published in 1932, expresses not only the developed political theology of Tillich's German period but also the culmination of his entire commitment to socialist politics. Typically abstract though it is—for Tillich saw his role in politics, as indeed in theology, in very Platonic terms—the book is a deliberate attack on the growing attraction of Nazism. Equally typical is the way in which this is part of his positive proposal of a new kind of revolutionary socialism. The book is, amongst other things, a study of political romanticism and of capitalism. For him, the very nature of capitalism, with its inner tension of class and imperial ambition, demanded a socialist answer. Going back to the typology of political philosophy with which he had begun, he argued that socialism's pattern of social organization was a harmony of the religious significance of the myths of origin and the prophetic critique of those myths. This is where the influence of Marx (1818–83) is very obvious, as Tillich made use of Marx's analysis of economic development and his concept of the alienation which is the product of capitalism. Writing one of his most illuminating memoirs, he describes his attitude and his effort thus:

> In the central section of my book *Die sozialistische Entschei-dung* (*Socialist Decision*), I tried to distinguish the prophetic element in Marxism from its rational-scientific terminology and thus to make more comprehensible its far-reaching religious and historical implications. I also tried to gain a new under-standing of the socialist principle by comparing it with the tenets of Judeo-Christian prophecy. Marxists may accuse me of idealism and idealists may complain of my materialism, but I am actually on the boundary between the two. (OB, pp. 89–90)

Standing on that boundary between idealist theory and Marxist practice, Tillich made his plea for a socialism thus reconstructed as the only answer to the struggle between bourgeois liberalism and the romanticism which lent credibility to hysterical nationalism. Anyone who cavils at this negative attitude towards romanticism must bear in mind that we have moved far from the religious and political struggle of Romantics such as Wordsworth, Shelley and Keats. In fact, we have moved to a very attenuated and more sentimental attitude which would simply bask in the reflected glory of that tradition rather than take up its challenge to political and social reconstruction.

The religious socialism which Tillich had worked out in his German period remained his position throughout his American period. Inevitably there were certain changes in terminology, for, once having gained an adequate mastery of American English, he prided himself on his ability to express himself in pithy English by contrast with the prolix language that typified someone like Barth who had written only in German. Thus in the article 'The Church and communism' (*Religion in Life*, 1937), he speaks of 'communism' rather than 'Marxism'. It is, I think, the same kind of linguistic translation that explains his choice of language when he tempered his socialist zeal so as not to offend American ears. More than once he impressed on me that while we could share a common vocabulary, this was not the case in discussions in America. There is also room for debate concerning Tillich's political effectiveness and even possibly his political courage in the years of his American success. But, when all this biography and the works of the period have been carefully examined, I would still maintain that it would be quite wrong to think of the American Tillich as a fundamentally different political animal from the German religious socialist we have seen.

His important contribution to the Oxford Conference on Life and Work in 1937 is a very good example of the way in which here as elsewhere Tillich's thought displays a remarkable consistency. Like the good Lutheran he described himself to be, Tillich takes as his starting-point the Lutheran doctrine of the Kingdom of God; and, ardent socialist as he was, he saw this idea as providing the crucial perspective for the interpretation of recent history as the end of bourgeois society. History and the Kingdom of God are, then, the two poles of the 'applied theology' which he developed in this paper. History derives its meaning from the unification and purification of its events in a supra-historical realization which is the Kingdom of God. 'The Kingdom of God', he says, 'is a symbolic expression of the ultimate meaning of existence.' A very important aspect of this political theology was its balance of a concrete emphasis on history with events and an equal emphasis on the non-historical nature of the meaning. While there was no mistaking the socialism of the fierce critique of capitalism, there was not the slightest evidence that the theologian had sold out to a political ideology to become the time-server of a socialist swell. That is clear enough from Tillich's unhesitating rejection of Bolshevism.

One of the reasons why it is sometimes thought that Tillich's socialist convictions weakened as he settled in America is the silence of his early years there. Such a criticism forgets that those must have been years of sad trauma when he must have seen himself very much like the ancient people of Israel—how could one sing the songs of Zion in a foreign land? However, moving forward to the year before the Second World War we do find Tillich making his famous appeal to German Americans to oppose Nazism for the sake of Christianity as well as for Germany's sake. This powerful condemnation of anti-Semitism was continued in articles and broadcasts thoughout the war. Towards the end of the war, the socialist motif in Tillich's thinking reappeared as the Council for a Democratic Germany (a group of anti-Nazi German refugees which Tillich chaired) published a declaration of its vision for the reconstruction of Europe. The fact that this effort to encourage the reconstruction of Germany as a socialist democracy met with little practical support in America must have been another sadness to Tillich. Nor was he much cheered by the end of the war, which left his native land barely recognizable. Weighed down by such sadness, he could hardly stir up any great enthusiasm for involving himself in American politics. Besides, he remained very conscious of the difference between his German situation and his American one, always remarking to his European pupils in New York that they should remember that 'this is not Europe'. Another factor was the presence in Union Seminary of his friend Reinhold Niebuhr (1892–1971), whose influence on American politics was very significant. When NBC television regularly had Niebuhr commenting on the political situation, it was little wonder that Tillich should feel not only that he should be guided by Niebuhr but also that he should not trespass on an area where Niebuhr was so obviously at home. The American suspicion of anything called socialism was very strong in the 1950s—so strong that Europeans were counselled by American friends not to use the word lest they should be branded as communists or communist supporters. That contributed to Tillich's seemingly changing attitude in these years, when he would say that the accommodation of Marxism in religious socialism was impossible in America. If so, then the rather negative comments he generally made on the social and economic theories of religious socialism are less persuasive evidence of a change of mind than one might think. What is beyond doubt is that Tillich responded enthusiastically to the Social Gospel movement precisely because he saw similarities between it and religious socialism.

The Terry Lectures (*The Courage to Be*) are an indication of the way in which Tillich's political thinking became more and more a general social theory which was in many respects a mixture of social anthropology and ethical theory. What strikes one on first reading the list of contents is the domination that a philosophical ethics exercises on this investigation; the only relief from such metaphysical concern is the psychological excursus in the middle. Reviewing the book on its first publication, I remarked that Tillich's argument seemed suspiciously like a reduction of ethics to metaphysics. But, as so often with Tillich, within the abstraction of his formulations one finds very practical concerns and concrete comments. Thus in chapter IV he turns from his ontological discussion to a survey of the more psychological and social dimensions of courage and offers a very judicious commentary on the American way of life. In his usual fashion, he starts with a broad historical and intellectual picture but quickly homes in on the particular situation of the time. American courage, he says, is 'one of the great types of the courage to be as a part' (p. 109). 'The courage to be as a part in the progress of the group to which one belongs, of this nation of all mankind is expressed in all specifically American philosophies' (p. 110). Being a part, one necessarily conforms; and Tillich identified the way in which the pressure to conform was constantly strengthened by the development of twentieth-century America. His own growing interest in psychology, psychotherapy and radical existentialism made him attuned to those vitalist elements in the American attitude which were at odds with his outlook. Still, he thought, America lived in the happy inconsistency of accepting both attitudes. *The Courage to Be* is an important book in Tillich's development of his philosophical and theological positions; but its importance for an understanding of his political theology is simply that it illustrates the way in which that became subsumed under a theology of culture which itself had become more of a theology of high culture; and with such a theology went a general philosophical psychology which was part of the overall metaphysical picture.

Much the same kind of thing must be said of *Love, Power and Justice*. In exactly the same way as the argument of *The Courage to Be* leads inexorably to the foundation of courage in the nature of God as Being, that is Being-itself, so the analysis of the three concepts of love, power and justice leads to the uniting of the three in the unity of the infinite and the finite. As a portrait of Tillich the theologian, it is wonderfully revealing: learned, highly abstract and obviously still under the influence of nineteenth-century Idealism, he is very much the borderline theologian, harmonizing different traditions but also never avoiding the practical issues of power and the inalienable claims of justice. He argues against the reduction of justice to power—and reading this, one recalls the legend that he knew Plato's *Republic* by heart. Yet he is equally adamant that a genuine social ethic must abandon the distrust of power. Justice is in fact 'the form in which the power of being actualises itself'. Again he argues against the old tendency to make a sharp distinction between justice and love. Love is in fact the ultimate principle of justice rather than some extension or modification of justice. 'Justice in its ultimate meaning is creative justice, and creative justice is the form of reuniting love' (LPJ, p. 71). The ontological analysis of love is matched by a similar analysis of power. Here the Idealist philosophy which was Tillich's background is very evident. Hegel, as well as Schelling, is echoed in this analysis, as when he says that power is the capacity of being to overcome non-being. Indeed, the whole pattern of the discussion and not simply the occasional concept is Idealist. The aim of the argument is to demonstrate the unity of the three concepts, and the method is that of abstract analysis rather than the discussion of moral and social situations.

It is always the case with Tillich that at whatever point he begins his argument, no matter how concrete, the direction of the argument is towards the abstraction of ontology. Thus, though it must be said that in *Love, Power and Justice* he wanted to fulfil his brief as Firth Lecturer in Nottingham and *apply* the Christian faith and *relate* it to the problems of the modern world, he ended up producing an essentially ontological theology that seemed far removed from the world of politics. The impression which this slim volume leaves is that Tillich was finding the world of politics increasingly strange and that he even felt that, as he had little to say to his American public, so his European public too could not be helped with much practical counsel. It would, however, be unjust to him were we to say either that he had lost interest or that he had changed his mind. As we have seen, he was eager to be diplomatic and to temper the wind to the shorn lamb; but he did not sell out or abandon his convictions. What animated these lectures was the concern that politics could not be left in some godless vacuum: churchmen and theologians should be engaged in working out the three kinds of relations the fracture of which had brought about the tragedy of Germany. Because of this, there are occasions when Tillich swoops from his metaphysical heights to comment very illuminatingly on practical issues. For all its abstraction, then, Tillich's most mature political theology remained a source of inspiration for political action because his perspective was always that socialism which expresses the Kingdom of God and his intention here, as in his theology, was to offer a help in answering questions. Theory he knew it was; but he recognized too that practice was the heart of the matter. Hence it is that the power discussed in *Love, Power and Justice* is something quite practical and not intellectual. This is what gives the book its clear sense of the realities of politics. There was no longer—perhaps there had never been—in Tillich's attitude any utopianism as he recognized the way that power struggles remain but held out an essentially optimistic interpretation of the role of politics in human history.

3

A Phenomenological Theology?

Tillich's first work as a professional theologian typifies what he was later to describe as the border existence that was his as a theologian. He had stood on the boundary between theology and culture. His theology had been born of a particular social and political situation and was in effect a call to revolution; but it was something that he produced as a lecture to a philosophical audience, the Kant-Society. The philosophical background to Tillich's theology is an important key to his understanding of the task of theology as well as its nature and method. The temptation to which some critics succumbed—of seeing him as someone who had sold out to secularism—will be avoided if we bear in mind that this is the perspective from which we must view his work. Simple contrasts with Barth are, we have seen, misleading because they blind us to their common background. They are even more so when they suggest that Tillich in any way lacked the keryg- matic purpose and fervour of Barth. Just as much as Barth he was concerned to proclaim the Gospel; but, as he used to say, whereas Barth thought the Gospel should be thrown at man 'like stones at his head', he wanted to present the Gospel as an answer to man's question. This idea of question and answer is one to which we shall return; for the moment, what is significant is the way in which the theologian is seen as beginning his work with the human situation. This was so characteristic of Tillich's intention and method as a theologian that it led to serious misunderstand- ing of his work. Thus the complaint was very often made by some theologians that Tillich had in fact gone so far in restoring the practice of natural theology that he had created not a theology but an aesthetic philosophy.

The truth of the matter, however, is that his understanding of the theologian's task was very biblical in that, like the prophet and the apostle, he felt himself called to stand alongside his fellow man. As the intellectual task of theology was the knowledge and understanding of ultimate reality, he thought it could not avoid being philosophical. What then gave him a sense of fresh hope as a young theologian was the awareness that philosophically theology was made not only possible but relevant, since both philosophy and theology needed to begin with human experience. The great influence of Schelling on Tillich masks the complex influence of philosophy on his theology. As a young university student he was rumoured to have read Kant's *Critique of Pure Reason* when he was in the Gymnasium before coming to university. Many years later, as a teacher in Union Seminary, New York, he was reputed to be outstanding among that glittering constellation of scholars because he knew *all* Plato more or less by heart! His knowledge of Schelling was not only profound—he was one of the century's greatest Schelling scholars—but so sympathetic that, on more than one occasion, he would quote a remark of Schelling's as being his own. However, as we have seen, his intellectual development was not confined to his university years and the war years were very significant. It was then, as he tells us (OB, p. 27), that he discovered painting, which was 'a crucial experience'. His study of the history of art and the experience of art—especially the revelation experience of his first encounter with Botticelli's Madonna with Singing Angels during his last furlough of the war—led to a philosophical reflection on art which gave him some of his fundamental concepts. Equally important from a technical point of view was the actual philosophical study that engaged him as he gained a little more relief from his overwhelming exertions as a chaplain in 1917. The arrival of another chaplain to assist him in August of that year enabled Tillich to resume the scholarly interest of his earlier career as a minister with academic ambitions. He described in a letter to a friend how he had surveyed the literature of modern philosophy, having cut himself off from the war to enjoy some peace of mind. One of the philosophers who impressed him as most interesting was Edmund Husserl. In the summer before he died, Tillich was in Union Seminary lecturing and I was giving a course of lectures on his philosophy. During a discussion we had of what I was saying, he applauded my plan of beginning with Husserl's phenomenology, describing himself as one of a generation of thinkers saved by Husserl from naturalism. To see how this was so, we can briefly consider phenomenology.

Husserl had begun his philosophical work by considering the philosophy of mathematics, where his problem was to understand number in terms of the essences of the numbering concepts which consciousness produced. From mathematics he turned to logic, again applying the method of directly viewing the essences of things so that logic is distinguished from psychology. Logical forms are independent essences which are manifested in particular matters of fact and are open to inspection as phenomena. This generalization of the method was continued by Husserl in his writings, so that in the two volumes of *Logical Investigations* the method is made applicable to metaphysical problems and again the very notion of phenomenology becomes expanded. Conceived originally as a method of descriptive analysis of subjective processes, it becomes a science concerned with mental images capable of extracting essences from experience. For Husserl, the first of all possible philosophies was an essential theory which could work within the boundaries of absolute evidence; and this was transcendental phenomenology, the mother of all *a priori* sciences. Husserl is concerned not only explain how knowledge is possible but also to describe that knowledge. What this involves is first the inspection of ourselves in reflection. Central to his philosophy is the view that all consciousness is intentional; it is aimed at something and in all our awareness there are things we intend, both subjective and objective. Because of this emphasis on the descriptive function of philosophy, a typical slogan of phenomenology is 'Back to the data'. Yet the emphasis on the description as one of essences is equally important. Finally, it is important to remember a distinction Husserl made in his later thought between the scientific world and the world of life or lived world. It is the latter which he regarded as primary and the source from which the scientific world is derived. So one of the central tasks of phenomenology is the analysis of the world in which we actually live.

With this clarification of Tillich's philosophical background, we can not only understand how he later became so influenced by Heidegger that he was often called an 'existentialist theologian' but how he was led intellectually to the conception of theology declared in his classical lecture on theology of culture. There Tillich sought to address not only scholars but anyone who was interested in rebuilding the world that had been so cruelly shattered by the war. The year was 1919 and the young theologian fresh from the horrors of the trenches was not in the least inclined to retread outworn paths or to offer false hopes. He knew, as he says, that the whole house lay in ruins; and yet he could not escape his calling to expound the Gospel of Christ's Kingdom to the whole world. As he pondered that task, he felt not only that traditional theology had manifestly failed his country but that its practice now would be a positive disservice to that Kingdom. The language of traditional theology was like the Tower of Babel: instead of communicating the meaning of the Gospel, it merely created a gulf between the church and the world, between the theologian and the layman. Therefore he proposed that theology be recognised as 'the ... normative science of religion'. Its perspective was that of a concrete standpoint: the theologian cannot, in Tillich's view, claim anything more privileged than a particular historical perspective. The theology of culture he proposed was the successor to neither dogmatics nor apologetics but to the third traditional aspect of theology, theological ethics. For the young theologian there was only one test of theology and that was the real world. That world he saw as charged with God's glory. Describing that world by a phenomenological analysis was, then, the business of theology. It would be claiming too much were we to think that Husserl's phenomenology was the method Tillich employed; for any careful comparison of the Husserlian method of bracketing and Tillich's method would reveal as great a difference as that between Husserl's view of intentionality and Tillich's understanding of the relation between thought and reality. Yet the evidence of the language he uses as well as the biographical evidence suggest that the impact of that philosophy had helped shape Tillich's developing concern with rescuing theology from an arid, indeed atrophied, orthodoxy. The way forward for theology was to express itself in a way that revealed its concern with real lived experience, to find 'words in which the power of the word pulsated', to speak to the contemporary conditions of its hearers.

In his description of theological method some twelve years after the lecture on the theology of culture, Tillich specifically uses the term 'phenomenological'. Rejecting both the old authoritative orthodoxy and the modern method of an approach through psychology and history of religions, he suggests a new way. This is the method of 'phenomenological intuition' whereby we approach the whole of reality in an immediate fashion and 'seek to lay bare the level of reality which is intended by the religious act'. The real basis of theology is neither some sacrosanct tradition nor even the claim to some special access to what is beyond the world. Rather it is to be found in the actual existence of man. In this way he felt that he could avoid the impasse into which he thought theology had been brought. That impasse was the end for him of the very theology that had first kindled his own theological aspirations, Liberalism. Though he always spoke of Liberalism with profound gratitude and respect, he was keenly aware of the fact that Liberalism had been shattered by the developments of the twentieth century, discredited by the political compromises of some of its greatest representatives, and fatally weakened by the attacks of Karl Barth and his followers. He was often at pains to distinguish his own method of correlation from mere apologetics, fulminating against any use of 'apologetics' that would suggest apologizing for faith as if real faith lacked the courage to be and to proclaim its truth. Thus he would say that though Liberalism was dead all theology had to be 'liberal with a small "l"'.

There are many respects in which Tillich is the true heir of Liberalism and perhaps none more so than the conviction that theology must be related to the developments of present-day thought. Liberalism was a vigorous movement in the nineteenth century, with theologians adopting an eirenic attitude to modern science and seeking to express the 'essence' of Christianity in a new way. Without suggesting that the whole of Liberal theology can be easily characterized and summarized, it can be said that there were some three or four motifs that typified it. One was the understanding of faith as essentially a matter of morality. Ever since Kant this had been a recurring theme and the 'essence' of Christianity had been located in the ethical teaching of Jesus. Harnack's (1851–1930) celebrated claim that the Gospel was originally such a simple message as this which later became accidentally complicated by the alien influence of Greek philosophy represented such thinking. If this was the way Christianity was construed, then the historical Jesus was fundamental to theology and the quest for him was one of theology's basic functions. Thus Tillich spoke frequently and mov- ingly of the real advance which had been achieved in theology as it 'incorporated with itself a scientific method', that of historical criticism. The name of the theologians whom he regarded as the greatest of his teachers at Halle, Martin Kähler, suggests a very important dimension of this particular thinking, viz., the contrast between the Jesus of history and the Christ of faith. For Liberalism

53

the Jesus of history is paramount. One strange consequence of this kind of thinking in the Liberal tradition was the tendency for theology to construe the meaning of doctrinal assertions in metaphysical terms. That is, despite the rejection of the heritage of credal definition as so much theological encumbrance, doctrines such as the Incarnation and the Trinity became understood as metaphysical statements about the relation of God and man, or God and the world. There was indeed a powerful undercurrent of immanentist thinking which brought theology and faith back to experience and a view of this world. Above all, what could be said to characterize Liberalism and perhaps explain its name was its sense of being free from shackles, free in the glorious modern morn to proclaim the Gospel of freedom in the brotherhood of man. This last theme of freedom is taken up by Tillich in his important autobiographical sketch *On the Boundary*. His self-portrait is that of a wounded soul who has painfully won an individuality. Twice he speaks of freedom: looking at his temperament and then at the boundary 'between heteronomy and autonomy'. He was a son of an eastern German father and a western German mother and 'this double inheritance' was a fundamental part of his mental constitution. It gave him no composure and made him think of history as a struggle between two opposing principles. Truth is dynamic 'found in the midst of struggle and destiny'. In this language are surely the accents of a theologian who had been convinced that only an untrammelled spirit could fulfil that professional task. The task of the boundary between heteronomy and autonomy is a more obvious echo of the freedom cherished by the Liberal. Looking back at his father's powerful influence on him, he speaks of the guilt he felt at every attempt at autonomous thinking. Yet he had gone on to break the taboo and to face and surmount his inner obstacles. The answer he gave to the opposition of autonomy and heteronomy was his concept of theonomy, a divinely filled autonomy. But what is so clear about the way in which he saw this tension as running through his whole thinking, political and religious, is the high valuation of freedom. It would be true to say that at the end of his life, just as at the beginning of his theological career, there was for Tillich no authority in theology other than the truth which sets man free. It is this more than anything else which he would recognize as something which bound him indissolubly to Liberalism.

This said, we must also recognize that there are very important ways in which Tillich distinguished sharply between the Liberal tradition and his own perspective and method in theology. In his survey of the history of Christian thought, he refers at the end to the way in which Barth had criticized the synthesis of religion and culture which Liberalism had achieved. To his mind neither alternative was sound; and while rejecting any simple synthesis his retort to Barth is that there must always be an influence of culture on theology. He illustrated this in one of the lectures on systematic theology by saying that any neo-orthodox refusal to recognize a source and authority other than the Bible forgot that this Bible was the product of culture. When Luther translated the Bible he gave the German Christian the benefit of the sixteenth-century heritage of European culture. Again, his stand on the significance of historical criticism should not blind us to the very significant difference between him and Liberals on the issue of the Jesus of history. As we shall see, his treatment of this is extremely subtle and was often hailed as a solution of the problem which Liberalism had bequeathed to theology. Whereas the Liberal could identify the historical Jesus as the basis of doctrine, and indeed the essence of theology, Tillich wants to sharpen the distinction between history and faith while at the same time emphasizing the historicity of Jesus. Finally, this most metaphysical theologian was at pains to distinguish the events of faith from the metaphysical assertions with which he felt his theology had constantly to grapple. His Christology was a highly metaphysical creation but he rejected any suggestion that it could be reduced to some metaphysical assertion. Furthermore, if the metaphysical tendency in Liberalism led to a stress on immanence, Tillich's thought tended in quite the opposite direction. Those who heard him lecture, as well as those who heard him preach, can testify that all his utterances were imbued with a sense of the tremendous transcendence of the holy God.

One brief final word on this matter of background will be useful. The fact of Tillich's reaction to the Liberalism from which he had sprung will bring to mind the question of his relation to Karl Barth, a matter of some complexity which is often misunderstood. Despite their different perspectives and despite the criticisms Tillich levelled at Barth and vice versa, they were in fact quite close. To begin at the end rather than the beginning, it was a great joy to Tillich to have resumed friendly relations with Barth, whom he visited in December 1963. Their personal relations had been difficult at times, but there was a profound concord between them dating back to 1919: in September of that year, they shared the platform at the three-day conference of European religious socialists in Tambach. A voracious reader, Tillich would doubtless have read Barth's commentary on Romans and would just as certainly endorsed that concern with 'a word from the Lord'. In a very real sense, then, their theologies developed away from a shared concern with the living revealed word of the Transcendent and with those social virtues demanded by God of man. Yet in 1919, there was no doubt that they stood shoulder to shoulder in opposing the tendency to allow everything to remain as it had been in spite of the destruction of all the old illusions. What was necessary and what must be sought now more than ever was 'a truth in the midst of error and lies, a justice in the ocean of injustice, a living action-force in the feebleness of spiritual movement's unity in the division within our society'. These are not Tillich's words but Barth's. They were indeed brothers united in the struggle. One thing more needs to be said and that is that it is not sufficiently realized that Tillich's intention in *Systematic Theology* is at least very nearly the same as Barth's in his *Church Dogmatics*, if not exactly the same. Tillich was never perhaps as much of a churchman as Barth. The strangely fashionable preacher in Union Theological Seminary, New York, in the 1940s and 1950s was not a figure much seen in the city churches or in any other pulpits. Even so, the intention of his great work was to be faithful to the classical (an adjective he preferred to either 'traditional' or 'orthodox') message of the Gospel. In that sense there can be no doubt that his theology is just as kerygmatic as Barth's. The difference between them that became so obvious is easily summed up in his own words: 'While Barth thinks that the Gospel should be thrown at people like stones at their heads, I want to present it as the answer to the question of man's existential situation.'

Tillich's earliest published works were in the field of ethics or political theology and philosophy of religion, and the great work on systematic theology was not published until the 1950s. However, it is quite obvious that he had always envisaged his life-work to be the production of a theology. He spoke of himself as having taught theology when he was in fact Professor of Philosophy, and in the Preface to *Systematic Theology* in 1951 he declared that this had been his intention for 'a quarter of a century'. In fact, the conception of a systematic theology went back further than that: he first sketched such a theology in 1913, and the full sketch of the 72 propositions was made by his friend Richard Wegener. This long-standing intention is important to remember, because it is something that helps us understand Tillich's thought in his final years. What kind of thing is, then, this theology so long considered and finally produced as more or less a completed work? He tells us at the outset that, though it is meant to serve the needs of the church, it will interpret the truth of the Christian message for a new generation, something that theology must do to every generation. As such, theology oscillates between two poles: tradition and the present situation. To be faithful to both these demands is difficult: there can be an over-emphasis of the one at the expense of the other, or indeed it can be the case that neither is properly fulfilled. Kerygma and situation must, then, be held together in creative tension, and great theology always corrects the relativities of the 'situation' by appeal to the kerygma and avoids the decline into orthodox rigidity by correcting itself in the light of the situation. It is in that sense that he recognizes the necessity of apologetics: it is what complements a kerygmatic theology and makes a properly rounded theology. Having said this, however, Tillich is very anxious to explain what is meant by 'apologetic' when he thus speaks of its necessity. It is 'answering theology'. 'It answers the questions implied by the "situation" in the power of the eternal message and with the means provided by the situation whose questions it answers' (ST, vol. 1, p. 6).

The phrase Tillich uses to describe this approach is the famous 'method of correlation' and it is important to grasp that it is a *general* description of the system. It is in this context of distinguishing his approach from Barth's that Tillich first uses the phrase in *Systematic Theology*. It is necessary, he says, to find a method 'in which message and situation are related in such a way that neither is obliterated' (ibid., p. 8). His answer to the problem is the adoption of this method, which 'tries to correlate the questions implied in the situation with the answers implied in the message', neither deriving the answer from the questions nor elaborating answers without reference to the questions. These are the errors of a merely apologetic or a merely kerygmatic theology. By contrast, a theology of correlation 'correlates questions and answers, situation and message, human existence and divine manifestation' (ibid.). I have deliberately used the phrase 'theology of correlation' rather than 'method of correlation' because I want to indicate the tradition in which Tillich then wants to stand. He had used the phrase 'method of correlation' as early as 1924 to speak of the relations between religion and culture in theology. In *Systematic Theology*, he declares that if this method does indeed effect the proper balance of message and situation, then it solves 'the two centuries old question of "Christianity and the modern mind?"' By adopting this method then, Tillich wants not simply to align himself with those—such as the Liberals, for instance—who wanted to harmonize Christianity and the modern mind and to expound it in such a way that 'the cultured amongst its despisers' might see its truth and worth (like Schleiermacher), but to stand in an even older tradition. For the reference to two centuries is hardly the slip of a pen or a historical miscalculation. The problem of modern theology for Tillich was the problem taken up at the end of the eighteenth century. If knowledge has as its content the world of our finite experience, how is it that theology gives us understanding of the revelation that God has given? In this, as in many other contexts, it is illuminating to look at Tillich's early writings. In *What Is Religion?* the three views of religion analysed and evaluated are those of Kant, Hegel and Schleiermacher; and this would suggest that in his development of a philosophy of religion, though he was obviously and profoundly influenced by Schelling, the starting-point was the problem which Kant defined for all future theology. Moreover, we know that Tillich himself was ready to admit that as you scratch an English philosopher and find a Hume, so scratch a German one and you will find a Kant.

If the method of correlation is thus inspired by a longstanding philosophical problem, it would be as wrong to make it merely a reflection of critical agnosticism as it would be to limit it, which one is tempted to do, to the correlation of philosophy and theology in the system. What has been said about phenomenology already should disabuse us of the notion that Tillich is really some nineteenth-century agnostic, or even atheist, masquerading as a theologian. 'Back to the data' is for him a call to describe the facts of faith's experience. Things become clearer as we read what he says about the organization of theology. Ever since Schleiermacher, he points out, there has been a tendency to replace the old natural theology by philosophy of religion. This kind of approach can be seen in the titles of some classical books in philosophy of religion published in the first half of the twentieth century—'the philosophical bases of theism'. This will not do for Tillich; for if such philosophy of religion is autonomous, if it lies outside theology, it cannot properly determine the method of theology. This is where the method of correlation is for him a vital element in his theology. Such philosophical work as is done in philosophy of religion must be part of the very approach of the theologian *qua* theologian. The same issue is in effect the second and third problems of organization: the position of apologetics and that of theological ethics. His answer to both these is the method of correlation. 'The "method of correlation" applied in the present system gives pointed expression to the decisive character of the apologetic element in systematic theology' (ST, vol. 1, p. 35). This solution is equally valid for the problem of theological ethics. Theological ethics must be part of the system, or else both ethics and systematic theology suffer. What is especially interesting is that here Tillich broadens his understanding of the questions and answers concerned beyond even culture to relate to the issues of finitude and guilt. The conclusion is that 'an "existential" theology implies ethics in such a way that no special section for ethical theology is needed' (ibid., p. 36). So we see that the method of correlation is a matter of being an 'existential' theology.

More than once already we have seen how anxious Tillich is to see himself in the 'classical' tradition of theology: that is as true of his adoption of the method of correlation as of anything else. There is indeed a sense in which he is looking for a new way of expounding the kerygma; but the method is not some new invention—it is the method theology has always used (ibid., pp. 67–8). In passing, too, it is worth mentioning that Tillich is not guilty of making theology a pure matter of method. Method is for him a tool, adopted and practised if it is found adequate to the subject matter; method is an element of the reality itself which is being studied. It is because of what we already know about the total deliverance of theology, our knowledge of a world shot through with the glory of God, that he thinks we must adopt the method of correlation. That is to say, he views the theologian's task as like that of some mapmaker in a land that is there for us to know but the characteristics and patterns of which we have yet to understand. This is not something to be undertaken without, on the one hand, a grasp of the patterns we seek to understand or, on the other, a very profound understanding of those dilemmas and confusions which make us despair of under-standing. 'The method of correlation explains the content of the Christian faith through existential questions and theological answers in mutual interdependence' (ibid., p. 68). So Tillich makes clear that the questions are genuine problems put *to* theology while the answers are provided *by* theology. He explains the meaning of 'correlation' further by distinguishing three elements: (a) the correlation (correspondence) between religious symbols and that which is symbolized by them, (b) the correlation of the finite and the infinite, (c) the mutual interdependence of 'God for us' and 'we for God'. All three elements are part of what we are talking of in the claim that theology uses the method of correlation. While this elaboration of the concept is far from being a successful clarification, Tillich leaves us in no doubt that what he is seeking is a means of doing genuine theology, theology that is a serious concern with those problems of humanity in its actual existence and theology that is a faithful attempt to expound the revelation to humanity confronting its needs. 'The answers implied in the event of revelation are meaningful only in so far as they are in correlation with questions concerning the whole of our existence, with existential questions' (ibid., p. 69).

The questions from which theology takes its rise, then, are 'existential questions'. They are the perennial questions of mankind about itself: we ourselves are indeed the questions. Though Tillich says that this is something much older than existentialism, there can be no doubt that this is where we see the significant influence of Heidegger's existentialism on his theological development. The close interest of young Heidegger in Luther's theology of the Cross may be one of the main reasons why, in his Marburg days, Tillich was won from resisting Heidegger's thought to an arduous learning from it. That he was thus influenced Tillich readily admitted, and there are many specific notions, such as being and anxiety, which reveal this. What is important here is the more general notion that the main task of philosophy is asking the 'question of being'. For Heidegger, the original task of philosophy had been abandoned in favour of some pretentious search for what lay beneath things, substance. We need to get back to the very horizon in which any such question would be intelligible, that is, our own existence. The published part of his new ontology, *Being and Time*, concentrates on this new inquiry, the analysis of our Being, Being-here (*Dasein*). Such is Tillich's understanding of the first task theology needs to undertake, seeing that we are 'the door to the deeper level of reality', and this is the first sense in which the theology he essays is phenomenological.

There is, for Tillich, no escape from this phenomenological method. The procedure followed by the method of correlation, he says, is this: 'it makes an analysis of the human situation out of which the existential questions arise, and it demonstrates that the symbols used in the Christian message are the answers to these questions' (ST, vol. 1, p. 70). Calling this a phenomenological procedure rather than an existentialist theology helps us grasp what Tillich had in mind when he said that he was as much (or indeed more of) an essentialist as an existentialist. We are talking of a method which in the philosophy of Heidegger is called a phenomenology and has links with that analysis of life experience which Husserl had proposed. Moreover, the unease with a rejection of concern with essence which is expressed in that famous remark is the unease Tillich feels at the prospect of doing theology that is in any way less fundamental and less comprehensive than the aim of classical philosophy, on the one hand, and poetry or drama, on the other. So he wants his readers to understand that while he aligns himself with the radically contemporary concern of a Heidegger he sees his work as authentically classical in that the very point at which he takes up Heidegger's departure from traditional philosophy is something to be found in Augustine's theology (ibid.). Moreover, in all this he is determined equally to be a faithful son of the Reformation and tellingly declares his method to be exactly that pursued by Calvin (1509–64) in his *Institutes* (ibid., where Tillich refers to Calvin, *Institutes*, I, 48). The analysis of human experience which he thus commends as the starting-point of theology is an analysis of man's involvement in and separation from the world—'a part of it' and yet 'a stranger in the world of objects'. This is an analysis of immediate experience that is also a generalization about any human experience: 'the immediate experience of one's own existing reveals something of the nature of existence generally'. Tillich emphasizes this generality by saying that what this analysis yields is not a doctrine of man but 'a doctrine of existence as experienced in him as man' (ibid., p. 70). All this is very philosophical in both language and concern but it would be as wrong to confine the notion of correlation to the view Tillich has of the relation of philosophy to theology as it would be to ignore the urgent significance now given to philosophy as a part of the theological enterprise. It is quite impossible to understand the novelty of Tillich's work in theology if we do not see the method of correlation as his way of restoring the classical co-operation between the two disciplines. Handmaiden, guide or censor—these models for the role of philosophy were to him outmoded and useless. What mattered was the realization that every theologian who had seriously and honestly pursued his vocation began with a philosophical task. Once again he deliberately takes Calvin as his example—not in order to say that Calvin begins his work with some kind of traditional natural theology but rather to show that a thoroughly biblical theologian cannot absent himself from that initial analysis which is completely philosophical.

How did Tillich understand the relation of philosophy to theology? It can be argued that his exposition of that connection as a correlation is in the end far less valuable than it seems. Such was my early argument that the correlation is a matter of truth by definition and that the assertions Tillich has made become tautologous (see *Paul Tillich: An Appraisal*). However, what we need to see at the moment is how Tillich goes about this task of solving a problem which had become so pressing for theology in the mid-century. One of the strange features of Tillich as a theologian whose sympathies were so wide, sensitivities so acute and knowledge so immense, was his almost complete ignorance of the changes brought about by Anglo-Saxon philosophy in the period 1930–50, the heyday of linguistic analysis. Consequently, he was prone to see any and every British philosophy as thoroughly empiricist and any 'linguistic' philosophy as 'damned Logical Positivism'. What this meant, then, was that he went back to his Kantian starting-point. With that honesty which was for Kant both the beginning and the end of philosophy, Tillich sees the theologian as doing the same kind of thing as the philosopher. There are, however, two differences between them: the scope of the enterprise and the purpose that lies beyond it. In the first place, the philosopher's analysis of existence is part of a broader enterprise, while the theologian is to some measure constrained or limited by the theological concepts that his Christian faith provide. That is, the philosopher's range of material to be investigated has no such limits as those which the theologian has by virtue of the fact that he is concerned to explain God's being and scheme of the world's salvation. How far Tillich is misled by a wrong model of philosophy as a science is an important question; but, once again, we can see that there is point in saying that the theologian's map of language has a certain limitation compared with the completely unrestricted map which the philosopher employs. Tillich's second point is again very Kantian in that he recalls the way in which Kant's critique of pure reason was a limitation of knowledge which was proposed in order to 'make room for faith'. So he stresses the autonomy of the theologian's philosophical work and yet insists that, from beginning to end, theology is a matter of theological concern. There can be no *a priori* determination of either theological or philosophical truth, so that the work of both is in that sense open. Even so, the theologian pursues his task in the confidence that 'nothing he sees can change the substance of his answer, because this substance is the logos of being, manifest in Jesus as the Christ' (ST, vol. 1, p. 71).

There is a more fundamental reason for describing Tillich's theology as phenomenological. The very theological datum is something which he thinks should be approached phenomenologically. Recognizing both the inevitability of starting with experience and the problem of the necessary transcendence of experience in theology, Tillich admits that the empirical theology which had grown out of the American evangelical tradition had made an important contribution to theology. This is because it had shown that religious objects are not objects among others but expressions of a quality of our general experience. Here he sees a convergence of that kind of theology with the continental tradition of Otto which he calls 'phenomenological'. The question which the theologian poses is not one about the existence of an object, God, but rather one about the meaning of 'the holy'. The significance of this has generally been missed when the issue of Tillich's 'atheism' is discussed. The point he is making is that the only way in which theology can proceed is by giving a phenomenological account of what is meant when something is recognized as holy. This is not because there is any doubt about the reality of that which is beyond experience—because, after all, the aim of phenomenology is to give an account of essences. Rather, the point is that to begin by posing a question of the existence of something confines us within the realm of experience. This is how Tillich has transposed the old problem of natural theology. Instead of establishing that some divine entity exists and so can be further described by a theology of revelation, he wants in fact both to collapse a natural theology into a theology of revelation and yet to confront the neutral issue of meaning. By leaving the problem of God's reality aside and undertaking the task of describing the meaning of the holy, we shall see the universal meaning of revelation, which in turn implies the reality of God. This is the only way theology can proceed and by so doing it avoids 'the danger of filling in logical gaps with devotional material' (ST, vol. 1, p. 118). Each of the five parts of his system thus begins, he says, by describing 'the meaning of the determining ideas before asserting their truth and actuality'. His method is a critical phenomenology. It neither abstracts to the point of empty generalization, nor will it take some arbitrarily chosen example as the norm. In deciding the example of the theological datum, we are dependent on a revelation received as final but the phenomenological approach is preserved. This is what leads Tillich to talk of the theologian as working *within the theological circle*.

One further characteristic of theology according to Tillich needs to be mentioned before considering what he regards as the sources of theology. Clearly, Tillich attaches great importance to the rational character of theology as a creative effort; but he is at pains to deny that theology is derived from reason—'reason is not a source of theology' (ibid., p. 60). Faith is for him something rational in the sense that there is an element of knowledge in faith. This knowledge is an existential participation in what we believe, of course; but because we thus share in the truth of what we believe we have a knowledge which has nothing to do with the level of our intellectual activity. It is again important to notice how thoroughly kerygmatic Tillich's stance is even when he is talking about the rationality of theology. Again and again in this section he refers to belief in the New Being, that is to say, the revelation in Christ. Where the theologian stands, then, in his view is in Christ. Rather than working from some rational foundation towards faith he sees the theologian's reason as grasped by the content of faith.

While recognizing that he does not thereby solve the problem of the rationality of theology, Tillich offers three principles as its outline: semantic rationality, logical rationality and methodological rationality. With regard to semantic rationality, Tillich was not advocating a special language for theology. On the contrary, he was very clear in his appreciation of the way in which the theologian must use whatever language is to hand. He rejected the idea that the theologian could, for instance, use only biblical language or use no language other than that of traditional theology. What mattered, he thought, was not where the language came from but that the theologian should be able to express his thought clearly by means of such language. This seems a very minor or a rather obvious point, but it is more significant than appears. For instance, Tillich was aware of the danger of a misleading expression of theology resulting from the use of language which had non-Christian connotations. Equally, and perhaps more significantly, he showed himself at this point able to recognize the way in which language can have a whole network of meaning. He uses the example of the word 'spirit', which has both philosophical and psychological and indeed magical connotations, and also the example of his own neologism 'New Being'. His exposition is tantalizingly brief but it does indicate a rare feature of Tillich's method which is generally governed by a more restrictive notion of meaning.

By logical rationality, Tillich meant something more than the element of formal logic in theology, important as that is. Theology should not concede its formally logical character in the face of either a philosophical or a scientific critique. However, true to his idealist inspiration, Tillich sees the logical character of theology as more significantly a matter of dialectics. This is very important for him because herein lies the ability of theology to express the way in which the Christian interpretation of existence is rooted in history and will. Again, Tillich is cryptic and does not explain what he means when he says that theological dialectics 'do not isolate the principle of logical rationality' (ST, vol. 1, p. 63). All that is clear is that, like Hegel, he would seem to view logic in a new way as an intellectual tool that enables the thinker to grasp both the dynamism of change and the essential unity within the change from the old to the new. It is very revealing that the example he gives is the doctrine of the Trinity, for this would seem to confirm that his inspiration here is Hegel. Yet, as is often the case with Tillich, in the very next paragraph he turns to a rather different style of thinking when he defends the rationality of theological paradoxes and says that in the end there is 'only *one* genuine paradox in the Christian message—the appearance of that which conquers existence under the conditions of existence' (ibid., p. 64). This is theology reminiscent of Kierkegaard and his stress on the Absolute Paradox as the heart of Christianity which emerges in the twentieth century as the Christocentricity of theology for Karl Barth.

Finally, theology is methodologically rational: that is, it must be a system because it is 'the function of the systematic form to guarantee the consistency of cognitive assertions in all realms of methodological knowledge' (ibid., p. 65). For Tillich, system and consistency are inseparable if not actually synonymous concepts, and a remark made here in volume 1 of *Systematic Theology* is one he repeated very frequently: a system is implied in the most undeveloped statement. Nor does the fragmentary nature of thought such as Nietzsche's make this claim less true in Tillich's eyes; in all of Nietzsche's fragments a system is implicit. He defends the possibility of system against three kinds of criticism. As against the contention that a system is a deductive scheme, he argues that theology has never attempted the impossible task of constructing a deductive system of Christian truth. His point is that it need not do so because a system is 'a totality made up of consistent, but not of deduced, assertions' (ibid., p. 66). Secondly, a system should stimulate rather than close the door to further research. By giving us a total view of the knowledge we have, the system enables us to see the implications of what we know. The illumination that we gain from such a result and from the very execution of the task opens up new questions. Lastly, we should not succumb to the emotional identification of a system with some prison-house for thought which destroys its creativity. Rather than ruling out adventure, it can afford the opportunity for adventure; such, says Tillich, was the experience of classical Greek philosophers, on the one hand, and nineteenth-century theologians, on the other. More than an essay, because it deals with a group of problems, the system is yet not a *summa*, because it does not deal with all actual problems. A *summa* being now impossible, we need a system all the more.

More than once it has been said in the course of this exposition that Tillich saw himself and his work as Christian. The system is a Christian theology. Yet it is well known that during the last decade of his life Tillich was very much concerned with the relation of Christianity to other religions. This has led many Tillich scholars and others to claim that if Tillich had lived he would have given this late interest in non-Christian religion a formal expression. The claim is given some credence by the fact that his last lecture had as its topic 'the significance of the history of religion for the systematic theologian' (*The Future of Religions*, pp. 80–94). So, the argument goes, Tillich was considering afresh what was a problem inherent in his theology, viz. the apparent contradiction between maintaining a Christocentric stance and method and yet holding a non-exclusivist position with regard to other religions. It is further argued that it was Tillich's intention to rewrite his systematic theology giving greater prominence to the history of religion and making religions rather than merely the Christian religion the basis of that theology. Before considering the theological problem, it might be best to deal with the biographical one. It is certainly true that Tillich was profoundly dissatisfied with various parts of *Systematic Theology*, especially the final volume. As a result, he told several of his friends and pupils that he wanted their help in rewriting that volume; but as late as the end of August, only two months before his death, he did not indicate—at least to one such would-be assistant—that he had in mind a radical revision of its content. It thus seems highly unlikely that Tillich had changed his mind about the nature of systematic theology and its relation to the history of religion. This does not, of course, mean that there was no problem which his now greater interest in non-Christian religions had exacerbated. However, if we read his last lecture—given the night before he suffered the heart attack from which he died ten days later—there is nothing to suggest any change of mind. What he did recognize was that, though his own systematic theology had a clear purpose and coherence, his interest in the history of religion opened up the possibility of a Christian theology developed on the basis of the insights gained from inter-religious dialogue. Such indeed he said was his 'hope for the future of theology' (*The Future of Religions*, p. 91). However, what he did not say was that it was his intention to rewrite his own creation in that way.

One reason why Tillich probably did not feel that this was necessary was his conviction that he had not adopted at any point in his work a position that was directly opposed to this kind of dialogic theology. Two features of Tillich as a theologian are demonstrated here. First, he had what was for his critics the annoying habit of absorbing criticism much as a boxer absorbs his opponent's punches. It is not that he does not feel them but that he is able to continue despite them. So Tillich almost ignored difficulties raised, or even acknowledged them but yet maintained his original position all the same. Secondly, there is about his whole work a quite remarkable consistency which shows that his thought was not only homogeneous but faithful to its own inspiration and intention in an extraordinary way. The fact that he wrote *Systematic Theology* in America does not mean that there is some disjunction between this and his work prior to 1933. The fact is that what he had maintained in his writings on religion and revelation during the years in Germany had not only been concerned with religion rather than Christianity but was formally consistent with what he would main- tain in *Systematic Theology* about the Christian revelation. From his first publication to his last, he was able to defend a Christocentricity in theology, though his understanding of theology had become more and more ontological. The pattern of his developing thought on religion and theology is thus one of a consistent but increasingly clarified notion of religion as both something that grasps man and a self-transcending human concern. Within that, an important place is given to theology. If we return to the point about Tillich's own sense of the consistency of his position, one of the matters that best clarifies this is his understanding of the sources of theology.

Discussing the method and structure of systematic theology in volume 1 of *Systematic Theology*, Tillich shows himself to be both close to Barth and yet very different from him. Just as much as Barth, he is emphatic that the norm of systematic theology is the revelation in Christ and that the Bible is the main source of systematic theology. Yet the difference is immense, as he insists that these are not exclusive claims. The Bible cannot be the sole source because the understanding of that very message of the Bible presupposes a preparation for it in religion and culture. This contextualization of the Bible is taken further by Tillich, as he locates the Bible in church history and relates the reception of its message to the contribution of the Church. It could be pointed out, incidentally, that in this way Tillich made one of the most significant contributions to ecumenical theology by moving the old debate beyond the opposition of Church and Bible and of Catholic and Protestant views. What is most relevant, however, to our discussion is the way he widens out this context to include the history of religions. The very general point that the language of theology has a background of religion and culture is the first point he makes. This contact with religion is 'unavoidable' and direct. What he means, then, is that in the very language he uses the theologian confronts a legacy of religions which he must affirm or deny as the means of expressing that truth which he wants to communicate. Above all, he must recognize that in that legacy there are 'existential questions' implied 'to which his theology intends to be the answer' (ST, vol. 1, p. 44). The discussion of the place of history of religion in the sources of theology is brief; but it specifically maintains that systematic theology depends on the results of a historical investigation of religion and even that the definition of the norm of systematic theology is influenced by it. This is one of the occasions when Tillich shows a healthy sense of the finitude of theology, as of the distinction between theology and the message of which it speaks. The history of religions is thus seen to comprehend Christianity itself and when used by the theologian affords him the understanding of the motives and types of religious expression and of the demonic distortions and new tendencies of the religions of the world. The discussion concludes with the explicit assertion: 'some materials taken from a theological history of religion appear in the present theological system' (ibid., p. 44). Viewed in that light, Tillich's system did not need to be reconstructed in order to accommodate his greater interest in non-Christian religions.

What has been said above can be reinforced in a way that will help us grasp the special character of the theology if we return to Tillich's concern with the phenomenology of the holy. In that final lecture, he uses the idea of the holy to express what is common to all religions. 'The universal religious basis', he says (*The Future of Religions*, p. 86), 'is the experience of the Holy within the finite.' This surely echoes what he had said at the beginning of *Systematic Theology* about the essentially phenomenological task of describing the holy which lay at the very base of his system. In terms of the system's key concepts, what we have is the correlation of revelation and experiential reason which produces a cognitive situation in which reason can grasp what transcends it. If then we move on from the opening of *Systematic Theology* to Part II, we see that it begins with a phenomenological description as promised. What is significant about that description is its identification of divinity and holiness. The doctrine of God that does not include this category, he says, is 'untrue' (ST, vol. 1, p. 239). This concept is what enables the theologian to use 'large sections of the history of religion'. The glory of Tillich's theology was its determined attempt at a phenomenology which was pursued in the conviction that if faith is faith in the ultimate, then the task laid by faith on the theologian was the awesome one of viewing all religion, even Christianity, in the light of the total demand made by the Holy.

4

God, Being and Existence

From the earliest period of his theological creativity, Tillich had displayed both a reluctance to regard religion as an end in itself and a powerful concern for God's transcendence. The lecture on the idea of a theology of culture had prefigured the critique of religion in his works on the philosophy of religion; and equally throughout his early writings there breathes an almost mystical sense of God's ineffability. Not to remember that this is the background to his very philosophical approach to the doctrine of God in the mature *Systematic Theology* is completely to misunderstand that doctrine.

Whatever else he was, Tillich was a genuinely philosophical theologian, and the concerns of the noun were as vital to him as those of the adjective. It is not too much to say that though the *theology*, the doctrine of God, developed in *Systematic Theology* was radically different from that of his friend Karl Barth, the origins of each were very close if not indeed identical. Tillich's debt to Schelling and Hegel has often been pointed out, but this should not be considered as something quite alien to the development of Barth's theology as well. Nor should it be forgotten that behind Schelling's Idealism lies Jacob Boehme's (1575–1624) mystical theology of ground and abyss. This was especially important for Tillich as he struggled to grasp the metaphysical significance of 'the experience of the infinite bordering upon the finite as one has it by the sea' (*Interpretation of History*, p. 7). There were, as we have seen, social and political concerns which played an important part in his early development as a theologian; but, for the moment, we can concentrate on the philosophical aspect even of these. He said that it was the philosophical influences which cleared his vision, and by this he did not refer to simply intellectual clarification: he was *saved* from an irreligious outlook. Having been saved from naturalism by phenomenology, he tended to regard the critique of Idealism by the later Schelling as making the same plea for freeing the essence of consciousness from its limitation to the facts of common sense. As he saw it, he had lived through the failure of Idealism which had been revealed to him in the horror of war and the subsequent social catastrophe that had befallen a triumphalist world-view born of the marriage of church and state. Now therefore he could not content himself with any outlook which canonized historical relativities.

This philosophical background to Tillich's theology is especially important for his specific doctrine of God; for it is in the very idea of God that Tillich seems to see the essence of what he often describes as the nature of theological method or the ideal of a proper theological approach, the method of complementarity. The human situation is for him not confined to the empirical and the finite; but neither is it one where man, angelic in his privileged position, can claim to be forever free of these limitations. Man lives on the border and is aware of the constant thrust of reason beyond all that technical reason can yield, aware of what he calls the depth of reason. This is the kind of fundamental metaphysical impasse that Kant describes when he speaks of the way in which the Cosmological Argument for God's existence remains something essentially flawed as any kind of logical proof or argument and yet brings the human mind to a point at which either the conclusion is admitted or we are confronted with an abyss. At the end of his days, Tillich readily accepted that Kant was a decisive influence on his thinking and the unusually eloquent words of Kant's *Critique of Pure Reason* seem a very apt description of his concept of the Unconditioned— that if we were to say that the chain of causes in the world led to a Cause who could say of himself that everything depended on him and yet could not define himself as unconditioned we are brought to a pure abyss of thought.

It is time to use Tillich's favourite term for describing his philosophical concern: ontology. That owes as much to early and classical Greek philosophy as it does either to nineteenth-century Idealism or to Heidegger. Not only was Tillich clear in his conviction that theology needed to be philosophical, but he was equally convinced that the Platonic tradition represented the proper trad-

71

ition in philosophy. He was fond of distinguishing his own attitude from an Aristotelian one, attributing failure to understand his position or criticism of it to an excessive influence of Aristotelianism. 'You are too Aristotelian', he would say to his pupils, as if he were blaming them for an impetuosity or some short-sightedness. Coupled with this was an assumption that the ontological philosopher did not make any artificial distinctions between philosophy, religion and science, so that what was understood as the object of ontological speculation was identical with the object of religious worship. What makes Tillich's little book *Biblical Religion and the Search for Ultimate Reality* so important is that it contains the clearest statement of this conviction. There, for instance, he shows that ontology is for him the essence of philosophy. While in *Systematic Theology* (vol. 1, pp. 23–4) he had protested against the reduction of philosophy to epistemology, in this work he argues that philosophy is identical with ontology, that it is nothing else than the ontological quest of ultimate reality. Ontology, he says (*Biblical Religion*, p. 6), is the word he prefers, because it is the centre of all philosophy: it is 'first philosophy', as Aristotle termed it. In the light of what was said above about Kant's critique of the Cosmological Argument, it is interesting to see Tillich go on in this discussion of philosophy to compare the 'child's restless question "Why is this so; why is that not so?" and Kant's grandiose description of the God who asks himself "Why am I?"' (ibid., p. 9). Then he says 'Man is by nature a philosopher because he inescapably asks the question of being'. Both here in this book and in other contexts beside *Systematic Theology*, Tillich insists that it is impossible to do theology without philosophy. This is a very important and extremely useful contribution which he has made to theology, and the interesting thing about his work is the fact that the way in which he did so was equally important. He was fond of pointing out that the error of an anti-philosophical theology was not to realize, or to forget, that the escape-routes from philosophy which the theologian then adopted were themselves philosophical. That is not the point we are here considering but rather the very different point that the idea of God as such is philosophical. The being-itself which is the 'ultimate reality' of philosophical investigation is God.

Such being Tillich's perspective on theology, he begins his discussion of the question of God in *Systematic Theology* with a description and analysis of four levels of ontological concepts. First, there is the basic ontological structure, by which he means the structure of being as a subject–object relation. That implies that we not only understand the world as a correlate of the self but understand that structure of self–world as fundamental, something which is prior to all other structures in terms of our experience as well as logic. The second level is a classification of concepts which are employed in the description of this basic structure. Because that basic structure is a polar relation, these concepts will also be polar relations. They are: individuality and universality; dynamics and form; freedom and destiny. These are the concepts which describe being as 'part of a universe of being', says Tillich. Translating that into a more intelligible language for twentieth-century philosophy, this is a matter of saying that such concepts describe being as constituting a universe, a complex of patterns of relations that describe what constitutes our world. The third level is the characteristics of being which are the conditions of existence. Here Tillich uses a concept which he once described as Platonic but which probably owes more to Schelling: that of power. Being has the power to exist: and the account of being must then distinguish between essential and existential being. The whole history of ontology for him illustrates this necessity of distinguishing essential and existential being. The definition of their relation is what is offered in the analysis of freedom. This too is a polar concept and so it presupposes that of destiny; for existence can only be understood in terms not of freedom pure and simple but of 'freedom in unity with finitude'. An analysis of being is thus for Tillich some kind of intellectual or abstract drama, the story of being becoming existence through freedom; and this story is that of the relation of finitude to infinity as well as the relation of finitude to freedom and destiny. Finally, following the Kantian tradition, he identifies categories as the fourth level and points out incidentally that his use of the term, though wider than Kant's own, is that of 'the post-Kantian schools'. Four such basic forms of thought and being are important for theology: time, space, causality and substance. These are the categories of finitude, and it is finitude that raises the question of God.

One other ontological concept needs to be mentioned before we consider the doctrine of God as such, and that is the concept of non-being. As we have seen, ontology is for Tillich an inescapable activity and he says that this involves asking the question of non-being. That question, as much as the question of being, he says, is and always has been part of ontology, though one might try to dismiss it as either a logical or an ontological mistake. Logical negation is meaningful, he argues, only if this non-being has ontological significance. Moreover, he maintains that it is impossible for us to think of a world if there is in fact nothing but being. These are two positions which he seems to maintain as one, and he maintains them in the face of modern logic and metaphysics. This concept of non-being, which he aptly describes as referring to a mystery, is one which has its roots in early and classical Greek philosophy. The 'genius of the Greek language', for Tillich, is its capacity for a distinction between absolute and relative non-being, what he calls the non-dialectical (*ouk on*) and the dialectical (*mē on*).

The concept of a nothingness which has a dialectical relation to being is an important element in Tillich's doctrine of God. It will play an important part both in his conception of the world that God creates and indeed in his view of the very nature of creation. Also, he sees the very idea of God as such as one which involves this idea of non-being. If God is the sole ground of everything and of the creativity of life, one has thereby refused to countenance any other principle of explanation. How then, he asks, can one avoid speaking of God as containing within himself some dialectical negativity? Being, 'limited by non-being', is finitude; and finitude is something that is understood by means of the categories. Also something of which we are aware is the state of anxiety, a concept which various twentieth-century disciplines, together with existentialist philosophy, recovered for us. A philosophical or a theological understanding of finitude is possible only by distinguishing between essential and existential being, what being is in essence and what we know it to be as fact. This is the presupposition of any distinction not only between the ideal and the real but also between the true and the erroneous, the good and the evil. How the distinction is made does not matter so much as the fact that the question of its possibility is raised in ontological terms—that is, whatever way we distinguish, say, between the good and the evil, the ground of that distinction is seen to be a matter of essential and existential being. Tillich freely admits that the distinction is not easy to understand because of the ambiguity of both terms. Ever since Plato, the terms have referred to value as much as logic; and the distinction is not only between what reality is and the fact that it is, but between 'the original goodness of everything created' and the 'fallen world'. In Christian theology, the distinction refers to the split between this created goodness of things and the distortion of their existence, that created goodness being the essential nature of all reality. In relation to the history of philosophy, the theological distinction steers a middle course between the Platonic and the Aristotelian traditions.

As we have already seen, for Tillich the religious outlook is man's response to the mystery revealed in the world. So he is very anxious to stress that belief in God should not be tied to the old debate about whether God's existence can be proved or not. In fact, he goes so far as to say that it would be beneficial for theology to confine the notion of God's existence to the Christological paradox, a view that recalls Kierkegaard's comment that God is and exists (that is, in time) in Christ; and, indeed, this is a view that is as old as Augustine (354–430). If Tillich's doctrine of God were seen in this very Augustinian perspective there would be less pointless discussion of his so-called atheism. Concerning the traditional proofs, he says that their lengthy and inconclusive history can only be explained by the recognition that their defenders and attackers were not arguing about the same thing. 'They fought over different matters which they expressed in the same terms' (ST, vol. 1, p. 227). The attackers, he says, attacked the 'argumentative form' of the arguments or proofs whereas the defenders 'accepted their implicit meaning'. It must be said that this view of the history of theistic proof is very simplistic: for instance, it makes nonsense of either Gaunilo's or St Thomas Aquinas's criticism of St Anselm's (1033–1109) Ontological Argument. Only the vagueness of the expressions which Tillich uses lends this contention any credibility. The fact of the matter is that Tillich is not interested in this historical issue, however much he may have wanted to say that he had history on his side. He is concerned only to illuminate what he sees to be the significance of the arguments and to expose the error of relating the notion of God to either argument or the concept of 'existence'. There is, he thinks, no way in which the existence of God can be defined in a non-paradoxical way that is consistent with the Christian view of God as the creator of all things. Rather than being an important or necessary tool for theology, the idea of existence contradicts the very notion of God as creator, 'the creative ground of essence and existence'. His point is that he regards the use of the term 'existence' as indicating the reality of some particular thing. So he thinks that to speak of the existence of God is to suggest that God is just one more item in the list of the universe's contents. By contrast, mediaeval theologians such as St Thomas (c. 1225–1274) saw that God's existence was the same as his essence and they were right to make this the way in which one speaks of existence in relation to God.

It is typical of Tillich that he ignores the complexity of St Thomas's view on this matter and says quite simply and categorically that even when the mediaeval theologians argued in favour of God's existence they did not mean 'existence'. They meant, he says, the reality or the truth of the idea of God; and to one's puzzled question whether this is not the same thing he would answer simply that it is very different. For him to assert that God exists is to say that God is something or someone who might not exist. The error of saying that God exists, then, is that of saying that something which is necessarily true need not be so or that some being which necessarily exists might not exist. That each of these statements is a contradiction in terms is clear enough; but what is not clear is which of these two statements Tillich means to assert and what he understands by 'necessity' in either case. His actual exposition of the doctrine avoids the kind of obvious ambiguity now stated because he suggests that the concept of existence is inapplicable inasmuch as God is 'beyond essence and existence'. God is being-itself, an assertion that manifests Tillich's profound devotion to the ontological approach to both philosophy and theology. A paper which is not only one of his most important but also one of the most self-revealing is 'The two types of philosophy of religion' (*Theology of Culture*, pp. 10–29). There he makes clear (p. 25) that the power of being 'is the *prius* of everything that has being', that one cannot approach being in any other way than by starting with the concept of being-itself as the power of being.

In following Tillich's philosophical analysis of the notion of God, we must not forget that what lies behind this is the phenomenological description of encountering the holy as that which concerns man ultimately. When in *Systematic Theology* he is engaged in the discussion of this phenomenology, Tillich shows not only that he is very consciously working within the historical tradition of religious philosophy, but, more particularly, that the basis of his thinking is the tradition of Christian philosophical theology. The discussion is a very scholarly excursus which has an aim that is in one sense very simple. His purpose is to show how philosophical questions coincide with religious ones and in particular to illustrate that the idea of God is a philosophical expression of the living awareness of the dimension of the holy. Thus he sees this idea of God as ultimate concern to be 'the abstract translation' of the First Commandment: 'The Lord God is one Lord and you shall love the Lord thy God with all your heart and with all your soul and with all your might' (Deuteronomy

6:45). It is interesting that one of the sources of this view of the nature of religion is Kierkegaard, the great opponent of Hegel's transformation of Christianity into a philosophy. Though it might be said that this only goes to show how Tillich managed to combine in his thinking influences that were so different as sometimes to be radically opposed, it is in fact an indication of how he saw his own theological stance to be anything but such a transforming attitude as Hegel's. His view is that, apart from references to our religious life as the existential encounter with the holy, the idea of God can be spoken of only as being. He is 'being-itself' or 'the power of being whereby it resists non-being', this latter being an idea which, Tillich says, is as old as Plato. Any theology which does not make this identification ends up making God less than God because 'its superlatives become diminutives' (ST, vol. 1, p. 261). If God is not being-itself, he is, in fact, in as much bondage as the old Greek gods were in bondage to fate—a King indeed but only a puppet-king.

Apart from the ontological assertion that God is being-itself, then, there is no theological assertion that is literally true. 'Being-itself' and its synonym 'power of being' are thus *definitions* of God, and all the descriptions of God which make up theology are symbolical statements. To understand this, and especially to understand that it is by no means a strange position, we need to grasp Tillich's individual view of symbolism. Whether he was right or wrong to make the claim, his oft-repeated assertion that his position was the same as that of St Thomas reveals his conviction that his position is perfectly orthodox. Before considering what Tillich means by symbolism, it is as well to note that he makes two exceptions to the rule which we have just uncovered. In the Introduction to *Systematic Theology*, volume 2, he refers to criticism of his theory that all theological language is symbolical and concedes that as any symbolical language must have a non-symbolical anchor, so there must be a non-symbolical anchor to our language about God. There is, in fact, he says, one such non-symbolical statement over and above the definition of God as being-itself, and this is the statement that all other language is symbolical. As I have shown elsewhere, this way out of his difficulty will not work, because he has not understood the logic of description. The second exception is that there are words which seem, as they are used in theology, to have the power of definitions or to act as names and so to be symbols of a special kind. These are such terms as 'eternity' and 'unconditioned', which would seem to be synonyms for being-itself (cf. ST, vol. 1, pp. 217, 265, 306).

The symbolic nature of religious and theological language is mentioned quite casually early in Tillich's elaboration of his doctrine of revelation in volume 1 of *Systematic Theology*. The casualness of the reference is indicative of how axiomatic Tillich took this position to be. This emphasis on symbolism in language and on the necessity of symbolism is something that goes back to his early philosophy. In *System of the Sciences*, he maintained that the concepts employed by metaphysics are symbols. The symbol affirms and paradoxically protests against its expression of the Unconditioned. Already, then, Tillich envisaged symbolism as a characteristic feature of metaphysics as such and therefore of the kind of thinking which he felt theology to be. Influenced no doubt by the fashionable concern with symbolical expression, Tillich also contributed to the popular understanding of theology as symbolism in a number of papers. Later, he went so far as to describe this as the centre of his doctrine of knowledge and he also claimed that in this he was at one with St Thomas—what Thomas meant by analogy was what he meant by symbol. This latter claim was analysed by more than one Catholic critic and the important differences between Tillich and St Thomas laid bare. Notwithstanding these differences, there is one very revealing thing about the claim that is worth noting. Just as St Thomas was concerned not so much to elaborate a theory about analogical meaning but simply to emphasize the meaningfulness of language about God, so, for Tillich, the primary purpose of his doctrine of symbols is to defend the meaningfulness of the language of religion and theology. Coming from this background of a very general metaphysical enterprise with this profound theological concern, he seemed to many to be the best answer to the destructive effect of contemporary philosophy.

We can usefully think of the role played by the theory of symbols in Tillich's theology by comparing it with that of the view of religion as feeling in Schleiermacher's theology: it is a way of appealing to sceptics, the disillusioned 'despisers of religion' among the intellectuals of the time. Responding to critics in his introduction to volume 2 of *Systematic Theology*, Tillich sets out his view of a religious symbol. It is a piece of ordinary everyday experience used to speak of God by its ordinary meaning being both affirmed and denied. A symbol is to be distinguished from a sign because, though, like a sign, it points beyond itself to something else, its relation to that is an 'inner' one—it 'participates in the reality which is symbolized'. There is a sense in which all language is a sign; but religious language is not only a sign but essentially symbolic. Frequently in his writing and when teaching, Tillich protested against the tendency to speak of something being 'only a symbol' when we should recognize that if we have a symbol we have everything. Symbols can be non-linguistic, as, for example, the flag and the crucifix. Sometimes Tillich used the expression 'participates in the power of what is symbolized' to indicate the nature of the symbol in such contexts of use. The symbol 'opens up' for us dimensions of reality which would other- wise be closed to us. There is no substitute for a symbol, whereas we could choose whatever we liked to act as a sign of something. 'The flag participates in the power of the thing or the nation for which it stands and which it symbolizes.' That is to say, there is some connection between the symbol and the thing symbolized beyond that which is assigned by a choice which could be simply random. Finally, if symbols are thus not chosen but are perhaps uncon- sciously accepted by us and are irreplaceable in this way, they can be said to be born and they can disappear only because they die. For instance, only if a nation breaks up and its history passes into night can its flag cease to be its symbol.

The central symbolic statements about God are that he is 'living' and that he is 'personal', that he is 'the creative and abysmal ground of being' and that he is 'Spirit' or 'Love'. Life is 'the process in which potential being becomes actual being'; but in God there is no such distinction, because he transcends both potential and actual being. So the assertion that God is living contains a negative element; but God is the ground of being and as such can be described as living. 'Ground' here does not mean cause or substance in the literal sense but something which underlies everything and whose relation to things we then *symbolically* describe as causation or substantiality. Any cause is also an effect, a link in a causal chain; but God is not so conditioned. Substance and accidents are related to each other in a logically necessary way, but God's relation to man is free. God is not a thing or an object: he has selfhood. Yet even that distinction does not give us the precise distinction we want; for 'self' implies separation from and contrast with everything that is not self, whereas God, since he is being-itself, is not separate from anything. He is the 'absolute participant' so that we cannot understand the assertion of his selfhood literally. He is superpersonal, and yet, necessarily, we speak of him as personal. God is free and yet he has a destiny—again in a non-literal sense, since in God destiny is 'absolute and unconditioned identity with freedom'. In no sense can we say that God exists, because existence necessarily implies being subject to space, time and causality. In this symbolical theology of his, says Tillich (*Theology of Paul Tillich*, p. 334), the two conflicting traditions of a theology of glory and a negative theology are unified. Using both terms of a polar description is the only way of giving a proper account of the nature of God.

Clearly, Tillich will have little sympathy with the classical so-called proofs of the existence of God. The notion of an argument for God's existence is for him fallacious on two counts: God does not exist, and is not the conclusion of an argument. However it is defined, the existence of God contradicts the idea of a creative ground of essence and existence. The only real atheism in Tillich's view is the assertion that God exists. The proofs are indeed important in theology because they are expressions of the *question* of God which is implied in human finitude. They are analyses of the human situation which show that the question of God is both possible and necessary. Thus the various forms of the Ontological Argument are various descriptions of the way in which potential infinity is present in actual finitude. They express the unconditional element in the structures of reason and reality. The Ontological Argument thus shows that the question of God is possible. The two cosmological arguments, as Tillich describes the Cosmological and Teleological Arguments, show that the question of God is necessary. 'First Cause' and 'necessary substance' are symbols which express the question implied in finite being, the question of that which transcends finitude and the categories, 'the question of being-itself, embracing and conquering non-being'. The Teleological Argument, the argument from design, moves from finite and threatened meanings to an infinite and unthreatened cause of meanings. The basis for the Teleological Argument is the threat against the finite structure of being, that is the unity of its polar elements. The *telos* from which this argument receives its name is the 'inner aim', the meaningful, understandable structure of reality. Tillich clarifies his rejection of traditional theism in *Courage to Be*, where he distinguishes three meanings of the word 'theism': the unspecified affirmation of God, the name of the 'divine–human encounter' and theological theism. Theism in the first sense, he argues, must be transcended because it is irrelevant, and theism in the second sense must be transcended because it is one-sided. Theism in the third sense, however, must be transcended because it is wrong. What is wrong with it is that God is conceived of as a being besides others and such a part of the whole of reality so that the distinctiveness of the notion of God is forgotten. Therefore, in *Courage to Be*, Tillich talks of the content of absolute faith as the 'God above God'.

As living, God is creative. He is creative because he is God and so it is meaningless to ask whether creation is a necessary or a contingent act of God's. It is neither necessary nor contingent inasmuch as God is not dependent on a necessity above him and creation is identical with his life. It is not the story of an event which took place once upon a time but the basic description of the relation between God and the world. That relation is symbolized by talking of creation as having taken place (originating creation), as taking place (sustaining creation) and as the future fulfilment of God's *telos* (directing creation). Originating creation has been defined as *creatio ex nihilo* (creation out of nothing). This clearly means the rejection of dualism—which was why the church so defined creation, thereby distinguishing its understanding of the world from other world-views, including heretical ones. The formula also means something else for Tillich: in the word *ex* he sees a reference to the origin of the creature. 'Nothing' is where the creature comes from, he says, and so the doctrine of creation has two further implications besides the rejection of dualism. The first is that the tragic character of existence is not rooted in the creative ground of being and so does not belong to the essential nature of things. Secondly, there is an element of non-being in creatureliness so that, though the tragic is not necessary, it is potential. Tillich rejects any deistic understanding of creation which would see God's action as simply originating and God himself as totally uninvolved in the world's continuing history. With Augustine, he holds that God is continually creative.

Referring to the description of God in the Nicene Creed as creator of 'all things visible and invisible', Tillich remarks that, once again, the doctrine distinguishes between a Christian view of the world and a pagan philosophy. The creator is not dependent on essences as he is in the Platonic doctrine of the creator-god who is dependent on the eternal ideas. When the doctrine of the ideas entered Christian theology, these ideas were said to be ideas in God's mind, themselves part of God's creativity. In God, there is no difference between potentiality and actuality, and the divine creation precedes the distinction or differentiation of essence from existence. Though later in his discussion of originating creation Tillich insists on the polarity of man and his world, saying that the traditional view as a microcosm should emphasize more the mutual participation of man and nature, he is really more interested in the creation of man than in the creation of the world. It is man's individual existence that poses for him the crucial problem within the doctrine of creation: how the creation can precede the differentiation of essence and existence. His answer is that man is grounded in the divine life but he is not kept within the ground. The doctrine of creation and the doctrine of the Fall join at this point. Being a creature means both that the divine creativity is the ground of its life and that its life is an actualization of the self through finite freedom. Creaturely freedom, Tillich insists, is 'the point at which creation and the fall coincide'.

In a brief discussion of the relation of creation to the categories of reality, Tillich takes time as the primary example. The idea that there was a time before creation is absurd, he says, because the idea of creation as an event is absurd. Since Augustine, it has been traditional to maintain that time was created *with* the world. So for Tillich, there is really no difference between this position and that which theologians like Barth maintain when they argue that, though there is no pre-creation time, creation is in time, co-eternal with God but temporal in its content because it is in God's time. For him, the solution to the problem of creation and time is to be found in the creative character of the divine life. If this world is created, then we cannot separate the categories as forms of finitude from the divine life: the categories do not indeed describe the divine life but it is the divine life which gives them their applicability to our world. So we must see time as part of that life, and as such time cannot have the negative character it has in creaturely existence. 'The divine eternity includes time and transcends it', he says (ST, vol. 1, p. 285). What this means for him is that in the divine life temporality is not a transition of past to future but a present. Our time is a time determined by non-being; but God's time is an eternal being.

As well as originating, creation is both sustaining and directing. What Tillich calls sustaining creation is traditionally spoken of as God's preservation of the world, even when philosophers like Descartes (1596–1650) recognized that the power needed for the original creation of the world is equally needed for its continued existence minute by minute. What Tillich dislikes about the termin-ology of preservation is the suggestion that in essence creation is to be understood in deistic terms. The world is thought of as an independent system with its own laws according to which history is unfolded. It is not only the traditional Deism which thinks in this way, he says, but even theistic views are guilty of such an error. Much better, he thinks, is the Augustinian view of preservation as a continuous creativity. This view—accepted by the Reformers and in particular articulated so clearly by Calvin—is what Tillich regards as the best way of protecting against the tendency to speak of God as a being alongside the world, a view he labels 'half-deistic, half-theistic'. What then is the difference between originating and sustaining creation? Tillich's answer is that sustaining creation 'refers to the given structures of reality, to that which continues within the change, as the regular and the calculable in things' (ST, vol. 1, p. 291). This abstract answer is not very helpful: it seems to be neither especially relevant nor indeed very clear. What he seems to mean is that whereas talk of originating creation is a way of defining the relation between the fact of the world and God, sustaining creation is how we conceive of the *nature* of the world to be related to God. That is, one could say that originating creation 'explains' the very existence of the world, how it came to exist at all; but sustaining creation 'explains' our confidence in the uniformity and regularity of nature. Sustaining creation is a symbol, Tillich feels, which is particularly relevant to the twentieth century because of its catastrophes and the expression of a sense of insecurity in philosophy and literature. If sustaining creation is a protest against the idea of God as a being alongside the world, what happens to the idea of transcendence? Quite clearly, Tillich does not abandon the notion which, as we have seen, is fundamental to his thinking. His answer is that we must penetrate beyond the spatial thinking which usually characterizes this symbol to the qualitative relation it expresses. We rightly say that God is transcendent to the finite world, but this transcendence is not a simple contradiction of the finite: rather, it is my encounter with a freedom which may conflict with mine and which also can reconcile the two. Finally, creation is directing. The divine creativity drives every creature towards the fulfilment in actuality of what in the divine life is beyond potentiality and actuality. Tillich rejects the concept of 'the purpose of creation': creation has no purpose beyond itself. Instead of 'the purpose of creation', we should talk of 'the *telos* of creativity'.

Traditionally, this is called providence, a concept which for Tillich has always had a paradoxical character. To assert that the earth on which we live is a part of providence is to make the paradoxical assertion that things are not what they seem: in spite of the incessant experience of meaninglessness, it yet asserts that historical existence has meaning. It is the triumph of the prophetical point of view, the paradigm of that triumph being the victory of Christ on the cross. The rational transformation of this notion of providence has been shattered by the history of the twentieth century but faith itself can yet be seen as the answer to this challenge. Faith in historical providence means that we are certain that all history contributes to the ultimate fulfilment of creaturely existence. The Christian notion of providence is a personal one: 'it carries the warmth of belief in loving protection and personal guidance' (ST, vol. 1, p. 297); but what is true for the individual is also true with regard to history. The apparent lack of fulfilment raises the question of the relation of God to the world's meaningless features, the question in fact of theodicy. The first step towards an answer is the recognition that creation is the creation of finite freedom, a risk that God had to take if he created and so created life. The final answer, Tillich insists, is a mysterious one: and he rejects all talk of theodicy that is not an expression of the kind of faith that is prepared to sit where suffering humanity does. The final answer is indeed a theology of the cross which speaks of the participation of the divine life in the world's negativities.

It is not only the profoundly philosophical character of Tillich's doctrine of God that makes it forbidding and difficult to grasp; the particular combination of so many philosophical sources produces puzzlement and misunderstanding. Having followed the elaboration of his doctrine from the very strong existential base, we have seen that in many ways he is essentially a kerygmatic theologian looking for the appropriate ways of expressing a theology of the *Gospel*. He is traditional and indeed orthodox in his view of God as the Revealer and Creator who triumphed on the Cross—and this despite the fact that he has been anything but traditional in his method and expression. The great attraction of Tillich as a theologian is his readiness to use philosophy and to cast theology in a language which—rightly or wrongly—he thought was intelligible to non-believers precisely because it was so often the language of modern philosophy. It could be said that one of his achievements was to have rescued the philosophical approach to theology from what he saw to be its decline in the mid-century. That his own philosophy was syncretistic, an amalgam of very different traditions, did not lessen his achievement in attempting a metaphysic in the teeth of the devastating critique of metaphysics in twentieth-century philosophy.

Nor did the confusions in his philosophical discussions invalidate the work he sought to do, which was to deal with the questions raised by the claims made by faith—without suggesting that those claims were themselves based on, and so challengeable by, philosophy. As we have seen, Tillich speaks of the idea of God as philosophical because this idea is of an absolute and there is no sense to such an assertion which is devoid of philosophical interest. When he offers his ontological definition of God, he does not want to suggest that there is any identification of God possible except in the encounter of Revelation. Here is an example of the unfortunate and misleading way in which so often he expresses himself. To say that the assertion 'God is being-itself' is a philosophical translation of the First Commandment is to say more than that; but two things need to be remembered, only one of which is that this is at least a statement that is *consistent* with the commandment. As has become very clear, Tillich was very linguistically sensitive but he had very little understanding of the developments in the philosophy of language, tending to dismiss all that as 'damned Logical Positivism'. It was not only that this was a translation of command into an interpretative assertion, but the language which was being translated was a biblical one. Wrong as he is to speak of translation here, he is surely nothing but orthodox in his starting-point. Similarly, his much-criticized 'atheism' turns out to be far less heterodox than appears. His understanding of mediaeval theology is as open to criticism as his grasp of the logical and epistemological issues in regard to proving the existence of God. Yet he most definitely wants to align himself with St Thomas and all the classical theologians who see the reality of God to be the basic axiom of theology. If by the non-existence of God he means no more than the assertion that God is not an empirical existent, then it is merely a rather paradoxical way of making an entirely unexceptionable statement. It is, of course, not the case that all seemingly radical suggestions in Tillich's theology are in the end harmless and indeed familiar positions or even banalities. He is often guilty of serious logical errors where such are of vital importance to doctrine. One example has already been discussed: the argument that the doctrine of a symbolical theology is guaranteed by the assertion that everything we say about God is symbolic has its non-symbolic anchor in that statement. This is a mistake as old as the paradox of the Cretan Liar and as such a distinctly unhelpful contribution to philosophical theology.

Tillich's philosophy was in his view very much a modern method:

the ontology was an ontology approached from and based on human existence. We have seen how in his discussion of creation an idea that is very familar to readers of Heidegger, the idea of Nothing, plays an important role. What is very interesting about Tillich's view of creation is that, though he speaks of man and the world as interrelated, it is human existence which is constantly discussed in the elaboration of the doctrine of creation. This is the existence that is brought to actuality by the divine creativity when it coincides with the split of essence from existence. That is the phenomenon which his ontology was to analyse and so show the quest in existence for the New Being, the providential reconciliation of the finite and the infinite life. To that analysis of fallen existence we turn next.

5

Existence and Estrangement

Following his phenomenological and ontological approach, Tillich offers in his theology an account not only of man's situation but also of his nature. The doctrine of creation has yielded a view of man as a creature which regards him as having a heritage of non-being. Post-Freudian as we are, we might think of this as some psychological analysis in terms of a death-wish; but, as we have said, this is an ontological account and Tillich is talking of the very nature of finitude. Man's being is limited by non-being, something which we have seen to be an important part of Tillich's account of the world's reality. The peculiar nature of man's finitude is his ability to experience the 'shock of non-being'. Whereas everything in the world shares finitude, only man is aware of it and, in that sense, is able to transcend it. As we have seen, Tillich regards non-being as something real and not as some purely negative concept of an absence of being or emptiness. This 'dialectical concept of non-being', as he calls it, has introduced a certain confusion into his doctrine of creation, because he both rejects the interpretation of the 'nothing' in 'creation out of nothing' as some kind of element in a Greek cosmogony, and yet he asserts that the 'nothing' is the origin of the creature. That the latter is not a piece of peculiar syntax is clear from the way in which he goes on to exploit this confusion by elaborating a doctrine of man which emphasizes non-being as an essential feature of his nature. In his typically etymological way of thinking, Tillich talks of finitude as related to 'that which is with a definite end (*finis*)' (ST, vol. 1, p. 210). The suggestion here seems to be that what is finite is what is of limited duration and so the finite is contrasted with being-itself which, because it is the power of being, can have neither beginning nor end. The logical basis of Tillich's argument, then, seems to be that limited duration of existence is necessarily related to non-being. Man is characterized by the heritage of non-being because as a creature he has a limited duration and his existence can be said to be bounded by non-being. This seems to be a strange combination of metaphor and a Platonic metaphysic of the process of change. My non-being before I was born is something in the way in which there was a chunk of marble which was then made or transformed into Michelangelo's David. Confronted with this, one is very tempted to dismiss Tillich's anthropology at this point as so much confusion. Yet it would be quite wrong to think that Tillich is simply perpetrating mistakes which have, in fact, often figured in the history of philosophy: he is making the valid point that man is a unique creature. His way of making that point is to emphasize, in much the way that Pascal did, the uniqueness of man's awareness of his own finitude. Man is aware of the threat of non-being and this 'inward' expression of his 'outward' finitude is the anxiety which is the fundamental character of his life. Anxious in the face of meaninglessness, man is estranged from the ground of his being. This is how Tillich interprets the significance of the Christian doctrine of man as a fallen creature, both reaffirming the doctrine and seeking to explain it anew.

The word 'existence' is, in Tillich's view, like so many words in that it is generally abused, and he criticizes the modern nominalist tendency to make words mere conventional signs. Words, he says, are symbols and so cannot be replaced at will. The theologian must recover their proper significance—their meaning and their power; and one way of doing this is to discover their etymology. So he begins his discussion of existence by indicating the root meaning of 'to exist' in the Latin verb *existere*, to stand out. To exist is to stand out of non-being or nothingness. Immediately, however, he says that existence 'does not completely stand out of non-being'. This is the definition of man as finite at which he had arrived in his doctrine of creation, so that this is the real basis for his argument about man rather than the spurious argument about the etymology of 'existence'. What exactly he thinks that etymology establishes is never very clear because he is hardly consistent in his view that the meaning of words is fixed—if only because he complains of the tendency to diminish their significance. Nor could anything be established from etymology that would be a proper foundation for an argument that is made up of metaphorical statements like 'everything that exists is in being and non-being'. Tillich's concern is to press home his conviction that existence reveals a split between potentiality and actuality. His mode of argument here in fact draws on more than one metaphysical tradition, talking as he does of essences such as 'treehood' which do not exist but have potential being. The tree exists because it 'participates in that power of being which is treehood' (ST, vol. 2, p. 24). The historical excursus in the argument is very interesting as a revelation of the background to Tillich's theology. Beginning with Plato, he moves to Romanticism and the protest against Hegel's essentialism which arose in nineteenth- and twentieth-century existentialism. The theological task is to demonstrate what this tradition has established about the meaning of existence, something the theologian does by attending to religious symbols which point to the human predicament. This should really give the lie to the charge, so commonly made against Tillich, that he transformed theology into an existentialist philosophy; and it is particularly unfortunate that he did not clarify the independence of the two enquiries, especially at this point where he sees them coinciding. What he has argued here is that there is a long tradition of philosophy which culminates in the existentialist movement, a movement stretching back to Schelling as he thinks, according to which man's existential situation is that of being estranged from his essential nature. Though it might seem a negative and a somewhat abstract account, this is the beginning of a theological account of human nature for Tillich, an account of the concrete reality of human existence in the light of the ultimate reality of God. We cannot—any more than Tillich himself—escape the difficult doctrine of sin.

It is no surprise, then, to find Tillich insisting on the symbol of the Fall not only as a historical legacy of Christian theology but as a necessary symbol of the human situation. We need to realize, he says, that the biblical story of the Fall of Adam has had important consequences for Christian theology because it has been interpreted literalistically as the story of what happened to humanity once upon a time. For him, however, the real significance is that here we have a symbol for the human situation universally (ST, vol. 2, p. 33). That is, we have here a truth about man at any time and in any place. His way of dealing with the traditional myth is not to reject it but to offer what he calls 'a half-way demythologization' of it. In other words, he does not want to go along with those who dismiss the mythical form completely but he wants to insist that this is no historical account and, to that extent, he is prepared to destroy the myth as the story of what once took place. His way of handling the myth is to retain the myth and yet to interpret it. The interpretation which he offers of the myth as 'the transition from essence to existence' does not remove from theology all traces of myth; for even this apparent abstraction still seems to carry some connotation of something that happened in time (a timeless transition being meaningless). Theology without myth never has been possible and never can be possible: for Tillich, this has already been established in his earlier analysis of theological language. Theological language is necessarily symbolical and, if so, it must be characterized by myth, since myth is a collection of symbols into a story. By this symbol of the Fall, then, Tillich sees theology engaging not only in the articulation of a religious vision of the human situation but in the kind of ontological analysis that has been obvious in Western philosophical thought since Plato.

To describe the transition from essence to existence, Tillich begins with the Genesis myth, 'the profoundest and richest expression of man's awareness of his existential estrangement'. It indicates four things: the possibility of the Fall, its motives, the event itself and finally its consequences (ST, vol. 2, p. 35). The possibility of the Fall is to be found in freedom, a concept which, in its polar unity with destiny, Tillich has already employed in his metaphysical account of existence. This concept he now refines, saying that freedom as such does not explain how the Fall is possible: man's freedom is finite. His freedom is limited by destiny, even when he is able by his freedom to contradict himself. In this way, Tillich builds up his answer to the question of the possibility of the Fall, and he sees this as an advance on the traditional theology of sin. The weakness of traditional accounts for him is that, though they rightly locate the possibility of the Fall in freedom, they regard that freedom as a weakness, 'a questionable divine gift'. Tillich, however, sees that possibility as part of the very nature of freedom; and he goes so far as to say that, without this divine quality, there would be no Fall—'it is the image of God in man which gives the possibility of the Fall' (ST, vol. 2, p. 37). If we speak of sin as man's weakness, then his weakness is identical with his strength which is freedom. It is this unique feature of the Fall which explains why theology has traditionally been exclusively concerned with the Fall as the Fall of man though it is also recognized that it is something cosmic. In terms of the story, though part of what happens is the prophecy that nature henceforth will resist him, the earth producing thorns and thistles, the central event is 'man's first disobedience'. What brings about this transition? To answer that question, says Tillich, one must have some notion of what the essential being of man is. In the story of the myth, this is some paradisiacal existence; and indeed this is the kind of thinking that is then carried on into dogmatic theology. However, the real problem for theology is not how what was once the case was changed but how what is always potentially true can be discerned in existential distortion. Tillich's answer is to employ a model derived from psychology. This 'original' state of man was one of dreaming innocence—though we must remember that man never was in a dream any more than he was at any particular time innocent. This state, he says, 'has no place: it is *ou topos* (utopia). It has no time; it precedes temporality, and it is suprahistorical' (ST, vol. 2, p. 38). What makes this model so useful is that a dream is at once real and unreal and in that respect can be said to resemble potentiality. Whereas the hymn says of ages past that 'they fly forgotten as a dream / dies at the opening day', Tillich is thinking of the future which is often part of our unreal but real dreams. Our hopes which are so real are there fulfilled in that comfortable unreality which is the dream. In the same way, the potential carries within it the actual. If the 'original' state is a dream it is unreal too as innocence; for innocence is like dreaming in that once we have experienced that of which we are innocent our very innocence has come to an end. The psychology of human or personal development is something which for Tillich makes this metaphor or model of 'dreaming innocence' very potent; and he takes the example of the development of sexual consciousness which, interestingly enough, features in the biblical story.

If we thus imagine man as in a state of dreaming innocence, then, says Tillich, we must continue the story that this state drives beyond itself. He rejects as not only misguided but nonsensical those theologies which characterize the paradisiacal Adam as perfect. To heap 'perfection upon perfection upon Adam before the Fall, making him equal with the picture of Christ' is absurd and renders the Fall unintelligible. 'The symbol "Adam before the Fall" must be understood as the dreaming innocence of undecided potentialities' (ST, vol. 2, p. 39). In this radically psychological interpretation of the doctrine of the Fall, Tillich follows Kierkegaard, and thus he goes on to point to anxiety as the motivation to the Fall. As man is aware of his finitude he is aware that his freedom is linked with anxiety, awareness giving rise to anxiety. Once again, Tillich turns back to the Genesis story and—like Luther—calls attention to the prohibition from eating of the tree of the knowledge of good and evil. He points out something that we tend to forget, viz. that it was necessary for God to issue such a command. The necessity for a command presupposes 'a kind of split between creator and creature'. That is, a command needs to be given if the other person is not likely to do what is commanded or if we need to be reassured that he or she will do so. This, says Tillich, is the most important feature of the story and in this again he follows Kierkegaard, who spoke bafflingly of a sin before sin. This is the desire to sin; and, by contrast with dreaming innocence, he calls this 'aroused freedom'. In this situation, man both wants to remain in the innocence of his dream and to move on to the actualization of the freedom he has discovered. The tension is broken by his decision in finite freedom to make his freedom actual. If we tell the story as one of man's anxious awareness of his finite freedom, it is the same story—and again the psychology of sexual development is illuminating. To be or not to be a fully actualized sexual person is the anxious decision that ends our innocence in the particular form actualization takes.

It is clear then, that, for Tillich, the Fall—or the transition from essence to existence—is a basic description of human existence. He calls it 'the original fact', 'a universal quality of finite beings' (ST, vol. 2, p. 42). In the mythical language of traditional religion, this is an event in the past, as in the Genesis story. Yet, once more, Tillich calls attention to this uniquely important story, showing how he was desperately anxious to do justice to the vision of concrete religion. He points out its psychological-ethical character and the cosmic myth that lies behind the psychological-ethical form of the story. So he comes to his own mythical expression of the transition from essence to existence, the myth of the transcendent fall. It is in fact no new myth, being as old as Orphism; and as such it has been given various forms: but, whatever the form, the myth stresses the pre-historical character of our fallen condition and also its universality. While Tillich does not elaborate the myth—here as so often making brevity a crucial virtue—neither does he indulge in any defence of its non-biblical roots. Sufficient for him is the fact that it does not contradict the biblical story which he has so clearly emphasized: it too is concerned with the ethical psychology of man as he finds himself in his cosmic context. Though he talks of the motif of the myth as the universal tragedy of existence and of the meaning of the myth as the implication by existence of the transition from essence to existence, Tillich does not propose any demythologizing. Rather, he is anxious to insist that without this myth in its two forms of a transcendent fall and an immanent fall it is impossible to understand the human situation. Understanding that, however, is to recognize the unity of ethical freedom and tragic destiny which is what the myth expresses. So Tillich pleads for a re-evaluation and indeed a reinterpretation of the classical doctrine of original sin, setting himself against the modern trend in theology to reject this doctrine because it was thought to presuppose a literalism of Scripture-interpretation and a negative evaluation of man. Rejecting the literalism of the biblical myth as it is used in traditional conservative theology, the theologian must, in Tillich's view, accept the humanist positive evaluation of man and so reinterpret the doctrine of original sin as revealing the estrangement of man as he exists. What is not very clear here is how Tillich understands the relation of this rediscovered meaning of the doctrine to the deliverances of psychology and sociology, on the one hand, and the biblical message, on the other. He speaks of the doctrine of original sin having 'an empirical basis' in psychology and sociology and yet it is very clear from what has been said that he is not *basing* his theology in these theories. His concern seems to be twofold: to stress first of all that this doctrine is true in that its balancing of freedom and destiny is a realistic picture of man, and, secondly, to emphasize that the truth of the doctrine is this ontological understanding which needs a myth for its expression.

By stressing the unity of the moral and the tragic elements of the myth, Tillich recognizes that he is treating Creation and Fall as coincident. This must be the case, in his view, if we do not accept a literal interpretation of the Fall. In all the myths of the Fall, he sees this unity of the responsibility of man for his situation and the tragedy of that situation. To emphasize only the responsibility is to lapse into the Pelagian heresy which classical Christianity has rejected in all its forms. If there was no point in time at which man fell then the notions of 'Man before the Fall' and 'Nature before the curse' refer not to realities but to potentialities. The doctrine is both a recognition of the tragic universality of existential estrangement and a rejection of the idealistic picture of man as guilty but Nature innocent. Our understanding of our history as evolutionary in its nature makes us better able to see this; for in the long development of man from animal 'there is no absolute discontinuity between animal bondage and human freedom' (ST, vol. 2, p. 47). Likewise, our understanding of the nature of responsibility makes it impossible for us to say that there is a particular moment after which the individual is responsible or that there are never any situations where man is not responsible. Equally, the modern psychology of the unconscious mind and of the social nature of even that aspect of human existence produces a better understanding of the unity of man and nature. Yet, though he is at pains to stress this unity, Tillich is emphatic that sin is not ontologically necessary. Creation and Fall are inter-related but they are logically distinct concepts. Whether he has succeeded in this fine balancing of the concepts of responsibility and tragedy is doubtful; for the problem is one, as we shall now see, that re-emerges in his interpretation of sin.

What do we mean when we talk of man as sinful? For most of the time, Tillich has spoken of estrangement, not sin; but he makes it very clear (ST, vol. 2, pp. 52–3) that they are not interchangeable concepts. What the word 'sin' implies is the responsibility of man for his condition, something which has not been part of the characterization of his condition as the fact of estrangement. The reinterpretation of sin which Tillich offers is an interpretation of the phenomenal characteristics of sin. By talking of estrangement, he thinks he can avoid the erroneous implications and associations of the traditional doctrine of sin.

The characteristics of sin for Tillich are threefold. The first is unbelief, which is not a matter of failing or refusing to assent to some theological doctrine or position but an act of the total personality involving emotion, knowledge and will. If we are to understand what this means, we must get away from the notion of belief as a weak form of knowledge and grasp that it is not of the knowing man but of man in his total being we here speak. This man has turned away from God towards himself 'and loses his essential unity with the ground of his being and his world' (ST, vol. 2, p. 54). So each of the aspects of the human personality is involved in sin: knowledge, emotion and will. Unbelief is thus more even than a denial of God, more than disobedience and more than self-love: it is all these. As Tillich puts it, man's unbelief is 'his estrangement from God in the centre of his being' (ibid., p. 55). Ultimately this, as Augustine saw, is indeed love turned away from God.

The second characteristic is 'hubris'. A term borrowed from Greek tragedy, here it indicates the presumption and pride that lead to downfall. No English word properly translates it but, says Tillich, we see the same thing described in the Old Testament—'the self-elevation of man into the sphere of the divine' (ST, vol. 2, p. 57). Man refuses to acknowledge the distance between himself and God's infinity: having turned away from God, he makes himself the centre of his universe. It would be wrong to think of this as the moral sin of pride; for hubris, says Tillich, can equally be a characteristic of humility. Once again we must realize that we are dealing with man in his totality. Hubris, then, is not one sin alongside others. Stressing its integral relation to the totality of sin, Tillich speaks of it as 'the other side' of unbelief, or man's turning away from the divine centre to which he belongs. No existing human being can avoid confronting this. Man, as not only consciousness but the consciousness that possesses the perfection of self-consciousness, is uniquely the image of God and therefore is confronted by temptation. The very perfection of the complete centredness of self-consciousness makes it possible for man to challenge the divine centre and make himself the centre of the world. Conscious of his potential divinity, he will not accept his actual finitude. This can be expressed in all kinds of ways, and so Tillich insists that calling it 'spiritual sin' is to be misled into thinking that it is to do with a special part of man. On the contrary, the metaphysicians who, like Hegel, confuse partial truth with their whole truth, show hubris just as much as the Pharisee or the Puritan who identifies his own limited goodness with absolute goodness, or again the man of culture for whom his cultural creativity is divine creativity. It can be seen in society because every human being has this desire to be 'like God'. Unwilling to acknowledge his own finitude, he is driven by a demonic structure to make his natural self-affirmation a destructive self-elevation.

Finally, sin is concupiscence, 'the unlimited desire to draw the whole of reality into one's self' (ibid., p. 59). Our self-affirmation has two aspects: the removal of our self's centre from the divine centre, which is unbelief, and the identification of our self and the centre of our world, which is hubris. So Tillich sees concupiscence as the very motivation of sin. Man is tempted to make himself the centre of his world because this puts him in the situation of drawing the whole of his world into himself. Neither a creature of the earth merely nor yet belonging totally to heaven, man stands between the two worlds of particularity and universality and wants to make himself universal on the very basis of his particularity. Concupiscence too is misunderstood if we identify it with some particular human weakness, as has often been the case in its reference to the sexual desire. Rather, it refers to every single aspect of man's relation both to himself and to his world—for example, physical hunger just as much as sexual appetite, knowledge, power and material wealth. In all these contexts, wherever there is an unlimited desire, there is concupiscence.

As he concludes his interpretation of sin, Tillich reveals his indebtness to a variety of thinkers: Kierkegaard, Freud and Nietzsche. All three have given a psychology of concupiscence, and Tillich notes the way in which Kierkegaard describes more than one kind of person to show how the unlimited desire is a world of inner emptiness. In Don Juan, just as much as Nero, the self-defying character of concupiscence is to be seen. Similarly, in Freud's 'libido' and Nietzsche's 'will to power' Tillich sees a description of concupiscence and regards these theories as having made an important contribution to the theological understanding of sin and to a general appreciation of the Christian view of human nature. Yet neither of these is a satisfactory account of humanity's situation, because both are concerned only with man's existential situation. They ignore the contrast between man's essential and his existential being. Interestingly, Tillich gives Freud high praise for his 'honest realism' (ST, vol. 2, p. 61), which is, he says, more Christian than the Christian or pseudo-Christian taboos against sex. It is evident that Freud's work found a ready response in Tillich's radical attitude to Christian morality. A theological interpretation of man is, he says, 'well advised to follow Freud's analysis'—up to a point. That analysis will not be adequate for theology, however, because of its concentration on the existential predicament. Thus it fails to distinguish between libido as concupiscence and libido as love. Its important contribution to theology is that it has shown man in thrall to unlimited desire which derives from his sexual nature, and that not even his spiritual nature escapes this. Freud has thus rediscovered important insights which characterized early and mediaeval Christian spirituality. Nowhere, for Tillich, does Freud show such understanding more clearly than when he talks of the 'death instinct': that is, a description of 'the desire to escape the pain of the never satisfied libido'. The pain of life at a higher level drives man toward the lower level from which he has emerged. The constantly unsatisfied libido makes him want to get rid of himself as man. Where, however, Freud went astray was that he failed to see that this is the predicament of man's existential being, not something that derives from his essential nature. The endlessness of the libido reveals man's estrangement. Essentially, the libido is not concupiscence but an element of love together with *eros*, *philia* and *agapē*. In all these ways, love wants the other being; but the distorted libido wants the other being only for its own pleasure, wanting *its own* pleasure through the other being, and this is concupiscence. The libido in essential man is a desire to be united with the object of love for the object's own sake. Luther is, says Tillich, in fact less ascetic than Freud in his view of man. Another important contribution to Christian theology was Nietzsche's 'will to power', a contribution that was indeed made through psychology, politics and social theory. This again is an account of man's existential condition. Partly concept, partly symbol, 'will to power' refers neither to the conscious act of willing nor to power as a social fact but 'is an ontological symbol for man's natural self-affirmation in so far as man has the power of being' (ST, vol. 2, p. 63). Self-affirmation as such is part of man's essential nature, not a characteristic merely of his estrangement. Nietzsche, however, like Freud, has confused man's essential self-affirmation with the unlimited driving power in all life which was Schopenhauer's (1788–1860) view of the will. The infinite constantly unsatisfied drive leads to self-negation. Nietzsche's will to power is devoid of norms and principles which can judge it and consequently remains unlimited, becoming demonic and destructive. So it is 'another concept and symbol of concupiscence' (ibid.).

If this is sin, what of the classical distinction between original and actual sin? Original sin is Adam's act of disobedience and the resulting legacy of sinful disposition. When theology has spoken of sin as original and hereditary, it was referring to 'the universal destiny of estrangement which concerns every man' (ibid., p. 64). That universal destiny is what is actualized in the individual act of sin. So, says Tillich, sin is fact before it is act. This is his cryptic but profound expression of what he has seen to be the correlation of freedom and destiny which is characteristic of man. My sin is my free act; and, as such, it is my personal responsibility, something of which I am guilty. Yet my personal freedom is part and parcel of the universal destiny of estrangement. The result is that we cannot describe the sin which, as Scripture says, so easily besets me without referring to that destiny–in Tillich's words, we cannot refer to the act without reference to the fact. Sin as fact as well as act is something of which I am aware in my experience of guilt. To describe the fact as

97

some deterministic pattern of mechanistic chain of cause and effect, as has been done in biology, psychology and sociology, will not be an adequate account of sin. This potent stress on the element of destiny in no way diminishes the responsibility that freedom implies. Christian theology must accept this emphasis on destiny as it appears in all these contexts of anthropology; but it must equally insist on the fact of finite freedom. The pattern of a realistic but coherent doctrine of man lies precisely in the balance of these different emphases. That estrangement is the universal destiny of man is not something that is easily asserted in the context of human freedom. Rejecting as nonsensical the simple assertion of sin as both human destiny and a completely free human act, Tillich insists that 'original or hereditary sin' is neither original nor hereditary but a universal destiny which is a more profound matter than mere history. In an orthodox doctrine of original sin, there is for Tillich an important realization that sin is something social which plays as significant a part in our personal life as the free acts of personal wrongdoing for which we alone are responsible. To deny that interrelation is to diminish the mystery of radical evil that characterizes human history. A sense of this radical evil must make us as aware of the psychological insight and educational practice of Catholic spirituality as it must bring us back to the understanding of sin as essentially and simply turning away from God.

By emphasizing the social nature of sin, Tillich is neither offering some sociological generalization nor supporting the idea of a collective guilt. That sin is fact before it is act is a metaphysical rather than a scientific statement: it is a more profound statement than the observation that most people or even everyone we know has done something wrong. On the other hand, it does not mean that I am responsible for the crimes of others or that there is any way in which guilt can be a concept that applies in a context other than where I speak of what is mine. Tillich is very clear about the logical difference between the nature of the individual as a person and society as a group. Even so he is anxious to stress that there can be no separation of the freedom which marks the individual from the destiny which is his as a member of a group. 'There is no collective guilt. But there is the universal destiny of mankind... Every individual participates in this destiny and cannot extricate himself' (ST, vol. 2, p. 67). The way in which this works out is that man's individual guilt becomes part of the destiny of others as well as myself. Such an understanding of the social nature of sin and guilt should, in Tillich's view, restrain the presumption of both individuals and nations in their attitude to and treatment of conquered nations.

The estrangement in which man and his world are to be found contradicts the created structure of both. This self-contradiction drives toward a self-destruction. It is nothing outside man, no external force which then produces the destruction that follows from estrangement: it is the very nature of estrangement itself which is a 'structure of destruction' (ibid., p. 69). This structure of destruction is what is meant by 'evil', and its basic characteristic is the fracture of the self–world polarity whereby man loses both himself and his world. Only man is characterized by this polarity of experience—a centred self and a structured world corresponding to it. Under the conditions of existential estrangement, evil is, in Tillich's view, a consequence of sin: to see evil as merely some kind of accidental occurrence in a human biography is to lose sight of both its context and its profound nature. This is why Tillich thinks that the age-old problem of theodicy needs a profoundly theological context, that of the doctrine of sin, where the very possibility of freedom implies the possibility of sin. While this argument might seem to create confusion rather than offer clarity, we can see that what Tillich aims to do is to show the way in which the analysis and explanation of evil must begin with the way in which it is involved in the very basic structure of the self. The basic characteristic of evil is that it is self-loss, the loss of one's determining centre, 'the disintegration of the centred self by drives which cannot be brought into unity' (ST, vol. 2, p. 71). This is indeed a matter of seeing theodicy in far more radical terms (both ethical and theological) than the traditional problem of God creating a humanity that then perpetrates moral evil. Tillich is calling attention to what *underlies* moral conflict or the pathological experience of the disintegration of myself and my world. We should not, he argues, think of evil as a pathology: the pathology when it occurs reveals the extreme expression of what is always present, namely the possibility of disruption. Man cannot take his centredness for granted: there is no such thing as a pure subjectivity and man must make his centredness actual by giving content to that basic form of his life. Self-loss, then, is the first thing to be noted about evil. The self that is in the grip of hubris and concupiscence comes to the point of disintegration because the overweening pride, self-assertion and lust that are seen in the attempt to make the finite self centre of everything lead to its becoming the centre of nothing. 'Both self and the world are threatened. Man . . . has lost his world' (ibid., p. 71). This is the first and the basic evil in man's estranged state.

The various evils of man's estranged history are the result of his basic loss of self and the world. That polarity broken, the other ontological polarities break up into their elements: freedom and destiny, dynamics and form, individualization and participation. As with self and the world, in each of these there is an interdependent loss. Thus freedom separates itself from the destiny to which it belongs and becomes arbitrariness—centre gone, there is no direction, only random activity. 'Under the control of hubris and concupiscence, freedom ceases to relate itself to the objects provided by destiny. It relates itself to an indefinite memory of contents' (ibid., p. 72). For Tillich, the story of every man is that once he has been aroused from his dreaming state of innocence, his freedom, which lay within his destiny, comes into conflict with his destiny. There is no longer the control which is afforded by the centredness of his being, so that one object is as good as another and there is neither meaning nor purpose in his choice. The pointers to meaningful, purposive choice which destiny provides still remain in man but his progress is wilfully blind to them. As freedom becomes arbitrariness, destiny becomes mechanical necessity, because freedom comes under the control of forces which move against one another. 'Parts of the self overtake the centre and determine it without being united with the other parts' (ibid., p. 73). This is what classical theology terms 'bondage of the will'—man wasting his freedom, and his destiny becoming the loss of destiny. The traditional debate between determinism and indeterminism is, for Tillich, a reflection of this story. Both theories are accounts of man's essential nature in terms of man's estranged nature. The way in which indeterminism views freedom is a matter of contingency devoid of responsibility; and in determinism freedom is not freedom but rather a mechanical necessity.

The same is true of the polarity of dynamics and form. In man's essential nature they are united; but under the control of hubris and concupiscence his dynamics are 'distorted into a formless urge for self-transcendence'. Essentially, man's dynamics are his vitality, which in that essential being is a directed drive towards self-transcendence. Because we are here talking of a *directed* drive, such self-transcendence of form has a form. By contrast, when man becomes estranged from his essential nature, intentionality no longer controls and directs his vitality. One can see this contrast, says Tillich, in the life of someone in whom grace is effective: the forms of self-transcending form are united with dynamics but these 'symbols of reunion' are in contrast to the existential disruption of dynamics. If we take St Paul as a concrete example, this is what he expresses when he speaks of 'pressing towards the goal' not as one who has arrived, or again when he speaks of 'the thorn in the flesh'. What this disruption of dynamics and form means is the loss of creativity; for since nothing is real without form, creativity becomes a meaningless novelty. This is the story of dynamics becoming an aim in itself: and the story of form without dynamics is the same story of destruction. Separated from dynamics, form becomes external law. Man's personal and social life becomes an empty chaos in which the only expression of meaning is the external law, a rigid legalism. Both the chaos and the legalism are self-destructive as man flees to legalism from chaos and from chaos to legalism. To understand man as essentially unlimited drive—which Freud does with his libido, or Nietzsche does with his unlimited will to power— is to describe such a situation of existential estrangement rather than the essential being of man. So whether we look on the matter as a perspective on history or as an issue in the philosophical account of human nature the point is the same: we confuse the nature of existential estrangement with essential being if we separate dynamics from form.

The final result of estrangement which Tillich notes is the disruption of the third set of polarities: individualization and participation. The essential interdependence of the two poles means that the more individualized a being is the more it is able to participate. Despite the fact that he is a being who is purely individual, man participates in the world, is *part* of a whole world. However, that singleness in solitary existence, which is essentially his, is distorted into a loneliness when man is in the state of estrangement—'man is shut up within himself and cut off from participation' (ST, vol. 2, p. 75). This loneliness is made worse by the fact that he is at the mercy of objects, which objectify him. We know the condition well, says Tillich, as something which has been described by contemporary sociologists and psychologists—a mood of the time. However, he is quick to point out that this is no mere fact of contemporary history but a universal human situation. The achievement of existentialist philosophy is precisely that it uncovered the nature of human existence as a loneliness which both creates and is caused by its being submerged in the crowd. Though obvious in extreme situations, the condition is a characteristic of all societies; for in talking of such a loss of self what we see is the separation of individualization from participation which marks estrangement. Such history is character- ized by the structures of destruction the source of which is the evil in all history. It is not only in existentialist philosophy that such an account of man in his estrangement is to be found, says Tillich. The idealistic philosophy which makes him a purely thinking being is equally an account of this fracture of the polarity of individualiza- tion and participation. Claiming to be an interpretation of man as he essentially is, idealism for Tillich gives in fact an account of estrangement. It deprives the act of knowing from any participation in the world as a whole. What is very interesting about this analysis is that Tillich is not content to see the deficiency of idealism as a neglect of the empirical world, a depreciation of what Kant called the sense element of knowledge. What for him is neglected is the pulsating passion of living man. Idealism, he says, removes the *eros*, the passion and sheer love that binds man to his world. True though it is that not all knowledge involves this, it is quite wrong to deny that this characterizes any knowledge. If, in fact, it does, then we have the situation of estrangement and the result is that man is just one thing along with the other things of the world. As a thing, man is a calculable object and it makes no difference whether our calcula- tion or quantification is done in terms of chemistry or of mechanics. In both cases, what has been done amounts to reducing the rainbow of human life to a rule and line. The insidious thing is that such a reduction of the human can be and is used as the basis for practical existence where men are treated as if they were mere things. Both theory and practice mirror the structures of self-destruction.

In terms that very clearly echo Heidegger's thought, Tillich goes on to spell out his understanding of the nature of human destiny: man is 'under the domination of death and is driven by the anxiety of having to die' (ST, vol. 2, p. 77). What Tillich does at this point is to turn from the *description* of man's condition which he has been giving to its *explanation*. Theology has traditionally explained death as the result of sin, and so Tillich's first point on this issue is that 'man is naturally mortal'. The idea that man is naturally immortal is something that he rejects as non-Christian. Having made this point, he returns to his description, saying that estrangement transforms man's essential anxiety about non-being into a 'horror of death'. What is a natural and so morally neutral experience has been transformed by guilt; for despite the fact that mortality is the common lot of mankind one experiences this as something for which one is responsible. Sin 'transforms the anxious awarenesss of having to die into the painful realisation of a lost eternity' (ibid., p. 78). The nature of death illustrates for Tillich the distinction between estrangement and finitude. The very desire for death in suicide illustrates this, because it is the attempt to escape the guilt one experiences by self-annihilation. He carries through this analysis by showing the same transformation in man's experience of the categories of finitude: time, space, causality and substance. Time is seen as a demonic power destroying what it has created; and man's answer to this is a desperate attempt to fill the moment with as many things as possible. 'It is not the experience of time as such which produces despair; rather it is the defeat in the resistance against time' (ibid., p. 79). Just as man thus refuses to accept time, so he refuses to accept space, seeing it as something that deprives him of a necessary place to which he belongs. The same is true, says Tillich, of the other categories. Man tries to make himself an absolute cause and to give himself an absolute substance. 'Without the power of being itself man cannot resist the element of non-being in both causality and substance, and his failure to resist is another element in the structure of despair' (ibid., p. 80).

As if to stress the comprehensiveness and generality of this description, Tillich insists that estrangement results not only in despair but in doubt as well. Doubt is not absent from man's essential state; for finitude must mark limits to his knowledge and it is, in any case, true that knowledge is born of the radical questioning of everything. There are various forms of essential doubt: the expression of the finite being's general insecurity, man's personal choices and self-doubt, and the doubt about being as being. So doubt as such is part of the good creation, where it is balanced by the certainty that is afforded by the dimension of the eternal. Man has in his essential being the courage to accept his finitude. However, in the state of estrangement that reassuring dimension of the eternal is shut out, with the result that 'insecurity becomes absolute and drives toward a despairing refusal to accept any finite truth' (ibid., p. 84).

Though Tillich makes clear (see ibid., p. 86) that his picture of man's existential situation is not entirely negative (inasmuch as he sees existence to contain structures of healing as well as those of destruction), it is despair which engages his attention as 'the final index of man's predicament'. That, rather than death, is for him the real boundary line of the human situation. It is 'the state of inescapable conflict'—and this is 'conflict, on the one hand between what one potentially is and therefore ought be and, on the other hand, what one actually is in the combination of freedom and destiny' (ibid., p. 87). Try as he will—and suicide is the most telling illustration of how he does try—man cannot escape; for he cannot escape from himself. These pages of the second volume reveal Tillich at his pastoral best as he analyses and speaks sympathetically of suicide, pleading for a less superstitious attitude towards it on the part of the church. Yet he is adamant that suicide can be nothing more than an expedient for removing guilt on the temporal level, leaving the dimension of the eternal unaffected. The very experience of despair points to its eternal context and to the same context as that of salvation which is the solution of the problem.

Such is the picture of existence which Tillich gives: one of man a stranger in a world of which he is part and a stranger to the eternal dimension which is his proper context. A very natural reaction to this on the part of theologians who are not necessarily conventional or fundamentalist is that Tillich has exchanged biblical truth for some fashionable existentialism or—if his views are to be interpreted in a more traditionally philosophical way—an old-fashioned ontology. It is true that time and again his language echoes Heidegger, but it is equally true that the Idealist tradition breaks through this language that seems so much that of the twentieth century. What he has to say about finitude is often unclear because one is not sure to which of the two contexts one should assign it. To that we shall return later; but it should be said that the most obvious point about this analysis is that it is much more a translation of Christian doctrine into an ontological account of existence than it is the phenomenology which Tillich set out to achieve. That is, the method which he has employed is more clearly that of what he calls 'the theological circle' than it is one of a careful description of the ontological structures revealed to an experience from which common sense and other such presuppositions are 'bracketed out' in phenomenological mode. This critical point is made not, indeed, to take issue with him; for, after all, it is a theological account that we would seek in a theological analysis of finitude. What this makes clear is that there is in Tillich a fundamental lack of clarity about his method, a lack of clarity that is to some measure born of his confidence that philosophy and theology are in the end engaged in the same task. To those more familiar with the movement of philosophy away from idealism and through linguistic philosophy to a renewed appreciation of idealism, this is enough to give them pause, and they might be tempted to dismiss the analysis as irrelevant. That would be a mistake because there is enough evidence of familiar lines to convince us that this is really a picture of the human situation.

If picture indeed it is, does it portray finitude accurately? Here is the difficulty that has been consistently felt about Tillich's doctrine of man. Putting the matter simply and bluntly, one cannot avoid the suspicion that, despite his constant assertion of a difference between finitude and sin, the analysis makes man's sinful condition part of what is meant by the nature of man—at least formally. The matter is not helped by the abstract language that Tillich uses, which—like the idiom, of abstract painting–tends to reduce even the familiar to lines that are unrecognizable. In that situation, one often feels that the account is less meaningful than descriptions which may fail to achieve accuracy but do convey partial enlightenment because they are concrete. The nub of the problem with which we are confronted is that in several ways Tillich insists on the universality, and so the necessity, of the transition from essence to existence. One example of this is the distinction he makes between man's 'original' and his fallen state in terms of potentiality and actuality. If that is how the distinction should be made, then it is difficult to see how he can maintain that the nature of the fall is moral—something for which man is responsible. I am responsible only for what it is that I cause to happen, what *I bring about* rather than what occurs in the nature of things. There can be no denying the profundity of his analysis at so many points, especially with regard to time and again the nature of suicide. As an attempt to explain the 'cash value' of the doctrine of original sin this is a remarkable achievement. That the explanation leaves us wondering whether the doctrine is more than an empirical generalization is one other example of how the ontology lacks clarity. The radical evil which Kant was obliged to recognize as a fact of human existence is something of which Tillich leaves us in no doubt; but it is far from clear what kind of thing this is and how we should understand its place in the structures of human existence. The one thing that is clear is that in developing his theological argument, Tillich saw himself as having posed the question to which Christ's life and work are the answer.

6

The New Being: Incarnation and Resurrection

The heart of Tillich's theology is his attempt at a new Christology. Here is not only the clearest example of his conviction that the theologian must work between the two poles of the kerygma, the unchanging message and the situation, the changing historical context: here too we have the articulation of what is for him the norm of theology. Because he sought to work out a philosophical Christology, some critics have been tempted to characterize his Christology as a departure from biblical theology. Likewise, his concentration on the metaphysical rather than the historical aspects of Christology gave rise to the suspicion that in the end he had cut Christology loose from its historical foundation. No interpretation of Tillich's work can, however, properly deny that he was as determined to maintain the historicity of Jesus' life and resurrection as he was to bring to their understanding a thoroughly philosophical perspective. To dub this a case of having one's cake and eating it, or a matter of ambiguity or even simple confusion, is too easy. Tillich neither set out to have it both ways nor was there anything simple about his occasional confusion or his tendency to exploit ambiguity. Just as there was nothing simple about his method, so there was nothing simple about the difficulty he faced in his Christology.

The point of departure, as well as the problem for him, was his clear understanding that 'Jesus as the Christ is both an historical fact and a subject of believing reception' (ST, vol. 2, p. 113). One of the interests and also one of the achievements of Tillich's Christology is the way he approaches it from his phenomenology of man's quest for salvation. The argument, or indeed the story so far, has been that the human situation of existence is one of estrangement where man's attempts at self-salvation end in failure. True to his conviction that it is wrong for the theologian to hurl the Gospel 'like stones' at his audience, Tillich seeks to explain what is meant by saying that Jesus is the Christ, the fulfilment of expectation and the bearer of our salvation. He does this by means of his concept of 'New Being', but unfortunately he never explains what exactly he means by this concept. The nearest he comes to doing so is in volume 2 of *Systematic Theology* (p. 92) when he speaks of the necessity of seeing the significance of Christ in terms of being—salvation is a historical fact, or we cannot speak of any historical consequences. In this way, he sought to hold together the metaphysical idea of a human desideratum and a historical situation with historical consequences. When I asked him whether he understood the term as a class with only one member, he simply dismissed the question as a piece of misleading Aristotelian logic, adding only that he was too Platonic to think that way and he was concerned with 'power' not 'class'. Yet this Aristotelian way seems to be the way in which we should understand the notion; and understanding it that way helps to clarify the difficulties which critics have with Tillich's view of the relation of history to Christology. The universality of the human predicament and of the uncertainty of any and every solution of that predicament means that there is in every religion and culture a quest for the New Being. This may take the form of a search for it beyond history or in history—a distinction that roughly coincides with that between Eastern and Western religion and culture. The distinctive nature of Christianity is that the New Being is seen to be actualized in history and that this reveals both the meaning of history and its future expectation. This is what is expressed by the term 'Christ', an idea the history of which Tillich does not confine to the biblical sources. Obviously, it is with the Christian use that one must begin to unravel its meaning; but the story pushes back beyond the Old Testament to the Semitic and Egyptian influences on Old Testament religion. Looking at that history—which is predominantly that revealed in the Bible, though it transcends it—Tillich shows how the historical character of Christianity was perceived by the church and how the theologian's task is that of demonstrating how this symbol is the expression of a universal expectation of a new reality whilst being also the name of a historical event. The historical character of Christianity 'must be defended in all periods, but in such a way that the universal significance of Christianity is not lost' (ST, vol. 2, p. 104).

This central assertion of Christianity is paradoxical, 'the only all-embracing paradox of Christianity'. Tillich is at pains to distinguish between the theological paradox and all those ideas of paradox which would make it illogical or irrational. Though he carefully sets out such ideas, his discussion is not very clear. What can be clearly said is that Tillich's understanding of the paradoxical nature of the Christological confession does not depend on any view of the paradoxical nature of all theological assertions. He is adamant that anything that is 'the destruction of formal logic ... must be rejected' (ibid.), and he is equally emphatic in making a sharp distinction between the mysterious nature of that to which theology refers and the rational nature of the tools of theology (ibid., p. 105). What, then, constitutes the paradoxical nature of the Christian claim? It is that it 'contradicts the opinion derived from man's existential predicament and all expectations imaginable on the basis of this predicament' (ibid., p. 106). This view of the belief that Jesus is the Christ—or, as Tillich always puts it, that the New Being has appeared in Jesus as the Christ—echoes Kierkegaard's view that this is the Absolute Paradox. It is unfortunately less clear than this doctrine of Kierkegaard because this is related to the paradoxical nature of religious and theological language in general and is to be seen as a special case of this inasmuch as we are uniting historical and eternal categories. For Tillich, the paradox of the Christian message that Jesus is the Christ 'is the only paradox and the source of all paradoxical statements in Christianity' (ibid., p. 107). This paradox, he insists, is 'not a logical riddle'.

In his analysis of the concepts used in speaking of the Christ, Tillich is especially anxious to offer a proper interpretation of what is meant by 'Incarnation'. To say that God has become man is for him a nonsensical statement; for this must mean, he argues, that God ceases to be God. It is not the 'becoming' that implies this but rather what he becomes, namely something other than himself. This argument is a very nice example of the way in which this great defender of symbolism would time and again concentrate on a very literal understanding of language when discussing theological positions. Escaping from such nonsense by talking of a divine being who has become man is dangerous because we seem to imply some polytheism and in any case we are employing the mythological notion of divine being changing into some other form. This kind of thinking is far removed from Christianity, and so he labels the unqualified use of the term 'Incarnation' as pagan or at least superstitious. He does not rule out the term altogether but regards as dangerous even the kind of thinking that follows St John's assertion that the Logos became flesh. It is, he says, practically impossible to avoid the superstitious connotations which the concept generally has. One of the misleading, if not indeed superstitious, connotations is the idea that it is solely for mankind's benefit that the infinite has entered the realm of the finite. We must remember, says Tillich, that the biblical expectation was something conceived within the context of the cosmos. For an age such as ours with an expanding view of the universe, this is very important, because this helps us understand more clearly what is meant by talking of the mediator and the saviour and indeed incarnation. 'Man cannot claim to occupy the only possible place for Incarnation' (ibid., p. 111).

It is only after such a phenomenology of the language that Tillich turns to the usual problem of the event of Jesus the Christ. Two points which he makes at the outset are crucial to an understanding of what he has to say. In the first place, it is Jesus *as the Christ* which he discusses. That is to say, we must begin with that confession, the characterization of the man as the Christ, rather than with some account of the biography. As he puts the point, 'Christianity was born not with the birth of the man who is called "Jesus" but in the moment when one of his followers was driven to say "Thou art the Christ"' (ibid., p. 112). Though Tillich is often thought to sit very loose to the historicity of Jesus and his biography and at times gives that impression very clearly, yet that is far from his attitude here. He is arguing very properly that the basis of Christology is the claim that was made that a historical individual is to be *characterized* in the way that the mythological tradition had characterized a special figure having a special function. It could indeed be said that in so far as he speaks of Jesus, Tillich presupposes a biography; but that does not alter the fact that the basis of Christology is the paradox that the historical figure is thus described, rather than some alleged biography from which that characterization is somehow inferred. The second point arises from the way in which this section of the system is described: the *event* of Jesus. The title Tillich uses for this Part is 'The reality of the Christ'; and crucial to the claim that the Christ is real is Tillich's conception of 'event'. In his lectures, he used to contend that 'event' *meant* both fact and interpretation, a mode of argument that was very typical of his fondness for stipulating what words meant either by reference to etymology or simply by legislative definition. To be fair, he also used to refer to the work of his colleague the New Testament scholar John Knox, whose Christology was founded on such a view of the event recorded in the New Testament. In *Systematic Theology*, Tillich's argument does not depend on definition. All that he contends is that by speaking of Jesus as the Christ, we are referring to both a historical fact and the 'believing reception', the interpretation expressed in faith's claim. Both are necessary for theology; and to stress the one at the expense of the other is to be led into mistakes. If there had been no biographical fact, the believing reception would have no reference. Conversely, if there had been no believing reception, then even a claim by Jesus to be the Christ would not have made him Jesus the Christ.

This brief summary is enough to show how difficult it is to understand the place of history in Tillich's Christology, so that it is no surprise to find so many critics arguing that he presents a Christ without Jesus. The criticism can be made in purely logical terms: that Tillich both asserts the necessity of history for faith and denies the relevance of history to faith. Again, it can be a criticism that fastens on the *theological* significance of what Tillich maintains, seeing in his position some tendency to the heresy of Docetism. Whatever form the criticism takes, it is based on the assumption that for Tillich the fact of Jesus is of no importance for theology. Exactly how he works out what importance it has we shall see; but, for the moment, it is the logical significance of what can be said rather than the content of those assertions that concerns us. What therefore needs to be said and clarified is that for Tillich, though the assertion of faith presupposes historical facts, it can never be reducible to these facts. This much he did say clearly in volume 2 of *Systematic Theology* and this is why he was so impatient and annoyed with those who attributed to him some kind of Docetism. Unfortunately, he did not maintain that level of clarity in his argument as he tried to resist the tendency of theologians to reduce or hide the gap between the historical assertions that Jesus lived and did such and such, on the one hand, and, on the other, the assertion of faith that he is the Christ. He complicates the issue and produces confusion in the first place by asserting an interdependence of fact and interpretation, whereas what he really means is that, though the interpretation does not make any difference to the fact, its presence is what makes the difference for faith. This is why he says again and again that the theologian has no interest in any neutral biography of Jesus because he is interested only in the biblical picture of Jesus as the Christ. Secondly, by insisting in this way that we cannot get beyond the biblical picture, that our knowledge of Jesus as the Christ is derived primarily (though not entirely) from that biblical picture, he suggests that it is not even theoretically possible for us to know anything of the concrete figure who was part of the historical scene between 6 BC and AD 26. What he wanted to say was that the picture is in fact all, or virtually all, that we have as historical evidence and that, despite its being a picture or a portrait rather than a biography or historical account, it is enough. It is indeed more than enough: this is a picture that produces not just knowledge but saving knowledge. Sometimes he expresses this very loosely, speaking as if it is the picture that is the cause of salvation; but the point is that he was thinking of the way in which a picture is very often more informative than historical accounts, and of our need to confront the past, especially in connection with God's revelation of himself. There is really no other *account* of Jesus and yet, he says, this picture which was evoked by faith and can be the means of evoking faith is also the means of *informing* subsequent generations.

Tillich raises two problems about the relation of Christ to history. First, he asks whether the fact that the confession of Jesus as the Christ demands a reception of the revelation by faith means that the validity of the message depends on the existence of the church. This is a problem which is made uncomfortably real for him by man-kind's capability of self-destruction. If mankind destroyed itself and there were a completely new beginning for the human race, would we be left with no memory of the event 'Jesus as the Christ'? His answer is that just as the revelation of the New Being cannot be confined to the space of this world, so there cannot be a temporal limitation. Yet the more important point is that faith cannot make any judgement about an end of history and what lies beyond it; in the nature of the case, this is something which cannot be a matter of historical knowledge. What faith does assert is that for the unique history of mankind, Christ is the centre. His second problem is the more concrete problem of modern critical history, that is, the theological problem raised by the modern scientific method of historical research with regard to the biblical narrative. Though the negative impact of historical criticism has been the most keenly felt, the real challenge of historical criticism for Tillich lies in its 'constructive-conjectural' aspect. The historian is concerned not only to assess the evidence but also actually to make out and, in a sense, reconstruct what actually happened. Hence we had the attempt to discover the actual event in this context, the celebrated 'quest for the historical Jesus'. Important as all the attempts, from Schweitzer (1875–1965) to Bultmann and his successors, have been, they must in Tillich's view be declared a failure. The end-result of this scientific investigation has been the discovery that the biblical picture itself is the only picture we can uncover, that the attempts do not yield for historical analysis any theory which can take the place of the data we have: the data are the only credible historical theory, despite such data being quite obviously no theory of historical explanation. Tillich stresses the logical nature of this failure. It is not that the scholars have failed where some day others might succeed. The failure is caused 'by the nature of the sources itself' (ST, vol. 2, p. 118).

This second issue, the relation of historical criticism to theology, is discussed at length by Tillich. He considers the various kinds of attempts to produce a 'Life of Jesus'. All such lives he describes as 'more like novels than biographies', adding that they offered no 'safe foundation for the Christian faith'. 'Christianity is not based on the acceptance of a historical novel; it is based on the witness to the messianic character of Jesus by people who were not interested at all in a biography of the Messiah' (ibid., p. 121). This argument is not very clear but Tillich thinks that it does clarify the nature of the failure encountered by historical research. So sure is he of this that he sees the whole enterprise to have been misled by what is fundamentally a semantic confusion. The term 'historical Jesus', he says (ibid., p. 123), is ambiguous—meaning either 'the results of historical research into the character and life of the person who stands behind the Gospel records' or the facticity of the event 'Jesus as the Christ'. Where Tillich complicates his position further is by asserting that faith guarantees 'the factual transformation of reality in that personal life which the New Testament expresses in its picture of Jesus as the Christ' (ibid.). After commenting on the benefits of historical criticism for theology—the appreciation of the difference between the real history as one might call it and the legend and myth in biblical literature, and the greater understanding of the development of the Christological symbols—Tillich once more confronts this problem. If we are to say that 'Jesus is the Christ' means that there is a *fact* beyond the New Testament, then what of the theoretical possibility that historical research would establish that the man Jesus of Nazareth never lived?

The note of insecurity and anxiety which this question introduces into the song of faith is something which Tillich appreciates and understands. It is not so much the likelihood of such a complete scepticism being validated that is the problem: the very thought of such a possibility seems destructive of the certainty which is a mark of faith's conviction—'I *know* to whom I have believed'. The need for certainty is something readily recognized by Tillich, and so he will not admit as basis something which is only guaranteed by the present failure of complete scepticism. Neither can faith itself provide such a guarantee against the scepticism which is an intrinsically possible result of historical criticism. Faith 'can guarantee only its own foundation', says Tillich (ibid., p. 131). This is his attempt at clarifying the ambiguity he discovers in the claim that faith can guarantee the existence of Jesus of Nazareth and the essentials of the biblical picture. Clarification and removal of ambiguity are not immediately obvious here; but one thing which does seem clear is that he does not want to say that faith can guarantee as true any statement of the kind that the historian makes, though he also insists that faith does guarantee that which is its own objective side, the reality which creates it. We cannot guarantee details such as the name—all this is a matter for historical criticism to establish. However, the reality of the event which is the basis of Christianity is guaranteed by participation and not by historical criticism. 'He might have had another name... Whatever his name, the New Being was and is actual in this man' (ibid.). The argument is further complicated by Tillich's use of the Cartesian refutation of complete scepticism. Incidentally revealing his great knowledge of the history of philosophy, he places that refutation in the Augustinian tradition and says that it 'pointed to the immediacy of a self-consciousness which guaranteed itself by its participation in being' (ibid.). This, however, is one occasion when the erudition does not help the argument very much. The situation of faith—'I believe in Jesus as the Christ'—is very different from the absurdity to which Descartes drove a radical scepticism, viz. that I do not know that I do in fact doubt if I can say of a whole series of propositions X that I doubt X. What is important for the moment is not whether by that argument Descartes proved what he thought he did (an existing thinking self) but rather the difference between any such proof by reference to my 'participation' in being and the kind of thing with which faith is concerned, something which by definition has to do with someone or something else. This is perhaps the crux of Tillich's Christology, the metaphysical assertion that the quest for the New Being has been met in history by a revelation of it as historical reality. It is almost as if he had been guided by Fichte's principle 'Only the metaphysical saves' and then made the theological conviction that mankind has been saved the guarantee of the invulnerability of the salvific process to historical criticism. If we recall that he had always maintained that the theologian works within the theological circle, then we cannot blame him for producing a *petitio principii*, a circular argument. What he has done is to produce an explanation of the nature of his belief, rather than some kind of neutral and so non-theological proof. At times like this one feels that Tillich is not enough of an apologist, a man of our time speaking to his contemporaries in their own language.

The issue of scepticism leads Tillich to distinguish his position from that commonly attributed to Kierkegaard (which is actually a 'position' postulated in his overall dialectical argument): that the bare assertion of early Christian belief is all we need as the 'occasion' of faith. In fact, he changes Kierkegaard's statement slightly, removing it from Christian history to some abstract realm of historical knowledge. Faith needs more concreteness than the empty historical assertion that God sent his son in the years AD 1–30. This much is obvious and incontestable: only a concrete historical reality can be known as New Being if that is the name of an event. Then, almost imperceptibly, Tillich's argument moves from what Kierkegaard called the situation of the contemporary disciple to that of the disciple at second hand, someone in a later generation who believes. We now know, not an abstract statement about the history of AD 1–30, but the concrete reality of the power which has created and preserved the community of the New Being. This is associated with the picture of Jesus as the Christ which is given in the New Testament.

Much ink has been spilt over the problem of the *analogia imaginis* in Tillich's Christology. In the light of what has been said so far, we can take it as read that what for Tillich is the actual salvific agency is the New Being. Putting it crudely, he would never have said that even the Bible can do what only God in Christ does: to bring about our salvation. Yet, like Coleridge, he would be very willing to testify to the power of the Bible to bring to every generation and everyone wherever that light has shone the revelation of the Divine Word.

What makes his argument so difficult to interpret accurately and criticize justly is that it moves on so many levels. It is an analysis of the nature of the historical information needed by faith but it is also an account of the way in which a historical tradition refers to that initial faith. Then again, it harks back to the fundamental problem of how we can speak of God. This is where he compares his *analogia imaginis* with the traditional theory of *analogia entis*, and this is confusion worse confounded. Rather than follow that discussion, it is better to concentrate on the fact that for him there is something about the biblical picture which guarantees that it is a true representation of the actual personal life of the Redeemer. This is why he is at pains to reject the notion that the risk of faith is synonymous with the kind of uncertainty that is part and parcel of historical judgment (ST, vol. 2, p. 134). The risk of faith is existential. One final thing can be said about Tillich's notion of *analogia imaginis*: he was much influenced by aesthetics as he sought to set out what the basis of faith was. At its historical root there lay, he says, a picture, not a photograph. The distinction is not as clear-cut as he would suggest; for even a photograph has a subjective element and there is no empirical account of a historical person without such an element. However, to return to his argument, the New Testament account as a picture is no 'painted projection' of profound religious experience but rather an 'expressionist' portrait. The Expressionist painter paints 'the reality and the meaning of his subject matter', neither reproducing some photographic likeness nor idealizing the image. It is in this sense that the picture is a real picture of Jesus.

Because Tillich strove so anxiously to single out the non-historical content of the Christological claim and to show the inadequacy of all attempts to make theology synonymous with history, he laid himself open to attack. He was commonly thought to deny a historical Christ and charged with presenting a form of the Docetic heresy. In fact, as we have seen, his concern was to hold in balance the two sides of Christology, the historical and the transcendent. His solution of the problem was to claim that the basis of the Christian faith is the historical picture of the revealed transcendent. The talk of an analogy of the imagination was an attempt to show how historical validity can be claimed about a statement which as a non-verbal expression is also not a photographic record, and that this historical certainty is the basis of a conviction about reality itself and not just history. Was it a successful attempt? That would be too much to claim: one of Tillich's obvious mistakes was his failure to address the theoretical problem of what guarantees the validity. How do we know that the Expressionist painting represents the reality and meaning of the figure? Again, because he was seldom prepared to work out a detailed argument and contented himself with finding the big building-blocks of a discursive scheme, he moved easily, too easily, from talking of 'meaning' in aesthetics to 'meaning' in ontology. So the connection between faith's valuation of Jesus and the historical assertions about Jesus is left unclarified. To say this is not to minimize Tillich's great achievement in mapping out the various relations that constitute the parameters of Christology. True to his Christocentric emphasis, he stressed the way in which theology, if Christian, begins with the revelation in Christ as this is recorded in the New Testament. This is something that belongs to the present history of faith and is not confined to past history, and that is why there is much point in comparing the response of faith to the aesthetic experience of looking at a portrait. Yet because the portrait refers to a datable piece of history, the issue is also obviously very much like estimating the truth about a history of this or that movement and evaluating the justice of a particular biographical portrait. Seeing all this, Tillich also saw that the judgement we are here making is not whether this man was wise or good or anything such, but whether he was the revelation of God. Hence he consistently referred to the category of the New Being.

What the discussion so far has shown is the way in which Tillich was a perfectly traditional theologian working out the traditional problems of Christology. However, what was most obvious was his determination to break loose from what he regarded as the mistaken constrictions of traditional Christology and to offer, in the words of the title of one of his most important articles, 'a reinterpretation of the doctrine of the incarnation' (*Church Quarterly Review*, 1949). What was wrong with the traditional doctrine of the two natures was not the use of a metaphysical category as such but the inadequacy of that category. The Council of Nicaea had in fact saved the Christian faith, but with inadequate tools, thereby creating a legacy of problems for theology. The most prominent and also the most disastrous is the misunderstanding of the paradoxical nature of the Christian message as a logical paradox of the uniting of two opposites. That misunderstanding leads to a quite erroneous sacrifice of the understanding when we should instead be contemplating the fulfilment of reason in the concept of authentic humanity, the New Being. This is one of the reasons why Tillich rejects the idea of a

Christian philosophy: it would reduce the Christian revelation to one competing theory alongside the other speculative views on offer to man. For him, however, the concrete *logos* revealed in Jesus as the Christ is identical with the universal *logos*. If the use made of metaphysics by Nicaea was inadequate, the solution was not to abandon metaphysics but to think in terms of new categories. In his development of the theological system, Tillich did not start here; but there is a sense in which the system's neat pattern of Being–existence–New Being is a reworking of theology that starts with the fact of salvation. That is, Tillich can be interpreted as having found the justification for his ontological interpretation of the doctrines of God, Creation and the Fall in the very nature of the saving event. If the saving revelation is a human history, then the categories for construing the scheme in its entirety are those of a philosophical anthropology.

Clearly, Tillich's ontological Christology is something that is very easy to misunderstand. As has been made clear, his warnings against an over-easy trust in history did not signify any desire to abandon history or to play down its crucial importance for Christology. Similarly, what is very far from the truth is the picture of him as a theologian who transformed the doctrines of God, man and Incarnation into some version of Heidegger's existentialism. It would be much more accurate to see him as a latter-day St Thomas Aquinas who sought to use competing philosophies to correct the anti-Christian tendencies in each and used a new philosophy to correct the philosophical mistakes of traditional theology. Sometimes he is criticized as being in the end an unreconstructed Liberal. Profoundly indebted as it was to that tradition, his theology was in fact quite the opposite. For him there could never be a distortion of the biblical message by a genuine ontology—the biblical quest had the same goal as the ontological, viz. ultimate reality. This was why a Christology could not avoid using ontological categories if it would express the full meaning of the christological claim. Not only would Tillich agree with Whitehead's judgement that Christianity, though not itself a metaphysic, has always been in search of a metaphysic, but he would go further and insist on the metaphysical challenge that Christianity represents. It is exactly on this point that he parted company with the Liberalism that was his background; for he would see the search for a metaphysic as part of the very nature of the Gospel.

To conclude this account of Tillich's Christology, we need to look at what he has to say about the Resurrection. In a sense, this is again Tillich the traditional theologian dealing with the issues of the historical life and death of Jesus, issues which arise because of the valuation of the event of Jesus as the Christ as being unique. He reminds us that we are concerned with the dogma because there is here a message of salvation. There is a universal significance attributed by the Bible to the picture of Jesus, and this is expressed by means of myths and symbols. Unlike his friend Bultmann, Tillich did not want to get rid of the myths: to do so would be to deprive religion of its language (ST, vol. 2, p. 176). What makes his approach quite immune to some fancies of myth-making, in his view, is that the myths and symbols of Christology are corroborated by history. It is in this way that he is here returning to the problem of faith's historical foundation. That sense of keeping his feet on the *terra firma* of history lends a profundity to his remark (ibid.) that the two central symbols of Christology are the 'Cross of Christ' and the 'Resurrection of Christ' because the former expresses the subjection to existence and the latter the conquest of existence. He is adamant that we are referring to two historical facts: if they were not, then it could not be said that the Christ had entered existence and had overcome it. However, he is not very clear in his description of these facts as historical. He speaks of the probability of the historical reference of the New Testament stories of the Cross, calling it a 'highly probable fact' (ibid., p. 177). By contrast, the event of the Resurrection is not something that happens in the public domain: it is 'the mysterious experience of a few'. Even so, the interdependence of these two symbols means that they are both symbol and reality: in both cases, he thinks, 'something happened within existence'. He points to the symbolic and mythological elements in the talk about the Cross and goes so far as to say that the disciples' claim that Jesus had been raised 'was dependent in part upon their belief in Jesus who, as the Christ, became the Messiah' (ibid., p. 178). Yet this is not, he says, the stuff of mystery cults and their mythological symbolism. What makes it different presumably is that *this* mythological symbolism refers to a concrete historical event. Yet, while Tillich is so obviously right in saying that 'the character of the event remains in darkness', one wishes that he would have said more clearly how or why the symbol *must* refer to a concrete historical event. It is very difficult to see why the interdependence of the two symbols guarantees this, unless there is prior knowledge of the one as historical. On the other hand, it could be said that it was quite typical of Tillich that he should think of the logical relation between the two concepts as indicating an ontological relation which necessitated a certain pattern of history.

As for the historical event of the Resurrection, establishing this by historical research could not be seen as a primary concern of faith. Despite that, historical research will necessarily be engaged in the delicate task of isolating a factual element here, as with the case of the crucifixion. Several times Tillich insists that what such research can deliver is never more than a probability which is, by definition, less than the certainty that faith requires. Such certainty is given by the very foundation of faith in the experience of being grasped by the power of the New Being, 'the certainty of one's own victory over the death of existential estrangement' (ibid., p. 179). The possible theories of what was the historical probability Tillich reduces to a basic list of three (ibid., pp. 179–82). First, there is the 'physical' theory, the story of the empty tomb, which is a theological rationalization of the event. That is to say, because we think of a living person as having a body, then to say that a person who has died has been 'raised' from the dead we imagine that the body which was a dead corpse has become capable of removing itself. 'Then the absurd question arises as to what happened to the molecules which comprise the corpse of Jesus of Nazareth. Then absurdity becomes compounded into blasphemy' (ibid., p. 180). The second alternative is the 'spiritualistic' theory, which works on the basis of the spiritualist's experience of dead souls appearing from 'the other side' or 'the spirit world'. This theory thus points to the New Testament evidence of Jesus' Resurrection appearances and treats them as similar communications or encounters. This theory also is given rather short shrift by Tillich, who regards it as too general in its interest, too much a matter of immortality and the possibility of post-mortem communication. This, he says, is a very far cry from the particular and very concrete matter of 'the reappearance of the total personality which includes the bodily expression of his being' (ibid.). Finally, there is the 'psychological' theory, 'the easiest and most accepted way of describing the factual element in the Resurrection' (ibid.). As a theory, this fits the evidence of the New Testament because not only was what the disciples knew as the Resurrection something which was 'an inner event' in their minds, but also the Resurrection appearances mentioned by St Paul as well as his own encounter with the Risen Christ can all be interpreted psychologically. Tillich is most anxious to make clear that such a theory is not synonymous with saying that the experience was either a hallucination or a piece of mere imagination. Even so, this theory 'misses the reality of the event which is presupposed in the symbol—the event of the Resurrection of the Christ' (ibid.).

Having surveyed the three possible types of theory or historical explanation, Tillich demonstrates both his conviction that there was some objective event and also his readiness to see that made a matter of historical investigation. He does this by proposing his own view of what happened, a view which is indeed a refined form of the psychological theory. Fundamental to this is an insistence on the unique nature of the reality as the converse of the uniqueness of the negativity which it overcomes. That negativity is the disappearance of him whose being was the New Being (ibid., p. 181). In other words, for Tillich even historical criticism in dealing with the Resurrection must recognize the universal ontological significance of the person raised. That conviction led him to offer what he calls a 'restitution theory' (ibid., p. 182); but he instantly distinguishes between this probable statement and the certainty of faith. This is less confusing than it seems: he wants us to bear in mind that even a reconstruction of what in fact happened at the first Easter cannot ignore the confession of faith, and yet its fullest and most informative statement will fall short of what is known by faith. For that faith, the indestructible unity of the New Being and Jesus of Nazareth is the corollary of the experience of the New Being. What Tillich thinks happened at the first Easter is, in effect, a repeatable experience, the experience of Christ's 'living presence here and now' (ibid., p. 181). To that extent, he would seem to reduce the Resurrection to something psychological; but he regards this mental event as something historical because it was a unique resolution of the tension between the disciples' conviction that Jesus was the bearer of the New Being and their disappointment at the turn of events which seemed to contradict this. 'In this tension something unique happened. In an ecstatic experience the concrete picture of Jesus of Nazareth became indissolubly linked with the reality of the New Being' (ibid.). However, Tillich will not admit that this presence was a bodily one in any sense—it 'does not have the character of a revived (and transmuted) body, nor does it have the character of the reappearance of an individual soul; it has the character of spiritual presence' (ibid.). This theory is, he thinks, faithful to the earliest evidence in 1 Corinthians 15, and in his concluding comments on it (ibid., p. 182), he even allows the possibility 'that the restitution of

Jesus to the dignity of the Christ in the minds of the disciples may precede the story of the acceptance of Jesus as the Christ by Peter' (ibid.). This throwaway remark will probably strike New Testament critics as a case of painting the lily of historical scepticism. Yet it does show very clearly to what lengths Tillich was prepared to go in order to accommodate both the corrigibility of historical theory and the unshakeable certainty which faith claims.

Not even Tillich's most ardent admirers can describe this view of the Resurrection as free of difficulty, if not, indeed, confusion. It is important as an attempt to bring historical criticism face to face with the difficulty of establishing and describing an event which is at once a historical event and also the effect of a transcendent cause. What it does not do clearly enough is to show the process of historical reconstruction and its result. That is, one can be pardoned for feeling that we still do not know what *happened*, or indeed whether anything did. That ambiguity as to whether anything *actually happened*—was it all like the reappearance of someone lost or the revivification of someone feared dead?—remains. What is worse, it is compounded by Tillich's further remarks about the 'symbols corroborating the symbol "Resurrection of the Christ"' (ibid., pp. 183ff.) where he describes the story of the Resurrection as an event 'anticipated in a large number of other events'. With a scholarship and a sensitivity that would have done honour to the Myth and Symbol tradition of comparative religion, Tillich looks at the various symbols which are connected with the Resurrection in the New Testament narrative, beginning with the mythical symbols of pre-existence and post-existence and culminating in the Second Coming only after the more proximate ideas of miracles and the rule over the church through the Spirit. This is one of the points at which Tillich's eagerness to be economic in his sketching of the System is tantalizing. In the early 1950s, he used to boast that he would complete his *Systematic Theology* in two volumes, not the endless series that seemed to be making up Barth's *Church Dogmatics*. This ambition, more or less fulfilled, is at least one reason why he did not spell out the very difficult issues which all these symbols raise for a theology of the Resurrection. To say that this discussion shows how little concern in the end Tillich had for historicity is to miss the point. That he was reluctant to *identify* the Resurrection with any historical event, however tenuously linked with publicly verifiable facts, is certain. I well recall his dismissive reply to a question of mine as to whether the factuality of the

Resurrection did not imply that the tomb was empty—'I am not interested in ghost stories even if you are'. Yet we would ignore not only a repeated stress but an actual example of historical explanation if we deny that Tillich's doctrine of the Resurrection saw it as having a basis in historical fact. It could be said that he was having the penny and the bun; but the truth of the matter was that, in his view, a real understanding of the bun left you with an unspent penny in your pocket. The real issue for him was the matter of what the Resurrection secured for mankind: through this history of Cross and Resurrection came the conquest of estrangement, what is traditionally called 'salvation'.

7

Christus Victor and the Conquest of Estrangement

Few aspects of his theology better illustrate its catholicity than Tillich's discussion of the doctrine of salvation. In the first place, however philosophical his view of the whole area of Christology, he had always stressed that Christology was to be seen as indissolubly linked with soteriology. This was at least part of what he meant by the constant emphasis on the interconnections between doctrines and the *systematic* nature of theology. It was also one reason why he would become incensed when one concentrated on the logical nature of his system; for, to his mind, he was indeed following out logically the consequences of axiomatic principles, but only because these soteriological principles were axioms. Also, it could be said that, having worked out a new doctrine of the Incarnation which made such liberal use of philosophy, he turned to soteriology as the problem of explaining the nature of his starting-point. That is, if Christ's significance is to be seen in terms of the new being which he bears, the answer to the human quest, then the completion of that explanation is the elucidation of how Christ imparts that new being. Very often, in reading Tillich, it is easy to miss the way in which his phenomenological approach to theology shows a profound concern with the personal, because he is so anxious to make the different parts of his theology fit into a scheme. Thus it might be thought that in his interpretation of the Atonement he has sold out to an Idealist philosophy and has moved from the reinterpretation of incarnation as New Being to the reunion which that implies in an Idealist scheme. However, Tillich's achievement in fact was to show that there was an important connection between philosophy and theology in this area, because sin has an epistemological significance. The apparent match of an Idealist scheme of thesis, antithesis and synthesis which can take on a much more theological colour when we look at Hegel's picture of a reunion of the estranged divine life is thus less significant as the motive force of Tillich's thinking at this point. His use of philosophy in elaborating a doctrine of Incarnation was profoundly theological because he was concerned with the personal significance of that conflict between essential and existential being. In the third volume of *Systematic Theology*, he points out that this is peculiarly true of personal existence, though all things share in eternal blessedness.

These comments about the relation between philosophy and theology at this point will help explain why his discussion of atonement starts in an apparently unbiblical fashion. Instead of going back to the biblical story, Tillich relates the meaning of salvation to ontology (ST, vol. 2, p. 191). Salvation is the universal significance of Jesus as the Christ, his victory over existence after being subject to existence. Characteristic of Tillich's aim and method in theology is his insistence that calling Christ Saviour, Mediator or Redeemer is to use language that needs clarification, clarification that he offers only after trying to explain the context and the content of meaning which the term 'salvation' has; for there are as many kinds of salvation as there are things or situations from which we need to be saved. Applying the test of theological meaning which he himself had laid down at the beginning, he singles out ultimate negativity and what leads to it as that from which we are to be *saved*. This is explained as the loss of the inner purpose and meaning of one's being. 'The tremendous weight of the question of salvation is rooted in this understanding of the term. It becomes the question of "to be or not to be"' (ibid.). Salvation in this sense could be said to be the goal, and so salvation can be understood also as meaning the way in which that goal is achieved. This is a nice distinction and it is clear enough; for one could equally speak of the payment of a debt as being the solution of my financial problem in the two senses of my bank balance no longer being in the red and of the actual payment of that debt. The effect of the distinction is that Tillich then proceeds to list the various ways in which salvation has been understood in the history of Christian theology. As usual, he interprets its original meaning by invoking etymology: it is a healing and that is an adequate way of interpreting this notion. If then we ask from what

124

we need to be healed, we must think back to the basic characteristic of existence as estrangement. Salvation is the reuniting of what has become estranged—which is to say, man and God, man and his world, and man and himself.

It now becomes clear that there is an important sense in which Tillich's view of atonement is what leads him to his distinctive Christology so that, as was said earlier, his ontological approach there was determined by a very properly orthodox theological concern. If the unassumed is not healed, then, in looking at the nature of salvation as healing, we need to consider afresh the nature of being and the answer to the 'question' posed by its existential condition. Indeed, Tillich himself says as much in this opening section—'Out of this interpretation of salvation the concept of the New Being has grown. Salvation is reclaiming from the old and transferring into the New Being' (ibid., p. 192). He is quick to point out that there is nothing unorthodox in this interpretation, since it includes the various things which had been emphasized in traditional theologies. So the truth of his argument for him lies precisely in the inclusiveness of his view; and lest it should be thought that he is making the term mean anything at all, he makes clear that there is a norm. For the glory of this understanding, he thinks, is that it includes the Liberal view of salvation as moral fulfilment precisely by putting that in the special perspective of the original idea of healing.

One further implication of the clarification he has offered is noted by Tillich: the very important point that salvation through Christ is not to be separated from the other historical processes of salvation. This gives the lie to those interpretations of Tillich as some kind of crypto-conservative whose contemporary language hid an old-fash-ioned theology limiting salvation to Christianity. The argument of this section is not very clear, because he distinguishes between a history of salvation and a historical continuity which is the context of salvation. These are not in fact his terms, his own terminology being the distinction between the history of revelation and the history of concrete revelatory events (ibid.). However, the point of the argument seems clear enough: there is a definite continuity of revelation and salvation in history. Yet we misunderstand religion and Christianity too, he argues, if we reduce the Christian revelation to a moment in some ongoing process of revelation which is the increasing enlightenment of mankind. Revelation is not a matter of gaining information about the divine: it is God making himself known, within all the emotional and life-giving impact that the discovery of his person has—'the ecstatic manifestation of the Ground of Being in events, persons and things' (ibid.). And when God makes himself known, he saves. In this way Tillich's very brief discussion of atonement is perhaps the most powerful expression of the kerygmatic nature of his theology. He never forgot that what he was concerned with was the salvation of the human person in its totality and in the totality of its context. His contention, then, is that as there was a history of revelation which the Christian theologian interprets as having its centre in Jesus as the Christ, so we cannot limit salvation within that history. Where there is history of revelation there has been in that sense a history of salvation. So he goes on explicitly to reject as *unbiblical* the ecclesiastical view of salvation as either total or non-existent (ibid., p. 193); and the context makes it clear that what he is opposing is a conservative Christianity which would say that outside the church there is no salvation. He labels this kind of view in all its varieties of expression, whether Catholic or Calvinist, as an 'absurd and demonic view' (ibid.). Moreover, he regards any attempt at a universalism as doomed to fail so long as we think of an absolute disjunction between salvation and condemnation. This is where the understanding of salvation as healing is so illuminating and liberating. All men can share in the healing power of the New Being; they must do so or they would have no being. Yet no man can claim a totality of healing, and that is why the Christian doctrine of salvation has an eschatological dimension. In fact the doctrine of a cosmic redemption shows how fundamental this dimension is to Christian hope—and once more Tillich's philosophical instinct moves him to note the metaphysics here involved as he adds that we are moved to consider 'the relation of the eternal to the temporal with respect to the future' (ibid.).

The traditional terminology of theology needed clarification, Tillich had said; and he begins this by referring to the traditional distinction between the Person of Christ and the Work of Christ. In its traditional use this was a distinction between two doctrines: Christology and soteriology. Very properly, Tillich protests against the notion that what is at the heart of Christology is different or distinct from the concern of soteriology. The Person of Christ, he says, is not a reality in itself which is the kind of notion one might have if the Person is thought of in abstract terms as the composition of two substances. Rather, he says, what makes Jesus the Christ is something which has to do with the power of healing signified by the

New Being. We cannot understand what either the Person or the Work of Christ means if we remove the event from the historical context of those for whom he became the Christ, and that has no place in the traditional distinction. Tillich's discussion here is extremely brief but he makes some crucially important points about the doctrine of atonement. Most important is the principle he enunciates, that the being of Christ is his work (ibid., p. 194). It is a principle which could arguably be said to be too limiting a Christological perspective—too much of a Melanchthon-like stress on the benefits of the Gospel which could be something of a reductive analysis of the fullness of grace. In both the description of the incarnate Word given in the Fourth Gospel and the stress on inexhaustibility in Ephesians, there is a clear recognition that Christ is more than what he has achieved for us. Yet it cannot be denied that any understanding of the being of Christ which fails to take note of his work is not only artificial but profoundly unevangelical and a distorted theological perspective. It is not simply that it fails to see the wood for the trees, but that it describes the wood in a completely abstract and unhelpful fashion.

In accordance with the principle that the being of Christ is his work, Tillich affirms that Jesus as the Christ is the Saviour because of, and by means of, the universal significance of his being as the New Being. Thus he tries to escape the artificiality of so much atonement doctrine which seeks to develop models into distinctions and talk about different aspects of atonement as 'offices'—prophet, priest and king. While these have a useful place in liturgy, they are useless for systematic theology. It is the same principle that Tillich applies when he considers the term 'Mediator'. The roots of the term in the history of religion are deep and clear. The divine is transcendent and yet it must be near—that is the tension that generates the notion of a mediator-god. That such a being reunites what is estranged is an equally important element in the idea. These two aspects are in play when the term 'Mediator' is applied to Jesus as the Christ. 'In his face we see the face of God, and in him we experience the reconciling will of God; in both respects he is the Mediator' (ibid., p. 195). To imagine that the Mediator is some third reality alongside God and man is, however, an entirely erroneous notion against which Tillich here enters a protest. It makes no sense for him either in terms of the nature of Christ or the nature of our reconciliation. The rejection of such a Christology was 'the first great anti-heretical decision of Christianity' (ibid., p. 196) and it is just as important for a doctrine of atonement. For what it would mean is that God is not the sole cause of reconciliation, inasmuch as he is dependent on that third reality for the effecting of reconciliation. By contrast, the message of Christianity is that God's will is salvific and that he made the first move in this reconciliation of the estranged. The agent of salvation is God and only if that is clearly understood can we speak of a Mediator.

No word has been more common in doctrines of atonement than the term 'Redeemer'. With remarkable brevity, Tillich indicates the very rich background of its meaning derived from the Latin *redemptio* (buying back). In the ordinary use of the term there still lingers, he says, the old notion of a ransom being paid to Satan in order to liberate mankind from his power. Because this idea of liberation from demonic powers has been so prominent a part of doctrines of atonement, Tillich considers that it is justifiable to speak of Christ as Redeemer. However, once more he warns against a dangerous connotation; for here again we are in danger of thinking that God's activity in atonement is not entirely free. 'It can create an image of someone who must pay a price to the anti-divine powers before God is able to liberate man from the bondage of guilt and punishment' (ibid.). It is obvious that this is something which Tillich would rule out because of his insistence that God is the sole agent in the work of atonement. The fact that he does not comment on either the figure of Satan or the notion of punishment can only mean that he regarded these as pure mythology which must be assumed to be subject to a theological analysis.

With this background, Tillich gives us his view of atonement. He begins with a clarification of types of atonement doctrine. Once again the phenomenological approach is very much in evidence. He defines the doctrine as 'the description of the effect of the New Being in Jesus as the Christ on those who are grasped by it in their state of estrangement' (ibid.). We are not talking about the divine counsels or giving an account of something outside history. Indeed, our starting-point must be within our own experience and not even back in the history of Jesus. If, then, this is what atonement is, says Tillich, it has two sides: the agency of atonement and the human experience of the atoning effect. 'In the sense of this definition, atonement is always both a divine act and a human reaction' (ibid., p. 197). Without being distracted into any account of the history of the doctrine of atonement, it is perhaps worth indicating that Tillich's use of the term 'subjective' in this context is slightly different from the normal meaning of the term as referring to certain types of doctrine. Usually when we speak of a subjective theory of atonement, we have in mind a doctrine such as Abelard's which would make the atonement a matter of the psychological effect of Christ's supreme example of love. In Tillich's use, the term can be said to indicate the practical human effects of what he has described axiomatically as an act of God. The subjective element in atonement is the human reaction of accepting the removal of the barrier of guilt which separates us from God—in the words of one of his most famous sermons, 'accepting that we are accepted'. This subjective element, in his view, is the explanation not only of the absence of a dogmatic definition but also of the variety of types of doctrine which have been put forward in the history of the church.

Though Tillich's understanding of the subjective element in atonement is not exactly what has been meant by historians of doctrine when they speak of subjective types of doctrine, he does in fact see the division of types into subjective and objective as corresponding to his polarity of subjective and objective. He regards it as the basic division; and any possible doctrine can be classified by placing it within the spectrum of subjective and objective—'predominantly objective, predominantly subjective and stages between the two' (ibid., p. 197). Within the space of three pages, he summarizes the history of atonement doctrine, taking Origen (c.185–c.284) as the example of extreme objectivity, Abelard (1079–1142) as the example of extreme subjectivity and Anselm as 'the most effective' alternative. The survey is an important analysis of what is to be said in a doctrine of atonement. Thus he recognizes that the objective doctrine developed by Origen could be read as 'a cosmic drama—almost a comedy' with God and Satan playing a game. All of this seems to have little to do with man; but it is the experience of the conquest of existential estrangement that lies at its very root. Moreover, the concrete symbols of Satan and the Christ express the profound metaphysical truth that 'the negative lives from the positive, which it distorts' (ibid., p. 198). So Satan is bound to lose in the end. If, then, it is the *experience* of the power of the New Being that lies at the root of even the objective theories of atonement, there is little wonder, says Tillich, that someone like Abelard goes to the other extreme. Christ's perfect expression of love on the Cross evokes in man a response of love. In fairness to Abelard, Tillich recognizes that he gives a little nod towards the objective; but essentially for him atonement is the liberation which is man's in his knowledge that God is perfect love, a knowledge which comes with his response of love toward God. The weakness of this view is that it takes no account of divine justice and 'love becomes weakness if it does not include justice' (ibid., p. 199). The analogy of psychotherapy shows for Tillich the importance of an inward understanding of the guilt for violated justice and the need to 'pay the price', as we would say. In his view, the predominantly subjective theory failed to allow for this and so could not be accepted as an adequate doctrine of atonement.

So much for the extremes; but the compromise theory, if one can so describe the alternative, even though it is 'the most effective one, at least in western Christianity', proves not to be entirely satisfactory either. Since it moves from its formal objective starting-point to a clear recognition of the psychological element brought out in regard to Abelard, it obviously meets the requirements of the *formal* polarity. Tillich's summary of Anselm's theory is so brilliantly economic that it is worth quoting.

> It starts with the tension in God between his wrath and his love and shows that the work of Christ makes it possible for God to exercise mercy without violating the demands of justice. The infinite worth of the suffering of the Christ gives satisfaction to God and makes unnecessary the punishment of man for the infinite weight of his sin. Only the God-Man could do this, because, as man, he could suffer and, as God, he did not need to suffer his own sins. For the believing Christian, this means that his consciousness of guilt is affirmed in its unconditional character. At the same time he feels the inescapability if that punishment which is nevertheless taken over by the infinite depth and value of the suffering of the Christ. (Ibid., p. 199)

It is the powerful psychological appeal created by this dual recognition of a need for punishment and the liberation from it by Christ's substitutional sacrifice which has made this theory so influential. It has made an impression on spirituality and liturgy as well as theology that has hardly been equalled. For all that, Tillich wants to bring out its weaknesses very clearly, though quickly. It was a theory based on a legal code long since dated and abandoned. It viewed sin and punishment in a quantitative way that is clearly inappropriate—one can hardly say that cheating is the square root of murder or that the punishment for this sin is deemed by God to be twice that for some other. There are the points already made in connection with the ideas of 'Mediator' and 'Redeemer' which are equally obvious criticisms. However, the most basic criticism is that it ultimately ignores the subjective side of the process of atonement. Tillich quotes Thomas Aquinas with approval indicating that the doctrine needed to be corrected by adding the idea of the participation of the Christian in what happens to the Christ. The proper compromise between the two poles would be effected, Tillich concludes, by replacing the concept of substitution by that of participation (ibid., p. 200).

Throughout his discussion so far, Tillich has been remarkably impressive in his combination of thoroughness with extreme brevity. Not even his one-volume survey of historical theology, *A History of Christian Thought*, can be judged to be quite as compendious as these few pages of the second volume of *Systematic Theology*. It is as if he is preparing us for the surprise he has in store—he will refuse to elaborate a doctrine of his own. Several times he had been heard to say that, unlike his friend Barth, he had learnt the knack of economic expression which is the genius of the English language, but there is more to the refusal than this laudable claim, justified or not. He clearly felt that theologians had got themselves into too many difficulties as they tried to reduce the drama of salvation to some kind of building plan. Part of that problem was that theologians had not displayed an adequately modest reverence, and again they forgot the necessity for the phenomenological approach which tells what we can see through the glass darkly. Most of all, it would seem, Tillich could not avoid the feeling that the doctrine of atonement was something that might well disappear in the future development of doctrine. He says as much (ibid.); but he typically leaves the suggestion tantalizingly vague. It may be that he regarded the lack of dogmatic definition as something which, though perfectly understandable and indeed natural, was a hindrance rather than a help. One of the main functions he saw himself fulfilling as a theologian was the reinterpretation of dogma so as to give it a new, free and liberating life as the expression of ecclesiastical existence. Whether this is a proper explanation or not the fact of the matter is that volume 2 was brought to a close with the elaboration of 'principles of the doctrine of atonement' rather than with a new theory. Nor, when at the end of his life he was talking of revising *Systematic Theology*, did he suggest that this needed to be supplied.

Six principles are stated and their exposition is of varying length. Thus the 'first and all-decisive principle' is stated in two sentences amounting to five lines. It is that the atoning processes are created by God and God alone. The only explanation given is that God is not dependent on the Christ but that 'the Christ, as the bearer of the New Being, mediated the reconciling act of God to man' (ibid.). That God alone is the author of the atonement is axiomatic; but this bald ascription of authorship seems rather a thin statement of all that has been pointed out over the ages about God's salvific will as theologians have contributed to atonement theory. As for the point about dependence, it seems almost as if Tillich had fallen prey to the same kind of misconception and even nonsense which he had condemned in old-fashioned doctrines of atonement. What he clearly wants to say is that even when we properly focus on the activity of Christ, the life and struggle of Jesus up to Gethsemane and on Golgotha, what we have here is a revelation of God rather than human heroic tragedy.

'The second principle for a doctrine of atonement is that there are no conflicts in God between his reconciling love and his retributive justice' (ibid.). With this terse statement, Tillich dismisses as misguided all the lengthy discussions in the history of atonement doctrine about the conflict between mercy and justice. Presumably he makes no reference to these because it would distract him from the task of spelling out the special nature of God's justice. He protests against our tendency to limit what it means by rejecting the anthropomorphic notion of 'a special act of punishment calculated according to the guilt of the sinner' (ibid., pp. 200–1). That is to say, justice in God is what it can never be in us because we can only screw our determination to the point of a special act, something which, despite the fact that we are its agent, is nevertheless separate from us. It seems very much as if Tillich's intuition here is that of St Thomas, that God's nature is simple, so that in him there cannot be conflicting elements. Again, Tillich wants us to entertain a nobler concept of justice than that which W. S. Gilbert comically described as making 'the punishment fit the crime'. He goes on to use another mediaeval idea when he defines God's justice as letting the self-destruction of estrangement take its course. God's power is absolute in itself but as 'ordained' in creation it is expressed within creation's laws. For God to interfere with these would be for him to cease to be God. This familiar enough argument is given greater force by Tillich's further comment that he would cease to be love. Justice, he says, 'is the structural form of love'. The argument seems too neat to be convincing; but that is because Tillich has been too cryptic on the one hand and on the other too ready to adopt an easy answer like saying that without justice love becomes sentimental. The essential truth of his principle is that whereas in our attempts at justice we cannot achieve the honesty of a proper love, in God's work on the Cross love and justice are visibly and indivisibly one. Once again the poets have seen it all, as Wittgenstein said; and seldom did insight and understanding meet so well as in Isaac Watts:

Here his whole name appears complete
nor wit can guess nor reason prove
which of the letters best is writ,
the Power, the Wisdom, or the Love.

To some extent, Tillich's exposition of the third principle clarifies the second and establishes the argument which we have just developed. It is that 'the divine removal of guilt and punishment is not an act of overlooking the reality and depth of existential estrangement' (ibid., p. 201). Here he explicitly rejects anthropomorphism, branding liberal humanism as guilty of just such a mistake because the liberals seek to understand divine forgiveness as the kind of thing we know from our experience of human relations, a sentimental dismissal of the wrong. To appeal to the Lord's Prayer in defence of this is to ignore the essential difference between divine and human forgiveness. The central point here is what Tillich says next: 'In all human relations he who forgives is himself guilty, not only generally but in the concrete situation in which he forgives' (ibid.). This is the lesson taught by Shakespeare in such a tragedy as *Hamlet*. While in *The Merchant of Venice* the reciprocity of such ethical relations is well put by Portia in her description of mercy as 'twice blessed / It blesses him that gives and him that takes', in *Hamlet* it is less simple and less clear. Herein lies the whole agony of Hamlet's indecision. What becomes clear is that the retributive justice demanded and promised at the beginning of the play is effected only at the end, an end which has seen the death of both Ophelia and Hamlet. The third principle is not very clearly explained, though the closing sentence of the exposition makes the clear point that the ethical order contradicted by sin as separation from God is God himself. What Tillich wants us to grasp is the enormity of sin in exactly the way that the Psalmist did when he cried 'Where can I flee from thy presence?' (Psalm 139:7). Therefore, he says, God's forgiveness is no private matter.

In the fourth principle, Tillich gives some indication of why he thought that atonement was a doctrine which was capable of further and possibly transforming development. God's atoning activity must be understood as 'his participation in existential estrangement and its self-destructive consequences' (ST, vol. 2, p. 201). Tillich's language is formal and abstract; but there resonates through all that a clear sense of the way in which he has grasped and plumbed the depths of the tragedy which the Cross represents in human history. He does something more than reflect on the tragedy of a good man put to death by cruel forces; for his reflection on this matter is theological. If tragedy this was, it was a tragedy in which God was one of the *dramatis personae*, to put the point rather crudely. The self-destructive consequences are, he says, in a sense the very consequences God himself has ordained. So, to remove them is impossible—that makes no sense. But what is the sense of the only other alternative, viz. that he participates in them in such a way that he transforms these very consequences for those who participate in his participation? This is indeed, as he says (ibid., p. 201), 'the very heart of the doctrine of atonement'. The first answer, says Tillich, is the obvious general point about theological language: that it is a symbolic way of speaking. Having made that point, he reminds us that this kind of symbolism is found in abundance in biblical texts where God is said to be patient, to repent, to toil with human sin and even not to spare his Son and so on. All such expressions are indeed rather obviously language that is anthropomorphic and as such, he thinks, language which theology should avoid. In passing it is worth remembering how he always insisted that theology must remythologize as well as demythologize; but clearly theological remythologizing was not for him something that lapsed into or ever countenanced anthropomorphic language. The point about this kind of language in the Bible for Tillich is that it shows 'a freedom for concreteness in speaking of God's living reactions to the world' (ibid., p. 202).

Because this is the heart of the doctrine of atonement, Tillich's very terse exposition calls for more detailed clarification. The general theological point was so clear that it hardly needed stating; but the tension between the living awareness of the direct religious expressions of the Bible and the formal considerations of theology means that he is impelled to say more. What more can be said? Only that, however we understand God's suffering as he takes upon himself the suffering of the world, this is something that does not contradict God's eternal blessedness and its basis. That basis is the very nature of God as that which represents the ultimate, that needs nothing else for its existence and explanation, 'this being by himself and therefore beyond freedom and destiny' (ibid.). Having said this, Tillich remembers that when he had spoken of God as living he had said that the divine life represents a conquest of the element of non-being—an abstract formulation that clearly fits (as an abstract painting fits the concrete image from which its conception began) the doctrine of the atonement as the drama of salvation. In a rare moment of pure myth, Tillich speaks of the very life of God: 'This element of non-being, seen from inside, is the suffering that God takes upon himself by participating in existential estrangement or the state of unconquered negativity' (ibid.). That said, he retreats into his characteristic reticence on the subject of atonement—'Here the doctrine of the living God and the doctrine of atonement coincide'.

8

The Church as Spiritual Community

In his treatment of atonement which has been outlined, Tillich studiously avoided discussing the way in which the victory of the church is reflected in the historical context which is the believer's temporal history. This was for various reasons, and three of them are worth mentioning here. First, though he was always prone to indulge in very abstract formulation, he had the uncanny knack of keeping the concrete very much in view even when he failed to give expression to that concrete vision. So he wanted to make a direct transition from the *nature* of salvation to an interpretation of the community of faith, the social context of the confession of salvation, the church. Secondly, true to his metaphysical cast of mind he wanted to contextualize this talk of a redeemed humanity in an understanding of life. This is not simply a matter of the anthropological context but of a view of life as a whole, a whole which includes even the large tracts of existence, such as inorganic matter, to which we would not normally apply the term 'life'. Thirdly, as his theological vision was in this way synoptic and comprehensive, he wanted to portray the redeemed existence as a part of history. In a strange way, nothing reveals the essential comprehensiveness of Tillich's view of religion more clearly than this correlation of salvation with history and the Kingdom of God, because it is with history and not simply with Christian history that he correlates both the work of Christ and the Kingdom of God. In these ways, Tillich sought to locate his theology, as a systematic theology, within its appropriate context of the universal.

We begin the account of the church and the Kingdom, then, by outlining Tillich's philosophy of life (ST, vol. 3, chas xxii–xxiv). 'Life' is the term he prefers, as against what he regards as the more limited concept of 'process', a notion which had, of course, been very popular in American philosophy. The sense of the word 'life' is, he says (ibid., p. 12), the 'mixture' of essential and existential elements. The two are necessarily correlated in any understanding of life, the former describing what he calls 'the multi-dimensional unity of life' which is the basis on which one can speak of the existential ambiguities of all life. A unity which allows for a multi-dimensionality needs something more than the metaphor of level for its expression. Reality conceived by such a metaphor is a pyramid of ascending value, with each level having objects that are equal in value. Both the religious development and the political history of the modern world have consigned this hierarchical concept of level to the museum. It misleads us, whether we think of ourselves as body and mind or of our social existence as a matter of culture and religion. In neither context can we properly speak of some ruling part or of a higher 'level'. A much safer metaphor—that of dimension—is therefore Tillich's choice; for this is a metaphor that allows us to speak of one dimension interacting with another without any conflict. It is not that he wants to suggest that life has no conflicts but rather that he wants to emphasize that 'they are not derived from the hierarchy of levels' but are consequences of the ambiguity of all life processes (ibid., p. 15).

Tillich's purpose in distinguishing the dimensions of life is to show the multi-dimensional unity of life and the source and consequences of the ambiguities of all life processes. The first of these dimensions is the inorganic, an indefinite area of immense religious import but rarely considered by theology. Tillich wants to remedy this and offer a 'theology of the inorganic'. He rejects the positivist reduction of 'matter' according to which only the matter we encounter under the dimension of the inorganic exists. The sphere of the inorganic is that in which potentialities become actual in the spatio-temporal objects which are capable of physical analysis and are measurable in spatio-temporal relations. It is the first condition for the actualization of every dimension, and equally that into which they all dissolve. Even more obviously comprehensive is the dimension of the organic; for here everything that we comprehend under the term 'life' is included in the organic. The organic dimension is that of self-related, self-preserving, self-increasing and self-continuing forms—they are

137

'living whole'. It is essentially present in the inorganic, but its evolution requires specific conditions. The third and fourth dimensions are vegetative and animal being. Though very obviously universal in his vision and sympathies, Tillich stops short of sentimentalizing or indeed philosophizing metaphor in his talk of self-awareness. Given our ignorance about non-human self-awareness, he counsels a wise caution: '... it seems wiser to restrict the assumption of inner awareness to those realms in which it can be highly probable ... most obviously in the higher animals' (ibid., p. 21). As far as we know, the actualization of the dimension of inner awareness as the personal-communal or the 'spirit' is something that has happened only in man.

Despite what he regards as the misuse of the word 'spirit' in the English language, Tillich wants to use the word to designate the characteristically human dimension of life. A quick glance at the history of 'spirit' in its various linguistic traditions leads Tillich to declare himself opposed to the intellectualization of the word as meaning 'mind' and also to the attempt to dissociate that from intellect so as to make 'spirit' replaceable by 'mind'. Theology needs a new understanding of 'spirit' as a dimension of life, recapturing the sense of power which the religious use has helped preserve. That the need is desperate is evident, he thinks, from 'the fading of the symbol "Holy Spirit" from the living consciousness of Christianity' which is due in part at least to the abandonment of 'spirit' as the description of man. Other factors have contributed to the semantic confusion: talking of the spirit of a nation or of a law, the kind of angelistic doctrine which makes man a spirit within a body, a 'ghost in the machine'. The extreme point, in fact the nadir, of such confusion for Tillich is spiritualism, which, whether true or false as matter of fact, has 'no direct bearing on the problem of man's spirit or of God as Spirit' (ibid., p. 24).

The picture that Tillich draws is that of a historical evolution in which continuity allows for the emergence of a new dimension. Though history is usually conceived as a human matter purely and simply, there is, says Tillich, a proper sense in which there is history when there is anything at all—that is, the sense in which the universe has a history (ibid., pp. 26–7). Emphasizing continuity as he does, he inevitably rejects the doctrine that there was a particular time when humanity was created by the addition of an 'immortal soul' to a body. The multi-dimensional unity of life means that the dimension of spirit is related to the psychological in a much more organic fashion. Knowledge and morality are not merely psychological phenomena, but are impossible without these phenomena: we neither know without sense impressions nor act morally without our drives and desires forming the material of the moral decision. Consequently, though we can distinguish between higher and lower forms of life and regard man as the highest, it does not mean that we ignore man's 'liability to the greatest imperfection'. What is decisive is the self-integration of life. That is most clearly seen in morality, so that morality can be called 'the constitutive function of spirit' (ibid., p. 40). A moral act is one in which a potential person becomes an actual person, a being in control of the psychological life which is the given of experience. This is necessarily a social act, an act which has placed man in a community and in an environment which he must own as his world; and it is an act for which he is responsible. The moral law for Tillich, as for Kant, is the law of our essential being and as such is unambiguous. The ambiguity of life is to be seen in 'the unconditional character of the moral imperative, the norms of moral action and moral motivation' (ibid., p. 47).

Growth, too, is a universal function of life; but in all life we are aware of the ambiguity of self-creation and destruction. Life lives and grows 'by suppressing or removing or consuming other life' (ibid., p. 54), and thus a symptom of the ambiguity of life is struggle. Tillich speaks very feelingly of Freud's great discovery that there is a 'death instinct' in us just as there is a 'life instinct' and he compares it with St Paul's description of the sadness of the world (ibid., p. 60). With his habit of constantly referring to etymology, Tillich was inevitably led to think of culture (*cultura*) as something involving growth. The fact that this was a much earlier understanding of 'culture' than the contemporary use of the term illustrates the difficulty one encounters again and again in Tillich's thought. However, the important point is that as he analyses the various aspects of cultural creation, he emphasizes the distinction between the technological language, or what might be called our handling of the world, and the 'first' language of being in existence. Language is of fundamental importance, but it is not something that is significant only because of its cognitive power; for its aesthetic function is just as important. 'This is a tree' is an expression of our understanding of the term and our ability to classify things; but as Tillich says (ibid., p. 66), when Van Gogh paints a tree 'it becomes an image of his dynamic vision of the world'. Throughout that argument, Tillich's *leitmotif* is the thesis that the cultural act is ambiguous. It is both the creation and the destruction of meaning. Language separates mind and reality as it transforms reality into meaning. Knowledge is not only our contact with the world but presupposes 'the split between subject and object' (ibid., p. 74). There are various ambiguities of technical and personal transformation—the ambiguity of our being free but limited, the ambiguity of means and ends which is a matter of means becoming ends in themselves, our transformation of subjects into things—as well as the ambiguity of personal life which has its natural centre but is lived within a community for which there is no such natural centre. All lead to the quest for the unambiguous in the Kingdom of God.

Before coming to what may well be thought of as the proper topic of discussion at this point, it is as well to see how fully Tillich contextualizes this familiar concept of Christian theology. First of all, he emphasizes once more that his view of life is of a multi-dimensional unity. Morality, culture and religion constitute the unity of the spirit: as aspects of that unity they interpenetrate one another, none being separable or independent of the other. 'Culture, or the creation of a universe of meaning in *theoria* and *praxis* is essentially related to morality and religion' (ibid., p. 101). Religion is defined as 'the self-transcendence of life under the dimension of spirit' (ibid., p. 103), which means that it is not an independent function of human life. That is, one's being religious is nothing more than one's being grasped by revelation. On the other hand, religion as a human activity is a fact of life and an aspect of culture, however much one might say that by its own terms it negates such an existence. 'Religion as the self-transcendence of life needs the religions and needs to deny them' (ibid., p. 104). This view of religion as being itself ambiguous is one of the most important points to bear in mind for understanding what Tillich has to say about the church and again about the Kingdom.

Precisely because it is characterized by self-transcendence, religion is doubly ambiguous. At once the expression of the greatness of life in its highest form as holiness, religion is also the rejection of life's greatness as it desecrates the holy by its own idolatrous tendency. Religion is based on the self-revelation of the holy, and all its features, whether they be ritualistic or personal, demonstrate a self-transcendence. As Tillich puts it, they are transcendent towards the holy (ibid., p. 105); and he makes the crucially important point that when we speak of persons or things being holy we are not referring to any quality such as intelligence, wisdom or even goodness, but

rather their power of pointing beyond themselves. The first ambiguity of religion, then, is 'the presence of profanized elements in
every religious act'. These are of two kinds: the 'institutional' and the
'reductive'. First, there is the tendency of religion to become a self-
contained and self-justifying institution, which is not the same thing
as organized religion but a kind of transformation of religion into a
subtle psychological or social framework that refers to nothing
beyond itself. Secondly, religion always and inherently tends to be
reduced to culture and morality, because culture is the form of
religion and because religion is a significant piece of culture
inasmuch as it is moral. Rather than accepting the claim of religion,
this approach to religion explains it away as a mythical and pre-
scientific 'understanding' or as some otiose way of expressing moral
or aesthetic attitudes. 'Religion which in principle has a home in
every function of the spirit has become homeless in all of them'
(ibid., p. 107). The second ambiguity of religion that Tillich distinguishes is something that seems to be a similar reduction but is
different from what has just been discussed in that it has nothing to
do with a negation of religion. The difference could be described as
that between the relation of religion to the world in which it finds
itself and the relation of religion to the anti-divine forces within its
dealings with the divine, the distortion of self-transcendence which
occurs when a particular bearer of holiness is identified with the holy
itself. This goes on in every religion, says Tillich, even in Christianity, based though that is on the self-negation of the finite in the Cross
of Christ (ibid., p. 109). In fact, Christianity affords very good
examples of this kind of ambiguity, because the very form in which
that basis is claimed can contradict the nature of the basis itself. The
claim of Christianity is that the Cross represents a final victory in the
struggle within religion on behalf of the holy, and yet the church can
demonically arrogate to itself that unique status. In Tillich's words,
'That which is rightly said about the Cross of the Christ is wrongly
transferred to the life of the church, whose ambiguities are denied,
although they have become increasingly powerful throughout its
history' (ibid., p. 111). However, neither reductive profanization nor
the demonization of religion can remove the quality of ultimate
concern and the quest for unambiguous life.

One of the difficult points to grasp about Tillich's concept of
religion as an ambiguous phenomenon is that he wants to say both
that it is the features and tendencies within the phenomenon of
religion that are ambiguous and that religion as such is ambiguous in

that it is not an end in itself though also an indisputable means to that end. It will be evident that because of what he has said about religion Tillich would never identify the life of the church with unambiguous life: similarly, his refusal to make faith a matter of factual judgement leads him to distinguish sharply between the Christian hope and any historical expectation. As he moves on to his analysis of unambiguous life, he begins by emphasizing the way in which religion is by its nature anticipatory. Moses, we might say, always seeks the Promised Land from afar; or, as St Paul might say, though now we see things only through a glass darkly there will be a time when all will be clear. Though Tillich does not say it (for the point is part of his *theory* of religious language), one aspect of that anticipation is the symbolic character of religious language. He refers to three symbols of the unambiguous life: Spirit of God, Kingdom of God and Eternal Life. To avoid the kind of erroneous notion seen in talk of God as a being, he says that he wants to use the phrases 'Spiritual Presence' and 'the divine presence in creaturely life'; and it is only in this oblique way that he will offer a doctrine of the church. Though the Spiritual Presence must be seen as related to all life it is something that 'is directly correlated to the ambiguities of life under the dimension of spirit' (ibid., p. 115). What this does not mean, however, is something that is derived from what we know as a dimension of life: it is a movement from the top down rather than talking of the divine as merely something we already know in the human. As with 'Spiritual Presence' so with the other two symbols: the 'symbolic material' is taken from the experience that is universally human—historical and political or temporal and spatial. One of the regrettable features of Tillich's discussion (if not indeed its weakness) is that he no sooner grounds the symbol than he is borne on his metaphysical wings to talk about its *meaning*. The symbol of the Kingdom of God 'covers both the struggle of unambiguous life with the forces which make for ambiguity and the ultimate fulfilment towards which history runs' (ibid.). The symbol of Eternal Life 'does not mean the endless continuation of categorical existence but the conquest of its ambiguities' (ibid.). A reader could be pardoned for thinking that this is explanation that explains nothing, so abstract and general is the formulation of the meanings involved. The one thing we can grasp is that in his doctrine of the church as much as elsewhere Tillich wanted to break away from the tradition of doing theology which involved following old categories. The main—perhaps the only—sense in which he wanted to make a new start was that of asking what the dogmas, definitions and debates really meant in terms of faith's encounter with the divine, so that there would be a serious and honest effort of intellect to explain to the world outside the church what being in the church meant. All three symbols, he says (ibid., p. 117), 'are symbolic expressions of the answer revelation gives to the quest for unambiguous existence'. In effect, he says that the three symbols mean the same thing, or at least that they are interrelated and mutually involving.

At this point in his projection of a system, Tillich is caught in a difficulty. On the one hand, he wants to give a phenomenology of the Spiritual Presence and, on the other, he wants to address the interplay between 'Spiritual Presence' and the church as a fact, addressing the problem of the ecumenical debate in twentieth-century Christianity by asking what Spiritual Presence means as idea and fact. On the basis of what he has had to say—and bearing in mind that this is a theologically inspired view of human development—Tillich does not want to consider the problem of the Christian Church as something that is supernaturally isolated from human history as a whole. Two important qualities of Spiritual Presence are, then, to be noted: its universality and its extraordinary character.

As universal, it is something that fits rather than destroys 'the structure of the centred self which bears the dimension of spirit' (ibid., p. 121). This is again not a matter of dictating to theology what must be the case but rather a reading out of the implications of theology itself. 'God does not need to destroy his created world, which is good in its essential nature, in order to manifest himself in it' (ibid.). This is therefore a basic rule of Tillich's theology of the church: 'the Spiritual Presence's reception can only be described in such a way that ecstasy does not disrupt structure' (ibid., p. 124). Lest anyone should read this as a prescription for conservatism, Tillich insists that what he is engaged in a 'defence of the ecstatic manifestations of the Spiritual Presence against its ecclesiastical critics' (ibid., p. 126). Neither is this some kind of antinomianism: not anything and everything goes, because we are enjoined by Scripture to *test* the spirits. The norm to be used in that test, says Tillich, is the manifestation of creativity in the ecstasy that derives from the Spirit.

Tillich's approach to a doctrine of the church is in a way tangential and one that moves from the nature of spirituality more than from history. That is, rather than starting with the church as the historical given, he starts with the fact of the Spiritual Presence being communicated by Word and Sacrament. 'These are foundational to the church; for it is their administration that makes the church the church' (ibid., p. 128). It is the wide meaning of 'sacrament' as sacramental reality (which can then be progressively narrowed in more traditional uses) that is for Tillich the most significant and indeed the religious nerve of the concept of sacrament. In what might seem rather a paradoxical move, he protests against the reductionism of much Protestant resistance to a demonization of sacrament as magic. He anticipates his discussion of the church by using his formula 'Protestant principle and Catholic substance' to express his positive re-evaluation of sacrament, insisting that 'the Spiritual Presence cannot be received without a sacramental element' (ibid., p. 130). Also he refers back to his theory of symbolism, saying that the sacramental material is not a sign but a symbol. He skates over this issue, complicating his theory of sacraments by saying that it is both true that the sacramental materials are therefore intrinsically related to what they express and that 'it is not a quality of the materials as such which makes them media of the Spiritual Presence' (ibid., pp. 120–1). What he can be understood to have sought was a view that steered a middle course between the Catholic doctrine of transubstantiation and the Reformed doctrine that the sacramental symbol is a sign.

Sacramentality is not for Tillich something that can be divorced from language, so that 'the word is the Spirit's other and ultimately more important medium' (ibid., p. 122). When we speak of the Word of God, he says, what we are referring to is human words as media of the Spiritual Presence. There is no word of God in any language, whatever its history, as there is a word of some Greek author in a Greek text. Whether or not something is Word of God depends on its becoming the mediation of the Spirit. 'No word is the Word of God unless it is the Word of God for someone' (ibid., p. 123). Quickly and deftly, Tillich removes his concept of the Word of God from any biblical fundamentalism. On the one hand, he is prepared to accept the Bible as the criterion whereby we can judge any presumption of a human word's claim to the dignity of being the Word of God. On the other hand, though he does not specifically address the issue, he does recognize that there is a canon within the Canon by reminding us that the only adequate criterion is the New Being manifest in Jesus as the Christ. 'Nothing is the Word of God if it contradicts the faith and love which are the work of the Spirit and which constitute the New Being as it is manifest in Jesus as the Christ' (ibid.). Similarly, Tillich walks a tightrope in his view of the necessity of what might be called an objective word. He shows himself aware of, and sympathetic to, the strength of the argument that the Spirit needs no mediation, admitting that his own understanding of the Spirit and his argument about the work of the Spirit mean that the Spirit is free from any of the ambiguous forms in which it is received in religion. Yet precisely because of this truth and because of the powerful influence such thinking has exerted on theology, Tillich thinks that the dangers in such should be made clear. Just as there can be no divorce of the believer from the tradition of revelation, so—more importantly—we must recognize how utterly inappropriate the categories of 'inner' and 'outer' are when we apply them to talk about God's relation to man. From this it follows that we must deny the suggestion that God speaks to man without a medium. What he had said about theology's dependence on a historical tradition Tillich reiterates here in a different context and to a different, though related, purpose. No criterion of cognition, let alone communication, is possible without language: it is in words that we think. So all revelation—whether to the author of the biblical text or to the prophetic figures in Christian history—is given through language, and that means the language of tradition. But Tillich's motivation in this argument is far from traditionalist. What he is concerned to emphasize is the creative work of the Spirit in the continuity of the Spiritual Presence. As he is anxious to identify the concern of the Reformers as an anxiety lest we lose sight of the ultimate criterion of revelation, viz. the New Being in Christ, so he is equally prepared to point out how the principle of 'the Word alone' worked against this spiritual understanding.

As one follows Tillich's argument, there grows in one the suspicion that he was really trying to be all things to all men. That judgement would be unfair; for what we must remember is that here Tillich is both talking *within* the church and trying to *explain* the nature of the church in relation to what he has called the multi-dimensional unity of life. So he repeats the point that what is crucial here is the manifestation of faith and love. In the discussion of faith and love that follows he demonstrates his radical understanding of these terms. Faith 'is the state of being *grasped* by the transcendent unity of unambiguous life—it embodies love as the state of being *taken into* that transcendent unity' (ibid., p. 137). What is radical about it is that it wants to view the Christian faith's universality in an inclusive rather than an exclusive way. That is, he is as orthodox as can be in his understanding of Christ as a final revelation; but he will have none of the domestication of faith that has so often character- ized this doctrine in traditional orthodoxy. One of the fundamental weaknesses of that kind of theology in Tillich's view is that it makes the act of faith a matter of the intellect, will or feeling, and this he feels is a misunderstanding of the relation between man and God. The balancing act continues as he tries to do justice to both the transcendence of faith as God's reaching out to man and the obvious immanence of faith as something to do with man's psychological history. With his own emphasis on faith as this activity of God as the background, he offers another of his neat distinctions—'it is not *from* man but *in* man' (ibid., p. 141).

With the concept of love, as with that of faith, Tillich wants to keep that strong sense of the transcendent and to cut through much useless traditional debate. As he had done with faith, he removes the misleading connotations of 'love' in traditional theology. Though it contains an essential and important emotional element, love is not an emotion. It is active and effective in all three life processes: it unites in a centre, it creates the new, it drives beyond everything given to its ground and aim. Talking of love as an inter-personal relation—which is necessarily a moral relation—Tillich points to the impossibility of an unambiguous love (*agapē*) except as participation in the transcendent unity of unambiguous life. If we think in this way then we can, he argues, resolve the Catholic–Protestant controversy about the relation of faith to love. With Luther we will say that faith is receiving and nothing but receiving; but because faith and love have been seen to be inseparable as participation in the transcendent unity of unambiguous life, we will also affirm the Catholic emphasis on love. Will and intellect play their part in love as in faith, and here again the great temptation is to distort the concept by reducing it to either of these psychological functions. Tillich was as familiar as the next person with the ambiguities of love and its possibility of profanization; and so he speaks of the controlling power of love. It can unite the various kinds of love just as it can judge them. Perhaps because of the ambiguities of his own personal life, Tillich showed great psychological insight when he talked of love, particularly in his rejection of and warning against a sharp distinction between *agapē* and *eros*. He also displays his profound sense of the mystery of the relation between man and God by summing up his discussion thus:

'in relation to God the distinction between love and faith disappears' (ibid., p. 147).

This very lengthy discussion of the nature of the religious existence of faith has a very concrete perspective and purpose: it is the preamble to Tillich's treatment of the nature of the church and the Kingdom of God which the church proclaims. Typically he reiterates the theoretical basis of such a doctrine in the *general* history of religion; but that is clearly only the *background* for his assertion that the 'divine Spirit was present in Jesus as the Christ without distortion' (ibid., p. 153). That is the objective half of the equation of faith, because, Tillich says again, 'the Christ would not be the Christ without those who receive him as the Christ' (ibid.). In his lectures (up to the mid-1950s at any rate), Tillich used the term 'church' when talking of these issues; but he became less and less happy with this traditional and perhaps simplistic terminology, preferring the term 'Spiritual Community'. As he says (ibid., p. 159), 'We do not use the word "church" for the Spiritual Community, because this word has been used, of necessity, in the frame of the ambiguities of religion'. Because he prefers to concentrate in this way on the transcendent aspect of what we normally mean by 'church', Tillich says that he defers consideration of its relation to the empirical church. From the nature of the Spiritual Presence and its reception, then, he derives a threefold form of its creativity as Spiritual Community: its anticipation, its central appearance, and its historical reception. Though he does not actually put this in historical terms, the context does suggest that he sees the history of religion as centred on Christianity and that there is an anticipation of that central revelation and a history of reception after it. That he does not specifically speak of history is important—not because he is anxious to distance himself from the awkward questions of either orthodoxy or history, but because he wants to make clear that the problem of the nature of the church is fundamentally a spiritual issue. As the Spiritual Presence is unambiguous, so is the Spiritual Community, and similarly it is, in Luther's word, 'invisible': it is the creation of Spirit and so discernible only by Spirit. Almost in a paraphrase of the comment by Jesus to Peter after the latter's confession in Caesarea Philippi, Tillich insists on the cruciality of this principle. That is why for him the story of Pentecost has so powerful a symbolic content. Here are to be seen the five features of the Spiritual Community. It is the unity of ecstasy and structure; it is the creation of faith; it is likewise the creation of a caring love; it is the creation of unity; and finally it is the creation of universality.

The question of how this relates to the historical church must now be confronted. It was precisely the conviction that revelation in Jesus as the Christ was final which led Tillich to speak of the difference between the term 'Spiritual Community' and 'the church' (meaning by this latter term the churches) and to solve the problem of their relation by using the distinction between 'latent' and 'manifest' church. The change in his approach and the increased reticence which one might describe as an increasing emphasis on the transcendent did not lead him to abandon this distinction which he used for decades (see ibid., pp. 162–3). He makes clear that he does not view the distinction as a simple historical one between what could be described as the anticipation of something which then, at a later point in history, becomes historical and actual. There is indeed a preparation for the Gospel and a Gospel church which, because it is a historical phenomenon, enables us to identify the earlier phenomenon as a preparation. However, for Tillich, there are continually recurring revelatory moments, *kairoi*, and the latency and manifestation of the Spiritual Community apply here too. In other words, just as there was something before the New Testament period which points to the fulfilled history in the New Testament, the Incarnation and what is traditionally called the extension of the Incarnation, so again and again the organized churches are made aware of God's work outside them. This is to be seen in various kinds of organization and activity, and it can even be that these are secular opponents of the churches. The interest of this distinction and indeed of the argument—what could be called its Lutheran beauty—is the way Tillich emphasizes the fact that 'Spiritual Community' applies to both. 'Certainly the churches are not excluded from the Spiritual Community, but neither are their secular opponents' (ibid., p. 163). By applying the distinction between 'latent' and 'manifest' in this way, Tillich makes clear that he has no interest in extending the meaning of the term 'church' to cover anything and everything spiritual. Only what is partly actual as well as partly potential reception of the Spiritual Presence can be called a latent church. So once more, Tillich reminds us that this is not a distinction to be divorced from reference to the transcendent union of the unambiguous life 'manifest in the faith and love of the Christ'. He suggests too that we are looking at a distinction between a spiritual life that is anticipation of an ideal and the kind of self-correction that even a poor expression of that ideal has within itself by virtue of its explicit reference to that ideal (the unambiguous life).

Tillich's doctrine of the church is radical in the sense that it seeks to reinterpret the doctrine rather than simply to offer a variation of current doctrines. He does this by following out the universality he has identified in the Incarnation and also by adhering strictly to his criterion of the work of the divine Spirit in deciding whether anything can be called 'church'. What he is arguing then is the twofold thesis that if the church is Christian it is related to the New Being in Jesus as the Christ and is not constituted by some merely historical or social connection; and, secondly, that its life must be spiritual in its nature and judged accordingly. Viewed thus, what he has to say about the 'marks of the Spiritual Community' is a rephrasing of what he had in his lectures been accustomed to call the unity, holiness and catholicity of the church, terminology which was very obviously orthodox. His starting-point is the declaration that the nature of the Spiritual Community is determined by its origin as the creation of 'the divine Spirit as manifest in the New Being in Jesus as the Christ' (ibid., p. 165). His reticence in describing this origin is typical: the general tendency to ambiguity is here reinforced by his determination not to lose sight of the divine work. So our first concern must be with what the divine Spirit has done in history, not with a chain of historical events leading back to Jesus and some historical description of that sequence of events. The Spiritual Community is a community of faith and love, and the marks or qualities of such a community are then what Tillich would regard as the marks of the church. They are, in fact, the criteria by which anything can be identified as 'church'; and the language he uses at this point, calling the churches 'the actualization and the distortion of the Spiritual Community', suggests that his view of 'church' and 'churches' is very much in the manner of Plato and his view of the relation of the 'ideal' world to the world of things. This tension between the actual and the ideal is not the only tension with which Tillich is concerned. The term 'community of faith' carries, he says, the connotation of the tension between the faith of the individual member and that of the community as a whole. Though he does not clarify his meaning here, there is no reason to think that he has anything more than issues of doctrine in mind. Certainly, at any rate, they are there, because he speaks of beliefs in this context; but it must be said too that he refers to the 'indefinite variety of expressions of faith' in the Spiritual Community. As he thus seems to suggest a very open community in terms of doctrine, if not indeed general pattern of behaviour, Tillich also insists that the variety is possible only because it is the universal expression of faith. Through that faith the Spiritual Community is holy because it participates in this way in the holiness of the divine life. In a similar fashion, Tillich understands the Spiritual Community to have the quality of love, and in just the same way here too there is variety and an ensuing tension. Equally, his insistence on the dynamic nature of Spiritual Community leads him to describe this tension too as something that never amounts to fracture, multi-dimensional as this love is. Though fragmentary, it anticipates the perfect union to be found in Eternal Life. As with faith so through love, the Spiritual Community is holy. This sense of the now and the not yet, or the fragmented and not complete, as against the united and the whole, which expresses the dynamism of Tillich's ecclesiology, is perhaps most evident in what he says about unity and universality. Again, these are the necessary implications of the fact that the Spiritual Community is one of faith and love. Tillich always likes the different parts of doctrine to have this kind of logical relation. Unity is what is expressed by the unbroken nature of the tension created by the variety of faith's expressions. Universality expresses the fact that the tension between uniting love and the 'indefinite variety' of actual relations of love is never broken.

Before going on to follow Tillich's discussion of the churches, it is useful to pause and reflect on this characterization of the Spiritual Community. If some Catholic critics had cause to complain that Tillich found paradox everywhere, perhaps it is not surprising that one's reaction to what he has said is also paradoxical. On the one hand, it must be admitted and recognized clearly that there is a sense in which what he has to say about Spiritual Community is a perfectly orthodox ecclesiology, despite its unfamiliar language and despite its refusal to identify the concrete church in any form with Spiritual Community. On the other hand, it is not so much a lack of orthodoxy as a lack of content or significance that one wants to identify here. It seems as if Tillich wants to say that whether we call the church one or universal or holy, what is being said is that by faith and love the church participates in divine life. That is true enough but it does not make any specific statement about the character of the church. The judgement seems a harsh one and there are moments when, as one reads Tillich, it seems unfair. It could be defended by pointing to Tillich's tendency to formalism and abstraction as he develops his argument; or it might even be said that his primary interest was not in offering any revision of the traditional characterization of the church, which he accepted as true, but in pointing out how paradoxical this was in its relation to a context that is necessarily ambiguous. Either way, it is the case that the value of Tillich's fundamental ecclesiology lies in his vision of the church as the creation of the divine Spirit. In this way, it could be said, he continued to show the prophetic concern that had marked his very first efforts as a theologian when he had sought to lead his fellowchurchmen away from the religious, social and political compromises so cruelly exposed by the First World War. That he left so much doctrine untouched he knew very well, and the only detail he was prepared to give was the typically paradoxical discussion of 'the Spiritual Presence and the ambiguities of religion'.

Reference has already been made to the Lutheran character of Tillich's doctrine of the church, and this is again evident as he begins his consideration of the churches. What he means by 'Spiritual Community', he says (ibid., p. 173), is what the New Testament calls 'body of Christ' and the Reformation called 'church invisible'; and the important implication of this is that it is not one group amongst other groups—otherwise the term 'invisible' would be a nonsensical description. Its reality is what he terms that of 'a power and a structure inherent in such groups' (ibid.). As was evident in the discussion of symbolism and also in the doctrine of God which was offered, the notions of 'power' and 'power of being' are fundamental to his metaphysics. We may clarify their use here in this way. Since God is defined as being-itself and power of being is divine, there is an obvious connection between the divine Spirit and the Spiritual Community. In the same way, Tillich is able both to recognize a historical connection between 'church' and Christ, and yet to extend the divine connection beyond this. If the group makes the conscious historical reference to Jesus as the Christ, then that group is what we normally call a church; but it is the fact of its being grasped by ultimate concern that makes it or any other group whatsoever an example of the effective presence of the Spiritual Community. This is the emphasis already seen in the distinction between 'latent' and 'manifest'; and, in apparently repeating the point, what Tillich wants to do is to defend his standpoint.

Returning to the logical-metaphysical problem of essence and existence, he says that the Spiritual Community is 'essentiality determining existence and being resisted by existence' (ibid., p. 175).

He clarifies this extremely opaque explanation by pointing to two kinds of mistaken implications. First, this does not mean that in talking of Spiritual Community we are referring to some ideal which he describes much in the same way as empiricist philosophers used to talk of universals or general terms, something constructed by abstraction from examples. To imagine such an ideal towards which the churches as real are progressing is to put things the wrong way round—'Essential power must precede actualization' (ibid.). However strange it may seem, Tillich insists, we *must* see the church as 'the new creation into which the individual Christian and the particular church is taken'. And if this talk of essence preceding existence sounds very Platonic, some kind of Platonism is in fact the second mistake which he identifies. It is quite wrong to conceive of the Spiritual Community as 'an assembly of so-called Spiritual beings ... represented on earth by ecclesiastical hierarchies and sacraments' (ibid.). It may or may not be a useful piece of symbolism but this kind of theology (exemplified, he thinks, in some Greek Orthodox thinking) is a quite erroneous identification of the 'invisible, essential Spirituality' which marks out the church. It is this character of the 'essentialistic' that is for Tillich the most successful way of understanding Spiritual Community. In so far as he has now expressed a profound vision of the church as the sphere of God's spiritual activity he has achieved much, but his metaphysical clarification of it can hardly be called a success. It is the same point that he makes when he speaks of 'the paradox of the churches' (ibid., pp. 176ff.). That paradox is quite simply the apparent contradictions between the fact that the churches are an example of the general ambiguity of life (and of the religious life as a special instance of this) and, on the other hand, the fact of their participation in the unambiguous life of the Spiritual Community. What we are saying, he insists, is not that there are two churches but that there are 'two aspects of the one church in time and space' (ibid., p. 176). His explanation of this is less than clear because he speaks of this as an 'epistemological' distinction between the sociological and the theological 'aspects of the church'. What he seems to be saying is that a sociology of religion is perfectly possible and that this involves all the methods and concepts of sociological analysis. That would necessarily be a secular history of the church. A quite different view is that of the theologian which 'does not refuse to recognize the sociological aspect but ... does deny its exclusive validity' (ibid., p. 177). In other words, this is not a matter of two different theories of knowledge but a matter of saying that in a sociological description that is a proper account of the church there will be a recognition that there is in the phenomenon a reference to something that demands a different description. It is most unfortunate that Tillich preferred his abstract way of referring to this point, saying rather misleadingly that the 'church at the street corner hides the church spiritual from view'. This makes it seem that he is merely repeating his oft-asserted point that the church shares in the ambiguity that is the characteristic of all life.

One of the refreshing features of Tillich's work is the way in which he can swoop so quickly from heights of abstraction to the comfortable levels of ordinary experience. So after this very abstract discussion of the church, he refers specifically to the gap between Roman Catholic and Protestant views of the church. While the former does not rule out the possibility of critical judgement concerning any element of the church, it does reject critical judgement of the constitution as such and all that derives from it. The perfection of the institution is the basis of any critical judgement and cannot itself be regarded as open to judgement. By contrast, says Tillich, this cannot be allowed by any Protestant view; for the holiness which the church always exemplifies is expressed in a distorted fashion and every empirical church is a distorted church. For Tillich, then, it is a moot point whether there can be any far-reaching reformation within the Catholic church, since its basis in conciliar and papal decisions is defined as unchangeable, and those decisions involve matters of church structure. Even if there is agreement that the interpretation of decisions must change though the doctrines themselves are unchallengeable, there can be no guarantee that 'the principle of reformation will be effective'. That this is possible Tillich does not deny: the guidance of the prophetic spirit could produce a reforming interpretation; but there is no guarantee of this—and only the future can tell.

Continuing this consideration of the paradox of the churches, Tillich has similar things to say about unity. We cannot argue to the unity of the churches from any actual unity and we cannot deny their unity because of their disunity. It has nothing to do with the fact, present or future, actual or possible: it is true in spite of the churches' separation. Once more, then, for all his sympathy with the Catholic position, he distinguishes between it and his own position. Roman Catholicism regards its particular unity as synonymous with the unity of the church; and the various consequences of this are for him to be seen in the historical prohibition of religious co-operation with other churches. The greater degree of tolerance and ecumenicity witnessed in recent years does not, in Tillich's view, change the situation essentially. For Rome to change its understanding of the problem of unity would mean the abandonment of its absolute claim, and indeed a completely changed self-understanding. The radically different understanding of unity among and between the churches as a paradoxical matter is what Tillich sees to be character-istic of Protestantism. These two points, together with a fervent support of the work of the World Council of Churches as expressive of the predicate of unity, represent a significant contribution by Tillich to ecumenicity and an equally significant, though cryptic, contribution to ecclesiology. Whilst not in any way changing his basic insistence on the paradoxical nature of the unity which is characteristic of the church, he was able to perceive great benefit in the ecumenical movement. Its most important achievement in his opinion was the creation of 'a new vision of the unity of all churches in their foundation'. As with holiness so with unity, his view was that it was a matter of the church's basis in the New Being. The well-known words of Samuel Stone's hymn describing Jesus Christ as the 'church's one foundation' quite aptly express his view. So, while not expecting the ecumenical movement, or indeed any other movement, to produce an empirical unity of the churches, he regarded the ecumenical movement as having awakened a new awareness of the fact that the disunity of the churches had not destroyed their unity as church. It was the doctrinal justification of this in terms of the church's foundation which he regarded as the advance in doctrine. Other benefits of the ecumenical movement, he thought, were the healing of outworn divisions, the creation of a new attitude with co-operation replacing fanaticism, and the conquest of denominational provincialism.

The final aspect of the church, its universality, is again expressed paradoxically in the actual life of the churches. What Tillich had originally spoken of simply as the universality of the church he latterly described as the universality of the churches' foundation in the New Being which is effective in them. He showed a typical sensitivity to the popular meaning of words, and so eschewed the use of the term 'Catholic'. Yet, true to his profound sense of orthodoxy, he went so far as to assert catholicity as an essential feature of the church's professed faith. 'Although the word must be replaced, the fact remains that a church which does not claim catholicity has ceased to be a church' (ibid., p. 181). He speaks of the 'intensive' and 'extensive' universality of the church (a very interesting example of how much he was preoccupied with his old terminology and certainly with the essentially ecclesiological nature of this discussion of Spiritual Community). The distinction is not clear; but since Tillich seems to use the distinction between 'qualitative' and 'quantitative' as synonymous with this (see ibid., p. 183), we can claim some clarity for it, despite his own reluctance to abandon paradox at this point. What he seems to be saying is that if we are talking of a community as a church, then there is in the attitude of that community an inclusiveness which allows a place for everything. This is the intensive universality. The exclusive universality is not essentially different in character inasmuch as everything that could be said about the intensive could be said also about the extensive universality (ibid., p. 182). However, this time we are talking of the church's foundation being valid for all nations and social groups— something which Tillich regards as being especially and immensely significant for the twentieth century. It is important to remember— particularly in view of all that is often said about Tillich's secularizing tendency—that for Tillich the characteristics of the church as the community of faith and love presuppose that, as church, it sees itself grounded in the fact of Jesus as the Christ (ibid., pp. 184–94). Once again what seems to be a very ambiguous or ill-defined and dangerous understanding is given as much specific concretion and orthodoxy as anything such can demand. It is as if Tillich were reminding us that in talking of spiritual characteristics he is talking of actual virtues and real historical connections just as much as any traditional ecclesiology: but he reminds us too that these are not quantitative concepts.

As if to illustrate the last point, Tillich discusses the 'functions of the church' (ibid., pp. 194ff.); but in reading him one needs the courage not to be daunted by the formalism of his talk of three polarities of principles corresponding to the three groups of functions that he distinguishes. All that is necessary for us to remember is that he wants to see this aspect of systematic theology sharing the formal and philosophical character of basic or foundational theology, and that he insists on the ambiguous nature of this as of all human experience. Three functions, then, are listed: the constitutive, expanding and constructing.

By the first, Tillich refers to the receptiveness that is characteristic of the church as dependent on the New Being revealed in Christ. In other words, the church is brought about historically by the mediation of the New Being through word and sacrament—someone preaches the word and someone administers the sacraments, and so the church exists. This relationship is not a social transaction between someone who has a particular status and another whose status is different. As there is a historical relation which can be shown between the church at any historical point and the New Testament, so there is a logical relation between the church and the New Being as the source of its transcendent life. To return to the issue of status, the division between priest and laity can never for Tillich be complete (ibid., p. 202); for one and the same person is required to respond as well as to mediate. A preacher must preach to himself, and the hearer is similarly a potential preacher. All kinds of things come into this function of constitution: for example, pastoral counselling and worship (which includes adoration, prayer and contemplation).

The expanding function of the churches is implied by the universality of the Spiritual Community—and because Tillich sees a strict implication here between the nature of Jesus as the Christ and the faith of the Spiritual Community, he asserts categorically that 'every church must participate in the functions of expansion' (ibid., p. 206). The first function of expansion is missions, which go on all the time because active members of the churches are in fact missionaries of the church as they meet those outside the church. Willy-nilly, their 'very being is missionary' (ibid.). The second function of expansion is that of education. This is not to be understood in any limited way as mere instruction or awakening a subjective piety but the introduction of each new generation to the reality of the faith and love in the Spiritual Community. The last function of expansion is evangelism, which is directed towards those members of the churches who are estranged or indifferent.

Finally, the constructing functions of the church are those in which it builds its life by using and transmitting the functions of man's life as typically human. As necessarily constructive, the church cannot be alienated from culture—culture can be rejected only by the use of culture. Two kinds of constructing functions can be distinguished: the theoretical, which include the aesthetic and the cognitive functions, and the practical, which comprise the communal and the personal. That is, the church builds up the world's life by art and knowledge and also by its personal and social virtue.

Tillich's appreciation of the important role played by aesthetics in the life of the church sets him apart from most Protestant theology. Karl Barth may have been brave enough to venture the opinion that the music of heaven would be that of Mozart rather than Bach; but Tillich was unique in the catholicity of his response to all kinds of art and particularly in his valuation of art as a medium of revelation. What he has to say about religious art will suffice to show this. There is, he declares, an obvious possible conflict between the reasonable demand of the churches that religious art should express what they confess and, on the other hand, the proper demand of the artist that he or she be free to follow the dictates of artistic conscience. From this he derives 'two principles which control religious art, the principle of consecration and the principle of honesty' (ibid., p. 211). The former is the principle that we have met before, that of form-transcendence, which here is a matter of 'expressing the holy in the concreteness of a special religious tradition' (ibid.). That polarity of form-transcendence and form-affirmation, however, means that artists refuse to accept the old forms—and that assertion of artistic freedom is something that applies to the artist's public just as well. Both the artist and his public are under an obligation 'not to admit imitations of styles which once had great conscious possibilities but which have lost their religious expressiveness for an actual situation' (ibid., p. 212). The conclusion to which he comes after a rich, though fairly brief, discussion of religious art is that as a historical fact the expressionist style is what has best suited religious art (ibid., p. 214). As far as the cognitive function in the church is concerned, this is what we call theology, something which for Tillich is never absent from the life of faith. Though he clearly sees no need to discuss the matter fully—it having been the very starting-point of the system— he does emphasize that, like all functions of the church, theology stands 'under the principles of form-transcendence and form-affirmation' (ibid., p. 215). These are the meditative and discursive elements in theology. He sees the meditative function as a direct awareness of what the religious symbols signify, what he calls the penetration of their substance, whereas the discursive element is a matter of seeing how this is to be understood, the analysis and description of the form in which that is grasped. His conclusion here is that theology is 'infinitely open' in all directions and is not confined to any one set of symbols. So whatever the philosophical tradition that is in vogue—or indeed the philosophical tool or vehicle which is adopted by a particular thinker—theology is always possible. As with the aesthetic element, he once more offers an opinion about the element that has stood the test of history: this is the 'existentialist' tradition which stretches from Heraclitus to Heidegger.

In conclusion, mention must be made of the 'practical' constructing functions. These concern 'the interdependent growth of community and personality' (ibid., p. 217). Despite the fact that it seems to flee concrete discussion and become a tangle of abstraction, this discussion makes an important contribution to ecclesiology. We would hardly expect to find in Tillich discussion of ecclesiastical polity and minutiae of church government or even church social action. By this time his vision of theology was much too formal for that. Yet his constant use of the word 'concretely' suggests that his concern was indeed with the *praxis* of the church, the problem of what it means to *be* a church. One can be forgiven for forgetting this when the conclusion of the discussion is inevitably couched in terms of life's ambiguities. Even so, the discussion has a remarkable freshness and intellectual honesty because Tillich puts the issue in extremely basic terms. The problem, he says (ibid., p. 218), is quite simply whether justice can be preserved if the communal aim is to achieve holiness and whether personal saintliness does leave our humanity unimpaired. It might seem at first glance that this is a rhetorical question and that, by definition, these things are guaranteed. However, Tillich's own history had taught him that here things are not settled by definition. His point is precisely that we must in fact look at the actual life-fruits to decide the truth of the claim that the community which participates in the Holy Community overcomes the four ambiguities which can be identified in communal life: the ambiguity of inclusiveness, the ambiguity of equality, the ambiguity of leadership, and the ambiguity of the legal form. The churches' inclusiveness can become an exclusion of those who confess another faith; and here their very existence seems to lead them to an 'idolatrous adherence' to their own particular symbols. Equality—the very stuff of justice—can become in practice so ignored that there is in the life of the churches a principle of inequality. Leadership in the religious context has the 'same profane and demonic possibilities as every other leadership'. Legal forms— an essential of church history as of any other form of human history—can become tyrannical. It is these last ambiguities in particular that, says Tillich (ibid., p. 222), have led to the protest against 'organized religion'; and all that would be of very little consequence for a theologian were it not symptomatic of a *religious* protest against the ambiguity of religion. The personal functions in the church have to do with the ambiguity of self-determination and the ambiguity of the determination of others. The problem is the identification of saintliness with asceticism, which would make it the negation of so many human possibilities. Looking quickly at the various examples of asceticism in Christian history, Tillich acknowledges not only the inevitable tension that there is here but also the possibility of overcoming it. That is achieved when the ambiguity of self-determination is overcome by grace (ibid., p. 225).

If anything is clear from this discussion of how Tillich views the church, it is that he sought to be not only orthodox but also completely faithful in his vision of what it means to say that there has been and there is a church. Protestant he was: for this was in his view the principle of faith; Catholic he aimed to be, inasmuch as there could be no escape from the ambiguities which characterize history and also inasmuch as the substance of 'church' is Catholic.

9

History and the Kingdom of God

As we have seen, Tillich's theology had its origin in the practical situation of a theologian, involved in politics. Thus, though he was very much a philosophical theologian always ready to discuss the metaphysical significance of whatever issue was under consideration, he had a lively sense of the cruciality for the Christian church of the expectation of the Kingdom of God. The interpretation of history was indeed so much a theme of his work that the phrase formed the natural choice of title for one of his earliest English-language publications. To this area of his thought we can, then, now turn to round off a viewing of his work.

His view of history was in several ways the coping-stone of his system for Tillich. It was something which could not be avoided at any point in the development of his total argument, because it impinged on everything. Yet the essentially human reference of the term 'history' meant that it was advisable to treat it last and to that extent out of context. In placing the discussion at the end of his system, Tillich acknowledged (ST, vol. 3, p. 315) that he was partly governed by theological tradition, but he insists that there is a more important consideration. The discussion of history is particularly significant because the historical dimension is all-inclusive and because of the equally all-embracing character of the symbol 'Kingdom of God' which is generated by the faith in the conquest of life's ambiguities. What the section of the system sets out to achieve is a large programme, and one is thereby warned that the discussion will inevitably be very cryptic. It deals with the structure of historical processes; it is also an epistemology of history, an account of the logic of historical knowledge. It is an account of the ambiguities of historical existence, but also it must do something more theoretical in that it expounds the meaning of historical movement. So far the task seems very much a philosophy of history, but even so the essentially theological nature of the task is clear. What makes this clear is the purpose of all this enterprise: it is to show how the symbol 'Kingdom of God' illuminates the history of which we speak and explicates it by referring beyond history.

With his customary fondness for looking at etymology for guidance, Tillich's starting-point for his analysis of the doctrine of history is the ambiguity of the Greek word *historia* as carrying both a subjective and an objective meaning. From this he concludes that 'an "event" is a syndrome (i.e. a running-together) of facts and interpretation' (ibid., p. 322). Characterizing history, Tillich says that it is purposive, free and the production of the new with which the concepts of 'value' and 'meaning' are necessarily related. He glosses this description by insisting on the uniqueness of any historical event. Obviously, he takes a great deal for granted here and sketches only an outline theory of much else; but the essential point which then becomes the basis of his doctrine is clear. Though one can speak of history in various contexts—not least nature and the biological sphere in particular—it is only in connection with human life that we can properly speak of history. He does not diminish the significance of prehistoric human life, because evolution proceeds by both leaps and slow changes and there is no possibility of identifying a moment at which human life in the full sense appears. The same evolutionary thinking makes him chary of any easy talk of post-history. 'It is not by chance', he says, 'that the New Testament and Jesus resisted the attempt to put the symbols of the end into a chronological frame' (ibid., p. 328). Groups rather than individuals are the bearers of history: a history is created by individuals only in an indirect way, because history demands a centred power which has the authority to command individuals' support and the power to preserve itself in its encounter with other powers. Far from showing himself some enthusiast for the modern phenomenon of the group or the masses, Tillich insists (ibid., p. 333) that it is misleading to ask whether it is 'great' individuals or mass movements that determine historical processes. More to the point is an appreciation of their interplay. That interplay is clear once we understand the metaphysical interdependence of time and space

161

(and on reading this, those who are keen students of Idealism will note how deeply Tillich was influenced by its beginnings in Kant). History moves in the same time and space that are occupied by the inorganic but is not confined to it; for in history 'the creative act of the spirit and with it the time and space of the spirit are always present' (ibid., p. 337).

The structure of history was for Tillich a metaphysical window on the human consciousness of history as pointing forward to some ultimate situation. The characterization of such must be symbolic, and that is what is effected by the idea of a universal unity associated with the symbol of the Kingdom of God. Even so, Tillich hesitates before turning to the theological symbol and looks at history itself and its dynamic movement. Always in history there are unchangeable regularities, and even when it seems to be a succession of purely new events there are trends to be discerned. History, however, is no system of universal regularities—every historical situation is as truly a chance as it is a trend (ibid., p. 348). The creativity of history means that it is not a matter of necessity but equally of contingency: and the contingent character of events means for Tillich more than merely non-necessity. It means that there is in history the opportunity to change the very trend that would make what has happened predictable. It is for this reason that Tillich resists the attractions of talk about the dialectical structure of history. Well aware of the power of the idea over philosophical discussions of history and historical life, he warns against making it a law of history which he labels a 'quasi-religious principle' without any empirical verifiability (ibid., p. 352). His only unifying metaphysical perspective is that history, like life, exemplifies ambiguity. The ambiguities of history are indeed what pose the question to which the symbol of the Kingdom of God is the answer.

The whole movement of history, says Tillich (ibid., p. 354), is 'progressive'. Though he seems at first to be making rather a small claim, talking of progress as 'a step (*gressus*) beyond the given', he does have a very clear idea of a real though limited progress in history. Moreover, each of us is on our own but the cultural context of our moral action can reveal progress. This kind of analysis can be applied equally to art, philosophy and social justice, but especially to the history of religion. 'Obviously there is no progress in the religious function as such. The state of ultimate concern admits no more of progress than of obsolescence or regression' (ibid., p. 358). Yet, he asks, have we not already declared that there is indeed progress when the revelation in Jesus as the Christ is called the final revelation? The answer is not simple, and its subtlety is something that is crucial to an understanding of Tillich's position on pluralism and relativity.

It was not only in the Hegelian interpretation of the history of religion as evolutionary but in various Liberal and even anti-Hegelian theologies that Tillich saw a simple but misleading answer to this question. The error of this model of evolution, to his mind, was its neglect of the claim to absoluteness in each of the great religions. That is, it was not an exclusive pattern and so it must lead us to the cultural context of the religions. There clearly can be progress; but this does not mean that there is either a progressive history of revelation or a progressive history of salvation. When the Spiritual Presence is revealed in its saving power it is not quantifiable—'there is no more or less, no progress or obsolescence or regression' (ibid., p. 359). Even so, we cannot speak of this as historical except in a cultural context, and in that context progress is possible. Taking a very definite stand of Christian commitment, claiming the event of Jesus as the Christ to be the revelatory event that breaks the power of the demonic, Tillich yet rejects any absolutizing of the Christian religion. His reasoning is twofold. First, if the revelation in Jesus as the Christ is the decisive event, it is what it is because it unites all the potentialities in our encounter with the holy. That is, the very absoluteness which we would ascribe to this revelation must imply that it will be the truth of any religious encounter. In a strange way, Tillich can be seen to be turning the old patristic apologetics back on themselves. While the Fathers argued that if there was any truth outside Christianity it had been stolen from Scripture, Tillich says that if Christianity's revelation can be said to be final, then all that is true outside it has been subsumed under and contained within it. What this implies is that a theory of horizontal progress is false. Secondly, he reminds us that what we have been talking of is the revelatory event and not the religion. 'It is not Christianity as a religion that is absolute but the event by which Christianity is created and judged to the same extent as any other religion, both affirmatively and negatively' (ibid., p. 360). Once again, we can see that there is no easy answer to the question whether Tillich's theological development took him beyond the Christocentrism that had been his starting-point. The only safe or indeed accurate description of his standpoint on the history of religion, even at the end of his life, is in terms of this subtle balancing of Christian commitment and the theological conviction that religion *per se* is inherently true.

Summing up his views on the progressive nature of history, Tillich affirms four areas of progress (ibid., pp. 360–1). First, in technology, man's situation has become better and better, and this obvious development has indeed spawned the idea of a necessary progress. Secondly, in all the sciences there will be found a similar building on what had gone before, as tested hypotheses have become the basis for further research. This, says Tillich, is true not just of the natural sciences but of 'all realms of methodological research'. Thirdly, progress is real in the realm of education 'whether it is by training for skills, by the mediation of cultural contents or by introduction into given systems of life'. Social as well as individual education is a very clear example of such a development, as immaturity develops into maturity and improves its heritage. Finally, the advent of the space age reveals the increasing conquest of spatial divisions. In these four ways, Tillich sees a real but limited progress in history.

Already, in talking of progress, he has raised questions that are not answered in terms of quantity or pattern, questions that take us back to the problem of understanding history, of its interpretation and its meaning. So in looking at the problem of the interpretation of history, though he repeats a principle already invoked in his Christology, that all history is interpreted history, he recognizes that there are many levels of interpretation (ibid., p. 372). His marvellous sense of tidiness makes him link the point with the subject–object character of history, but unfortunately this does not help to clarify what he wants to say. The argument is in fact not very clear, because he wants both to emphasize the intrepreted nature of history and to see history as something that confronts man as relating to human concerns. Indeed, just like Marx, he thought that by this emphasis he could set out the claim of the true interpretation of history. That is to say, Tillich's view of history at the end of his life can be seen as the more theological formulation of the revolutionary outlook he had articulated in 1919: it had now been made into a metaphysical theory which was also distinctly theological in character. There were several ways in which Tillich was quite happy to remain under the influence of Marx, and this conviction about the meaning of history was one. Obviously he had rejected any kind of dialectical materialism; but it has been equally obvious how much dialectical thinking remained the governing factor in his view of history. More important was the view of history as teleological in nature, a process that moves towards a goal: and this view had somehow to make room for the perception that history is made by man. This is the perspective from which Tillich is concerned to tackle the problem of history. If it is a matter of human concern and also something of which it is sensible to ask what its goal is, then, he says, the real problem of history is establishing what the significance of history is for the meaning of existence in general. He concedes that his existentialist standpoint might be thought to raise a problem. For, if it is only from within existence that any philosophical analysis of existence can be effected, then some kind of relativism seems inevitable. His answer to this is not very clear; but he seems to be making a twofold answer. In the first place, he suggests that no standpoint can be acceptable which does not allow for a possible claim to universality. In the history of thought we can distinguish a classical Hellenism and a prophetic Judaism, but each will raise the problem of history *as a whole*. Secondly, then, he argues that it is the very appeal to a universal standpoint that justifies the circularity of the theological interpretation. That we have already used the key to understanding history is, he says, 'an unavoidable consequence of the "theological circle" within which systematic theology moves' (ibid., p. 373). His standpoint is clearly and unambiguously affirmed as that of Christian vocational consciousness: the Kingdom of God is the answer to the problems of history.

In the exposition of the Christian interpretation of history, there is for Tillich more involved than a simple articulation of claims. This kind of standpoint has a metaphysical dimension in that we are claiming something about the world rather than simply offering an ideology for a particular group. What is implied, he says, is 'an answer to the universal meaning of being' (ibid., p. 374). Once more he does not pursue this point as he presses on with his argument, concentrating rather on the notion of the Kingdom in relation to history. The universality of reference which the interpretation of history contains must mean, he argues, that the idea of the Kingdom must comprehend all history, human and natural, within its scope. No sooner has Tillich opened our eyes to the wider metaphysical ramifications of faith than he calls us back to the task in hand, which is the description and justification of the Christian view of history as having a definite purpose. The justification in fact precedes the full exposition and it takes the form of considering the alternatives, the negative and the positive answers to the question of the meaning of history.

The ambiguities of history have led to two contrasting interpretations of history: the non-historical and the historical, or negative and positive, outlooks. Tillich distinguishes three types of the non-historical: the tragic, the mystical and the mechanical (ibid., pp. 374ff.) The tragic, which was given classical expression in Greek thought, is the cyclical view of time which sees history as a circular return to its beginning. Both individuals and periods of time are marked by a pattern of decay from some point beyond the beginning, that decay being the decree of fate which is the only meaning that can be discerned in the process. 'Existence in time and space and in the separation of individual from individual is tragic guilt, which leads necessarily to self-destruction' (ibid., p. 375). Though in such a view there is an appreciation of greatness and glory, there is no hope for any kind of fulfilment of history. The final word, then, is that whatever glory there is revealed, there is no conquest of any of life's ambiguities. As for the second, the mystical, though it is found in Western culture, its most typical expression is Oriental religious philosophy. According to this, history has no meaning in itself. 'One must live in it and act reasonably, but history itself can neither create the new nor be truly real' (ibid.). Even when such a view talks of cosmic cycles of genesis and decay, there is really no sense of historical time. The emphasis is rather on the individual and the goal of individual enlightenment. What constitutes such enlightenment is the way of release from the ambiguities of life. Universal suffering evokes pity but is a signal for an escape from this pointless reality rather than a call to action. The final negative view is the result of the scientific revolution. We are led to view time as physical, and so history is seen as a succession of physical changes. 'History has become a series of happenings in the physical universe, interesting to man, worthy to be recorded and studied, but without a special contribution to the interpretation of existence as such' (ibid., p. 376). However much this kind of outlook may emphasize progressivism, it has no feeling for the greatness and tragedy of human historical existence, and certainly no vision of a goal towards which history aims.

For a tragic view of history Christian theology has no place; but equally, says Tillich, it cannot accept some positive theories—progressivism, utopianism and the 'transcendental' theory of two worlds. Each of these is an ideology but none more so than the progressivist outlook, which, for all that it was a genuine attempt at characterizing history, was a quasi-religious symbol. 'It gave impetus to historical actions, passion to revolutions, and a meaning to life for many who had lost all other faith' (ibid., p. 377). Progressivism proper is something which Tillich connects with the growth of Idealism in modern industrial society. For such an outlook reality is always dependent on the agent or knower and as such is the ever-open possibility of human creativity. There is no reality beyond this: and when Idealism gave way to positivism as a dominant philosophical outlook there still remained this conviction that human history was the self-consciousness of the universal law of history, that history was an infinite process of progression. So dated had this view become that Tillich felt that it was incumbent on him to defend what he thought was true in it, despite its being an inadequate view of history. Ironically, it was the second inadequate positive answer which had been the more fierce attack on progressivism, though it sprang from the very same roots as progressivism. The difference between utopianism and progressivism proper is that for utopianism history progresses to a definite stage, one where the ambiguities of life are conquered. Precisely because it is able to distinguish between the impetus to proclaim a utopian faith and the view that the utopian ideal is identifiable, the utopian faith will be characterized by the conviction that revolution will herald that final transformation of reality which is the ideal. With his customary sure sense of history, Tillich remarks that the various forms of contemporary secular utopianism have their source and inspiration in the ideas typical of the Renaissance. It is the 'I' who is captain of man's soul and master of his fate. Again, as with progressivism, the history of the twentieth century has made a mockery of such a faith, though here too Tillich is anxious to recognize that there are areas where the law of progress is valid. But there is something even more significant than this general characterization. Utopianism, says Tillich, was an insidiously mistaken view of human freedom inasmuch as there was no guarantee against what he calls 'existential disappointments'. What he has in mind as guarantee is the kind of realism that makes Wordsworth's mother say of him at his birth 'He will be a force for either great good or great evil'—there was no advance prescription as to which he would be. So, says Tillich, utopianism exacts its price: its idolatrous ecstasy results in the individual and social diseases that are the harvest of existential disappointment. The final form of inadequate historical interpretation is the view that there are in history two worlds, that of individual salvation which culminates in a post-mortem heavenly existence, and that of ambiguous power structures on the other hand. History is no longer the scene of salvation and so in history no progress or development can be expected. Three things can be said to be wrong with such a view. In the first place, it wrongly cuts off the individual and his salvation from the group and the universe, something which Tillich sees as a weakness exposed by critics such as Münzer in the sixteenth century and by the religious socialists in the nineteenth and twentieth centuries. Secondly, it is wrong to separate the realm of salvation from, and contrast it with, the realm of creation. Thirdly, the Kingdom of God is a message for those in history, not for immortal souls: it is a life to be dynamically expressed in time rather than something to be expected in eternity.

Setting aside such erroneous and inadequate views of history, we have still to ask what it means to say that the answer to the question of the meaning of history is the Kingdom of God. Of the three symbols of unambiguous life—Kingdom of God, Spiritual Presence and Eternal Life—this is the most comprehensive because it relates not only to what lies beyond history but equally to the very inner nature of history. Spiritual Presence is what reveals the inner-historical nature of the Kingdom, the historical dimension that signifies the way in which the divine 'rules' the temporal world of changing fortunes. And when the Kingdom 'has come', then we have life that is Eternal Life. The history of the symbol's use is a chequered one. Tillich notes that the sacramental emphasis of Catholic Christianity pushed it aside until it was rediscovered by the Social Gospel movement and religious socialism—only once again (partly by this rediscovery) to lose its power. In view of its prominence in Jesus' own teaching and the constant prayer of the church for its advent, this is indeed, he says, nothing short of remarkable. It can, he thinks once more become a living symbol because in the encounter of Christianity with Asiatic religions, and in particular Buddhism, it is the symbol which crystallizes the difference between Western and Eastern religions and culture. 'The symbolic material is taken from spheres—the personal, social and political—which in the basic experience of Buddhism are radically transcended, whereas they are essential and never missing elements of the Christian experience' (ibid., p. 382). The implication of these observations is quite clearly that in this dialogue the Christian contribution is a necessary element of any true answer to the question of history's meaning.

Four aspects can be distinguished in the meaning of this symbol of Kingdom of God. First of all, it is obviously political; and this matches the dominant role of politics in mankind's story and the unfolding of its history. Very briefly, Tillich points to the double character of the symbol in its various uses within the Old and the New Testaments. It is God's controlling power which is important in the Old Testament, taking precedence over any idea of the Kingdom as a special *realm* in which God rules. The latter thought is obviously there; and later it becomes more important, as the vision of a new reality in a new period of history is proclaimed. With such an expansion of meaning the context becomes cosmic but still retains the political connotation. What Tillich wants to emphasize here is the way in which the patristic confession of Jesus Christ as 'King for ever' was not a political ideology, while the very fact that 'King' is a political concept meant that the confession was a conviction about political control. Secondly, if it is political then it is by definition social; and as social it refers to virtues and aspirations of social life such as power and justice. In this way it is an idea that has the idealist thrust of utopian expectation of a *better* social life: but, most importantly, it shows the distinctive nature of this particular expectation by saying that these are the virtues that come from God. It is that essential moral implication of the presence of the holy. Thirdly, the symbol is essentially an absolute valuation of the individual person. The Kingdom comes not by the disappearance of the individual but by the fulfilment of humanity in every human individual. Finally, the Kingdom is indeed a cosmic and not merely a human reality. 'It is a kingdom not only of men; it involves the fulfilment of life under all dimensions' (ibid. p. 383). As there is a polarity of society and individual, so there is one of humanity and cosmos. Man and his society are there in the Kingdom, but the Kingdom is far more. This is indeed, says Tillich, what St Paul meant by saying that God will be all in all.

Again and again, Tillich stresses the fact that, though the idea of the Kingdom does refer beyond history, it has a very clear and immediate reference to history. So in his exposition of doctrine no less than in his early political activity he does not avoid the question: how is the Kingdom of God seen in the dynamics of history? It is not surprising that he begins his answer by reference to the technical notion used by modern theology of *Heilsgeschichte* (history of salvation). If you talk of salvation, he argues, then it is necessarily true that you are able to talk of revelation; and if there is a universal revelation, then there is a universal salvation. The next theological issue is the relation of history as man's work and achievements to the history of salvation. Classical Idealism and liberalism identified them; but that is a mistake because historical life, like all life, is characterized by ambiguities. It is these very ambiguities that are conquered in salvation, which then stands in judgement on history. 'Saving power breaks into history, works through history but is not created by history' (ibid., p. 387). The confession of this is the confession that the Kingdom of God is being manifested in history. This is no general theory of history but the concrete historical expression of a revelatory experience.

Though he has hedged his theology of history round with these denials of any ideological or theoretical claims, Tillich is emphatic in his declaration that Jesus is the centre of history. That notion, of course, has nothing to do with quantitative measurements. There is no point in history which is a 'middle between an indefinite past and an indefinite future', any more than there is some crucial conjunction of the cultural lines of the past in relation to the future. What he means by 'centre' is the moment in history that makes everything prior and after both anticipation and reception. Once again, he stresses that this is an assertion of faith, not a theoretical hypothesis, an assertion that does indeed risk being wrong but claims to be true because it is based on faith in a revelation. As this kind of assertion, it is the rejection of such theoretical claims as those of relativism and progressivism. It denies that history is a series of events each as significant or insignificant as the next. Nor will it accept that the centre is the result of progress, itself to be overtaken by more progress. There is no progress beyond the centre; and everything that follows it 'stands under its criterion and partakes of its power' (ibid., p. 389). As we have seen, not only does Tillich insist on the faith-element in this view of history but he is equally anxious to avoid any kind of triumphalism. He has no desire to claim for Christian theology some privileged position in the discussion of the meaning of history. Yet he also maintains that the Christian theologian is not offering a merely optional view of history. The theologian does not have all the answers but he is interpreting a revelation that is the stuff of history. His point is that the Christian view of history has about it a certain maturity represented by this revelation, a maturity that is itself the source of the recognition that revelation is not confined to the centre. 'In biblical and theological language', he says, 'this has been expressed as the symbol of the transtemporal presence of the Christ in every period' (ibid., p. 390). Such a view or attitude refers not only to the preparation for the centre but equally to reception from the centre. That is, Tillich conceives the history before Christ and the history after Christ in very similar terms: it would be wrong, in his view, to imagine that the former was markedly different from the latter in some such way as one maps the progress of a weather-system over an area.

What makes his argument a very distinctive contribution to Christian theology of history is that what makes such a view possible is the conviction that all history makes up one whole of which the event of the Christ is the centre. The very position that would seem to be denied by what he has said is thus said to be its justification. Though in this way he has seemed to some critics to have sold the pass in Christian apologetics and to others to be merely having his cake and eating it, his insistence is that he has articulated the distinctive nature of a Christian view of history. Herein lies for him the distinction between the Christian faith and such faiths as Judaism, Islam or Buddhism. He says quite roundly 'The appearance of Jesus as the Christ is the historical event in which history becomes aware of itself and its meaning' (ibid., p. 393). The New Testament description of that moment in which the event occurred as *kairos* was a concept that Tillich had taken up in his early career when he was involved with the religious socialist movement in Germany. There were various reasons for that choice. It reminded theologians that for the New Testament (and the Old) the character of that particular history was that it transcended its own history. For philosophers it brought the salutary lesson that any interpretation of history which sought a proper adequacy had to go beyond the logical analysis and the metaphysical description of history in terms of categories. Most of all, it matched the general feeling that the time was ripe for a new and fuller understanding of the meaning of history and of life. All this remained as a valid justification of the use of the term in systematic theology. What is significant as well as instructive about Tillich's use of the term is that he takes it to mean something that occurs again and again. In this he is not at all consistent, because he still regards the centre of history as *the kairos* or the 'great *kairos*' and the other *kairoi* as relative—the former being re-experienced through the latter. He speaks of the relation between them in two ways. The 'great *kairos*' is the criterion by reference to which anything is judged to be a *kairos*. He also says that it is the source of the relative *kairos*'s power. While it is unfortunate that he did not engage in any further explanation, Tillich cannot be said either to contradict himself here or to offer anything other than a perfectly orthodox theology. Both descriptions of the kairotic nature of history will work and are consistent with what he has said. The Christocentric emphasis of his theology means that the New Testament *kairos* is indeed the criterion—the very criteria of theology which were set out imply this. Also, we have seen how Tillich wants to extend the traditional notion of God's providential activity beyond the traditional limitation to the church. Thus Christ can be said both to be the norm or criterion of whatever can be regarded as the fulfilment of God's purpose and also to be the source of the power revealed in such moments of history.

Just as much as elsewhere, Tillich is at pains to distinguish between his theology of history and the kind of theory which could be developed from social psychology or sociology. We are aware of *kairos* only if we have the vision of faith. However, once more he confuses the issue by his fondness for making distinctions, saying that the difference is the contrast between 'detached observation' and 'involved experience' (ibid., p. 395). This would seem to make the difference one between two kinds of experience. Perhaps he was conscious of the confusion, because he goes on to qualify what he has said by admitting that observation and analysis are by no means excluded. He makes his point more clearly when he says quite simply that 'observation and analysis do not produce the experience of the *kairos*'. The fact that the 'great *kairos*' is a criterion must imply that observation and analysis are relevant—since a criterion is invoked only if there is some assessment or evaluation of what is known. For Tillich, as for the New Testament, every claim to the status of the Spiritual must be tested. Indeed, he illustrates this from his own experience of world history because, as he says (ibid., pp. 395–6), the term *kairos* was used not only by the religious socialists but also by the Nazis. While the former spoke in obedience to the great *kairos*, the latter were false prophets, advocating an idolatrous nationalism and racialism. The illustration clearly demonstrates the two final points he makes about *kairoi*: that they can be demoniacally distorted, and secondly that they can be erroneous. Even the 'great *kairos*' could be said to show this in that, at the very least, what we see there is the possibility of error in the human judgement about the time, space and causality involved. What he has in mind is clear from the New Testament narrative of Jesus' ministry from the story of the Temptation to the story of the Betrayal and the Passion. Though Tillich's exposition is rather confusing, we can fairly interpret him to be repeating his insistence that revelation is not a matter of empirical information, so that we should not be surprised if the very reception of revelation will involve erroneous factual claims. Predictions proved false; but the reception of the revelation changed the course of history. And this is a clear enough answer to the question which Tillich's caution might raise in our minds—does he really believe that there is a *kairos*? More than once we have seen how Tillich has attracted the suspicion that he has sold out, here attenuating the meaning of the term *kairos* so much that it is one applicable anywhere in history. His answer is an emphatic negative. Though the 'great *kairos*' has changed history, not all history is experienced as *kairos*. The Kingdom of God is always present, but it does not follow that human history is always aware of this transcendent dimension.

Tillich's answer to the question of history's *meaning* is, then, a very complex one. Though, like any theologian, he will want to say that there is a sense in which *all* history is summed up in Jesus Christ, he is forever warning against simplistic views of history. There are times when one feels that his mode of argument is so cautious that even a successful clarification of all the confusions he has consequently generated will not yield a clear argument. Yet this much can be said: he believes that the divine creativity in history implies that there is a real unity to history, but he does not believe that theology can offer a concrete interpretation of anything more than particular develop-ment. The notion that history is meaningful because of a pre-ordained design is a false mechanistic model to be rejected in favour of the basic ontological polarity of freedom and destiny. Indeed, Tillich rejects any and every idea of design, because design excludes freedom and contingency, which are the conditions of historical novelty. Nor is it only freedom and contingency which must be given a place in any proper theological account of the meaning of history as providence. Only a theology which takes into its idea of providence the 'immensity of moral and physical evil and the overwhelming manifestation of the demonic and its tragic consequence in history' has a right, he says (ibid., p. 397), to use the concept of providence. One of Tillich's greatest sentences is what he writes here—'no future justice and happiness can annihilate the injustice and suffering of the past'. His understanding of providence is thus both realistically existential and a very clear declaration of faith. History can only be understood as the arena of freedom, and that means freedom for good and evil. The very creation of good by man's free history brings about the possibility of evil too. What is claimed by the Christian answer that the meaning of history is providence is that the evil in history can never destroy the drive of history towards the divine. In a word, Tillich's view of the providential meaning of history is the vision of the Johannine prologue—that though it is in darkness that the light shines, yet the darkness does not overcome it. And, for all his sympathy with the Idealist interpretation of history, he rejects Hegel's assumption that we can know this meaning as some explanatory theory derived from a metaphysics. This is mystery and 'beyond all calculation and description'.

It hardly needs to be said that in the light of this Tillich wants to insist on the paradoxical way in which the churches are a representation of the Kingdom of God. The churches hide the Spiritual Community when they represent the demonic Kingdom which is clearly a distortion of the divine Kingdom. So the representation of the Kingdom of God by the churches is something that is as ambiguous as is the relation of the churches to the Spiritual Community. There are in fact two sets of analogies which Tillich has in mind here. First, there is the analogy of the ambiguity or ambiguities in the case of Spiritual Community and Kingdom of God. In both cases there is ambiguity by virtue of the fact that they are based in history. Secondly, just as the historical dimension includes all other dimensions, so the Kingdom of God includes 'all realms of being under the perspective of their ultimate aim'. History includes all other dimensions, because whatever aspect of existence we may be considering, it is always possible to speak of its history. So too the Kingdom of God is an overarching concept relevant not only to the Spiritual Community but also to everything else which is in God's creation. There is one other consideration which is very important for Tillich's thinking here: it is that the reality of even the distorted kingdom is derived from the divine Kingdom. He means more than some vague suggestion that there is some dependence on the divine, which could be no more than being given rope with which to hang oneself. The reality of the function is what he has in mind particularly, saying that 'the churches, which represent the Kingdom of God in history, cannot forfeit this function even if they exercise it in contradiction to the Kingdom of God' (ibid., pp. 400–1).

With this consciousness of the shadows of Eternity in the weaker glories of historical church life go Tillich's very strong sense of the mission of the church and his almost mystical sense of the church's embodiment of both the inorganic and the organic as elements of a sacramental universe. Because the churches see themselves as representatives of the Kingdom, they will express their commitment to it as *milites Christi*, soldiers of Christ who are struggling with the

174

forces of darkness. At the same time, the Kingdom is something which they expect to come and for the coming of which they pray, and in that sense not the victorious result of their struggle. This double reference is an important aspect of Tillich's view of the role that is played by the churches in history, because it very clearly illustrates his understanding of the moral and transmoral dimensions of the Christian hope which animates the church. The awareness of the Kingdom as the 'end' of history gives the moral commitment the unique quality of hope, and the commitment itself a resolution that is more than moral effort. The churches are able to be the means by which the Kingdom is furthered because their action is not a simple exercise of moral will: they are based on the New Being and, as grounded in the conquest of evil in Christ, their moral action is a work of grace. As well as this, the moral effort is inspired by the conviction that it is as it were on history's side—in the poet's phrase, going 'with the grain'. And in his exposition of this vision of history and the function of the churches Tillich briefly enters the plea for a cosmic understanding of the Kingdom. The Kingdom of God is a symbol that refers to the whole of reality and not simply to social history, however much we widen that concept. This is understood so much better, he thinks, by churches like the Greek Orthodox than by churches of the 'word'. So Tillich quietly but clearly criticizes the Protestant (and, in particular, the Reformed) tradition for the way in which the emphasis on law and individualism has resulted in not only a neglect of sacrament but also a depreciation of the cosmos.

One other way in which the problem of the relation of the churches to the Kingdom arises is in connection with their history as the history of the church. Because he has emphasized the positive as well as the negative side of the ambiguity which characterizes the church, Tillich is clear that the history of the churches is a history of the church—and this the one church. However, he rejects the inference that up to a certain time—whether that is said to be AD 500 or 1500—there was the one church, actual in time and space, and that it was then split into a plurality of churches. Whichever option of dating such an assumed change is adopted, the error is the same; and that, for Tillich, is a theological rather than a simple historical one. Presumably he would accept the historical argument that a 'Christian beginning' is a myth; but what he is arguing is that we cannot ignore the fact that the church or Spiritual Community always lives in the churches. If churches confess their foundation in Christ as the central manifestation of the Kingdom, they are the church, as we have seen. It is this distinctly ecumenical and Christocentric view which leads Tillich to the paradoxical assertion that church history can never be identified with the Kingdom and yet it can never be denied to be a manifestation of the Kingdom of God. He considers various 'riddles' (his word for problems in this connection) about the actual pattern of church history. Why has it been so largely a feature of a particular civilization? Why have scientific humanism and naturalistic communism flourished in non-Christian civilizations? How have the contradictory interpretations of the basis in Christ come about in the history of the churches? Tillich also identifies profanization as a great riddle, but says at last that the greatest is 'the manifest power of the demonic' in church history. When one reflects that the glory of Christianity is its claim that the demonic powers are conquered in Christ, this is an 'offensive riddle'. While he does not attempt to discuss these riddles, Tillich takes them all to raise one question: 'What is the meaning of Christian history?' (ibid., p. 407). His first answer is the negative one that church history cannot be identified with 'sacred history' or 'history of salvation'. Then, in what is now a familiar fashion, he goes on to say that sacred history is in church history but not limited to it, manifest in it but also hidden by it. Even so, he ranks church history above all other history because in so far as it relates itself at all times and in all contexts to the eternal revelation of the Kingdom in history it carries within itself the criterion by which its own history is judged.

The discussion of history and the Kingdom of God has taken Tillich far and wide. Problems about the writing of history and the analysis of history which are the usual concern of a philosophy of history have been taken up as he pursued his basic aim of seeing history as the locus of a final revelation and the shadow of the Kingdom. In following what he has to say and struggling with his constant tendency to formalize things into abstractions, it has been hard to resist the feeling that he has often made the confusion only more clearly confused. Yet there can be no denying the magnificence of his consistent grasp on two clear perceptions. He has made us see first that it is only the presence of Christ in history that gives us the ground for talking of church and Kingdom and indeed history itself as meaningful realities. Secondly, he has never lost sight of the fact that here we are dealing with mystery, so that the theologian's main task is to resist the temptation to reduce this to concrete assertions and thus gain a false security.

10

Tillich the Global Theologian

We have followed the story of Tillich's career and of his developing thought—a young, brilliant and promising theologian whose spirit, broken by war, was restored by the hope of a better world created by the political action of the post-war years only to be confronted by worse challenges as the twentieth century unfolded. The tragedy of the story does not need to be retold, and all that needs to be said is that we have seen the story of a life that in several ways encompassed the world. This, then, is the picture that one takes away from reading Tillich—a thinker who is aware of belonging to a total universe. Early in his career he came to the firm conviction that theology is a discipline that takes its practitioner into the world. That it was born of a church life and that it was tied in with a very definite intellectual and cultural background did not seem to him to limit the theologian's horizon or excuse him from the task of seeing reality and seeing it whole. His life-story can be viewed as an increasing awareness of the global character of his vocation.

Born in Germany, he spent nearly half his life in the USA; and to quite a significant extent he became Americanized. Yet he was always conscious of the difference in cultural background and attitude or outlook, as was clear when he remarked to me on one occasion 'You forget that Americans do not understand what you and I take for granted'. His church affiliation was inevitably affected by the change of continent; and his staunch Lutheranism became imbued with a real catholicity of ecclesiastical outlook. It was a standing joke in Union Seminary that, whether the topic was Luther or Calvin, Tillich's course on the Reformation was an exposition of his own understanding of the abiding significance of reform. The point of the joke was in fact that in changing continents more than a simple national change had been seen in his church and religious affiliation. Naturally, he became an American churchman and this meant widening his affiliation; but the more significant point was that in the American context the greater catholicity of his religious sympathies could be given expression in a new way.

There was indeed a new boundary on which Tillich found himself after he had gone to America which is not mentioned in *On the Boundary*, and that was the boundary between Christianity and other religions. While he had always been aware of and thought in the context of the study of religion and the history of religions, it is true that he did not have personal contact with other religions until quite late in his life. This has led many scholars to distinguish between his work up to his visit to the Far East and the work of his latest years. For the moment, the resolution of that debate does not concern us. What is important is simply that this was an even more fundamental way in which Tillich developed a worldwide, and in fact global, reference for his theology which was at least not explicitly stated before.

One last point can be mentioned before looking at these issues more closely. What has been a consistent theme—whether plot or sub-plot of the story—is the world of nature. His interest may indeed have been very romantic—that of a Wordsworth who could hardly distinguish between himself and the world of natural events and things in which he exulted. Certainly that is something which struck some of his friends as a nature-mysticism and other friends as the sentimental attitude towards a chocolate-box picture which recoiled at the very thought that there could be snakes in the countryside. Obviously, Tillich wrote his theology before the emergence of an ecological concern among theologians. Yet it can be said that beneath the social, political and physical concerns of these theologians there is a basic theological conviction about creation which Tillich shared and consistently expressed.

Because these issues have been contentious, I want to start this final description of Tillich as a global theologian by looking at some less contentious matters. One of the most familiar, as it is also one of the most widely discussed, aspects of Tillich's work is his appreciation of philosophy. His eclecticism and his wide sympathies make a simplistic judgement all too easy. Some authors (such as Wheat in his book *Paul Tillich's Dialectical Humanism*, Baltimore, 1971), have argued that this is the clear indication that Tillich was some kind of fifth columnist who sought to modernize Christianity by offering a philosophy instead of a theology. Others have seen his philosophical work as a genuine enough theological concern but one which was so all-inclusive and contradictory in its syncretism that it was irredeemably confused. In fact, it was with regard to his idea of philosophy that I first made the criticism that he was essentially a nineteenth-century thinker. This he rejected forcefully, saying that he was essentially the product of the twentieth century, though he was at the same time insistent that the roots of this influence were to be found in the nineteenth century. This seemed to me to confirm my view that what we have in Tillich is the same kind of view as is found in Hegel and Schelling. While I would not want to retract my basic criticism of Tillich's correlation of philosophy and theology, what I now think is worth saying is that the renewed interest amongst philosophers in the Idealism of the nineteenth century gives Tillich's work a new relevance. Tillich's philosophical achievement has not been much studied, critics generally being content to quote Georgia Harkness's famous remark that what Whitehead had been to American philosophy, Tillich had been to American theology. Whatever Harkness meant by that, I would see the analogy to signify that in both cases the concept of God was viewed as philosophically indispensable. It may well be that the two thinkers reveal the profound influence of Idealism of which we are becoming aware. In the summer before he died I shared a lecture programme with Tillich in Union Theological Seminary, New York, and my lectures were a discussion of his philosophy. My starting-point was the influence on him of phenomenology, and of this he approved very readily. He said that one of the basic lessons he had learnt in philosophy was the importance of the phenomenological method and that he still looked back at Husserl's work in logic as fundamental. His remarks on the latter were memorable: it was, he said, Husserl's *Logical Investigations* that had saved him and many of his generation from the materialism of nineteenth century naturalism. This I took to refer to Husserl's insistence on the priority of consciousness to any cognitive situation. I have tried to show the pervading influence of this philosophical approach on Tillich's theology. What critics of his philosophy tend to forget is the way in which Tillich managed to fuse different philosophical traditions precisely because he would see, for instance, the phenomenological approach as offering a *method* while the importance of Idealism was that it reminded philosophy of its proper vision. What I have tried to show is the great service Tillich did theology by demonstrating the relevance of philosophy for the theologian, whose starting-point was indeed quite different.

The global character of Tillich's philosophical style of theologizing is obvious if one considers his Christology. Without repeating our earlier discussion of the theme, we can pick out the themes of history and myth as an example of the way in which what might seem to be the exclusivism of a Christocentric starting-point and method in theology becomes in Tillich's work an invitation to a definitely inclusive theology. Whereas I have in the past said very often that with regard to history Tillich tried to have the penny and the bun, I am now inclined to say that he showed too little interest in the actual questions asked by historians as well as the intricate relations between ontology and empirical claims. Even so, he saw more clearly than most what was involved in the problem of the historical Jesus and that one did not solve the epistemological problem by simply talking of myth. Despite his admiration of Bultmann, Tillich argued that demythologizing was no more than a prelude to the theological task of remythologizing. When it comes to the matter of interpreting the doctrine of incarnation, Tillich offers an essentially ontological interpretation. In this way he showed how little is achieved in Christology by talking of myth; it is a concept that has only limited use. As I have said, Tillich was as eager as any orthodox theologian to assert the factuality of Jesus; but his wariness in regard to historical statements about the Resurrection, for instance, is born of an unwillingness to express the meaning of the Christological event in language that is so concrete as not to be universal.

Another theological topic where the increasing sense of globalism has been evident is the doctrine of the Kingdom of God with its inevitably political overtones. Tillich's theology was born of a political ferment, and his earliest theological work can be read as the manifesto of a political revolution—so much so that it disturbed his apolitical ecclesiastical superiors. Nobody can fail to see that spirit or fail to be moved by that idealism as one reads 'On the idea of a theology of culture'. This close contact with, and involvement in, politics during the years immediately following the First World War have been obvious in the brief account of his life-story. Beside the lecture just mentioned, there were various publications well into the 1920s which express this; and even the famous article of 1943

('Beyond religious socialism') continued the same enterprise and revealed the same attitude. However, by contrast, the work of his American period lacks the same sense of concreteness. Both *The Courage to Be* and *Love, Power and Justice* are important contributions to the analysis of and comment on the politics of the 1950s; but they show a formalism which amounts to abstraction. There is here a sense of distance from political action; and this leads one to contrast the early Tillich with the very theoretical Tillich of the late American years, in particular. Yet he never disowned his early conviction that theology is done in the context of politics, which it then serves because of its higher allegiance: and, for all their formalism, the works mentioned are, I believe, an inspiration to political theology. It has been argued that theology suffers from an over-readiness to canonize left-wing politics. However, it seems to me that biblical prophecy is nearer the tone of left-wing political ideology than the confidence in the status quo which marks right-wing politics.

In his political theology, as in much else, Tillich is closely linked with the heritage of Romanticism. Recent studies of the Romantics have made us aware of the way in which religion and politics were intertwined in their vision of the reformation that was necessary and for which they fought. Religion was in fact the primary arena in which the Romantics pitched battle with the power structures of their society. For this very reason, it is perhaps worth repeating the point that Tillich's political theology had a very distinct anti-utopian thrust. He warned against the utopianism of a world united by either fear on the one hand or vacuous hope on the other: both forms of utopianism are, in his view, an attempt to escape the tragic encounters of the political world. This was where he had parted company with his friend Emmanuel Hirsch, who had supported the 'German Christian' movement. The result of this utopianism, he argued, was Nazism. The phrase he used to describe his political theology was 'belief-ful realism', and what characterizes that is the transcendent Christian hope. Nothing expresses this combination of realism and hope so well as his views on the creation of a global community (*Political Expectations*, pp. 111–14). There are three ways in which he saw this being conceived: (1) the development of a global empire, (2) the delegation of certain sovereign rights to a supra-national community, (3) the birth of a higher community which surpasses national sovereignty. However, to the question whether one can envisage a viable political unity of all mankind, Tillich gives a very clear negative answer. Such a union would, he thought, end up by organizing life according to invariable repetitive processes. Life would cease to be self-transcending and creativity would disappear. As long as there is human history, the union of mankind is no more than some kind of Kantian Ideal of Reason, the schema for understanding a disunited humanity.

Talk of a global community brings us naturally enough to a discussion of Tillich's views of the religious future of the world; for there are few arguments as recurring, and few criticisms of religion so popular, as the contention that religion is divisive of humanity. It is worth reminding ourselves that one of Tillich's distinctive emphases as a Christian theologian was his insistence that the history of religion constitutes one among the various sources of theology. This was a position set out very clearly in the first volume of *Systematic Theology*; but it had been expressed much earlier too. As early as 'The conquest of the concept of religion in the philosophy of religion' (1922; *What Is Religion?*, pp. 122–54), he had argued that one should not regard Christianity as a religion which was, by definition, absolutely true as distinct from any other religion, which was therefore false. The argument had not indeed been put in these terms but it is clearly implied by the view of 'religion' and 'Christian revelation' there expounded. His thesis there is that any philosophical attempt to understand the Christian faith forces the philosopher to abandon the concept of religion. If the philosopher describes the fact of Christian faith, he must concede that the concept of revelation is not only decisive for Christian faith but is meaningful. Because Christianity affirms a revelation that is not contained within a religion, then religion is not a concept that describes Christianity. Now, whatever one makes of the argument as a piece of philosophy of religion, it is clear that it provides a powerful stimulus to religious tolerance and inter-religious dialogue. As a student of the history of religion just as much as an observer of the changing history of his world, Tillich would agree that the context of faith is always being changed, and that as much from beyond as from within its own boundaries, so that the history of religion, as that of humankind, is global. Certainly from the early period of his systematic effort in theology, if not indeed from the very beginning of his career, he had reflected the changed outlook of the modern world where there is no longer a 'we' and 'they' situation but a common humanity of religious faith. In the elaboration of the standpoint he took up as a systematic theologian, he saw no contradiction between this essentially universal outlook and the recognition, on the other hand, of the unavoidably Christian basis of his systematic theology. What I want thus to emphasize is that, no matter whether others might argue, there was a fundamental inconsistency. Tillich did not regard this as even an area of tension, let alone contradiction. The clearest indication that this was his attitude is that he did not single this out—as he did with Christology—as an instance of theological paradox.

If the background to Tillich's systematic theology was a distinctly human and, as has been argued, global view of religion, his development of that theology from the late 1950s onwards was very much in relation to other religions. This was given expression in the book *Christianity and the Encounter of World Religions*, which not only repeats his view that a conviction of faith is the presupposition of this kind of thinking but also insists that dialogue is possible only because there is a common ground between religions. This is another instance of Tillich's subtlety in understanding the nature of religion; for what seems to be a wide and undiscriminating view of religion that could hardly sit comfortably with a Christian claim to final revelation turns out to be something very different. It is the basis of a religion in revelation that gives it validity, as we have seen, and so Tillich's premiss here is that the criterion of judgement is something beyond the religion itself. This was a view of religion that early defined his understanding of the nature of theology as well as his stance in philosophy of religion. If there is any change in attitude in Tillich's thinking from the 1920s to the 1970s, it is the growing recognition of the difference between the situation of the present-day theologian and that of the Fathers. Whereas they had been engaged in the conquest of old concepts and their transformation into Christian terminology, dialogue is the activity of the present-day theologian, and this is 'a common inquiry in the light of the world situation' (*Christianity and the Encounter of World Religions*, p. 63). It has been argued by some scholars (e.g. D. Terence Thomas, in his edition of *The Encounter of Religions and Quasi-Religions*, Lewiston, 1984, and elsewhere) that Tillich's own first real experience of Oriental religion in its context produced so decisive a change in his outlook that he saw his whole theological enterprise in a new light. This seems a strange claim to make when these same scholars are obliged to confess that Tillich was anxious to remain a committed Christian. To add an autobiographical piece of evidence to the contrary, I can say that my last meeting with him in the summer of

1965, only two months before he died, gave no indication of this. He was engaged, he said, in a revision of all his work published in English and he was especially concerned to produce a revised edition of the final volume of *Systematic Theology*. Since we had been discussing some of the issues treated in that volume, he remarked that he found my constant complaint about his lack of clarity very useful. What I could do for him, he said, was to go through the volume setting out the areas that needed clarification and the precise clarification that was needed. The significant point about this is that neither in his account of what he was then doing, nor in the description of the work then envisaged, was there any suggestion that the revision he proposed involved a change in his basic standpoint. The truth of the matter, it would seem to me, is that while in some of his earlier works the language may appear more traditional and indeed exclusive, the position he took up was always the same. Here more than anywhere he demonstrated his extraordinary ability to balance very opposite tendencies and to live very happily 'on the boundary'. In this he made a unique contribution to the necessary task of inter-religious dialogue, one that demands of both believer and theologian a truly religious humility.

Tillich antedated the great concern with ecology that is so obvious a feature of present-day theology. However, it can be said that though the emphasis is not there, it would be wrong to conclude that his theology lacks an ecological dimension; and it is certainly true that where ecological theology goes beyond practical concerns to treat the theoretical bases of an ecological vision, what it treats is the kind of issue that appears consistently in Tillich's treatment of the idea of creation. Mention has already been made of his essentially Romantic attitude to Nature. If there were one Romantic slogan which he could be thought to echo it would be Wordsworth's cry 'We murder to dissect'. In his epistemology he had been anxious to plead for a more classical view of Reason than what he saw as the Cartesian legacy. The latter's influence he regarded as a modern malady which made us think of Reason as confined to the ratiocinative processes so evident in the quantitative calculations of modern science. This is what lay behind his important distinction between 'technical reason' and 'the depth of reason'. True to the Romantic vision that animated so much of his theology, he wanted to oppose not only the stifling of the human context which this produced but equally the disastrous effects it had on our understanding of the natural world. His message as a prophetic theologian was that if we restrict our cultural horizons to the limits of technical reason, then we shall end up not only with the failure of our cognitive quest but with the far worse fate of the destruction of the very object of our quest.

As with so many aspects of his theology, Tillich was content with adumbrating a vision and it is pointless trying to spell out this vision from what he says. Yet there were three respects in which this vision can be regarded as typical of his theology: it was first a Logos theology; secondly, it was a correlative theology; and finally it was a theology of Being. The role of Logos in Tillich's theology is difficult to define, because one can easily be tempted to see this only in relation to the Christology. It seems to me, however, that the real importance of the concept is its very general application. Very much as the Stoics had thought that here was a key concept for interpreting man, society and nature, so Tillich sees Logos as a concept equally applicable (*mutatis mutandis*, of course) to God, man and the world. In his characteristically large view of Philosophy, he thought this was what united nineteenth-century Idealism and Stoic metaphysics. If then he regarded Nature as *sharing* the distinguishing feature of God the Creator and man as knower and user, there could be hardly any more powerful motivation to an ecological ethic in regard to Nature, the object of man's cultural interests. Secondly, as a correlative theology, Tillich's enterprise was one of meeting the contemporary question. We have seen his clear awareness of the sinful, not merely secular, attitude towards Nature as something which is there merely for our exploitation. If *the* modern problem is that of understanding Nature as having an intrinsic rather than a merely utilitarian value, then Tillich's theology can be seen as a very modern exploration and articulation of the rationale for this desired attitude towards Nature. Brought up in a continent that had been the cradle of Romanticism and in an era when the approach to Nature was more respectful than exploitative, Tillich was inevitably aware of the very different attitude that characterized America in the 1950s and 1960s, if not perhaps before. Can we not read the picture he draws of man in *Systematic Theology*, volume 2, as such a reading of what confronted him? And if so, then it is very clear that what he goes on to describe as the theological definition of problem and answer is the kind of general foundations of ecological vision which have been claimed for him above. The final point is that Tillich's theology is a system with Being as its leading concept. He was a believer who had been launched on a metaphysical quest by the concrete concerns of the post-war world. So, however far he strayed in thought from these basic motivations, he felt his roots real and concrete. As he struggled with the problems posed by culture and history, he was convinced that Being was the key that unlocked the mystery, and the window on Being was man's existence, which was indissolubly bound up with Nature.

Tillich's definition of his aim in *Systematic Theology*, was to help those looking for answers. What can be said to be the greatest debt he laid upon those who have made a serious attempt to understand him is simply that he has taught us to recognize problems where we thought that we already had answers.

Index

187

INDEX

188